Science and Environmental
Decision Making

Pearson Education

We work with leading authors to develop the strongest
educational materials in science and environmental
studies, bringing cutting-edge thinking and best
learning practise to a global market.

Under a range of well-known imprints, including
Prentice Hall, we craft high quality print and electronic
publications which help readers to understand and
apply their content, whether studying or at work.

To find out more about the complete range of our
publishing please visit us on the World Wide Web at:
www.pearsoneduc.com

Science and Environmental Decision Making

Mark Huxham
School of Life Sciences, Napier University

David Sumner
Moss Park, Ravenstone, Whithorn

Prentice
Hall

An imprint of **Pearson Education**

Harlow, England · London · New York · Reading, Massachusetts · San Francisco · Toronto · Don Mills, Ontario · Sydney
Tokyo · Singapore · Hong Kong · Seoul · Taipei · Cape Town · Madrid · Mexico City · Amsterdam · Munich · Paris · Milan

Pearson Education Limited

Edinburgh Gate
Harlow
Essex CM20 2JE
United Kingdom

and Associated Companies throughout the world

Visit us on the World Wide Web at
www.pearsoneduc.com

———————————

First published in Great Britain in 2000

© Pearson Education Limited 2000

The right of Mark Huxham and David Sumner to be identified as
editors of this work has been asserted by them in accordance with
the Copyright, Designs and Patents Act 1988.

ISBN 0 582 41446 6

British Library Cataloguing in Publication Data
A CIP catalogue record for this book can be obtained from the British Library.

10 9 8 7 6 5 4 3 2 1
04 03 02 01 00

Typeset by 30
Produced by Pearson Education Asia Pte, Ltd

Printed by B & Jo Enterprise Pte Ltd, Singapore

Contents

Contents

Contents

Preface

There are many, many questions to which we do not have scientific answers
... these include almost all questions which really matter to us.

Ray Monk

In the Western world, we live surrounded by, and dependent upon, science
and its products. Scientific methods, discoveries and modes of thought are
perhaps the most distinctive and successful legacies of the last 400 years of
history. And yet our attitude to science remains one of wary ambivalence;
we are struck both by its wonder and its tragedy. The universe it opens to
us, of black holes and subatomic quarks, of coalescing continents and
dividing cell nuclei, is one of awesome beauty. Ours is a world infinitely
more wonderful than the most fantastic fiction, and science gives us the
eyes to see it.

But paradoxically, and tragically, just as science reveals these wonders, it
seems also to restrict our responses to them, and to alienate us from them.
Scientific discoveries are often kept behind walls of jargon, apparently
designed to exclude the outsider. If these discoveries have applications,
then to comment on their risks and benefits, on how they should and
should not be used, requires that we speak the language of science. Those
who cannot, or will not, use this language are left outside.

This exclusion would be less important if science existed beyond society.
But the romantic picture of the scientist as noble inventor, or humble
seeker after truth, striving only for the good of humanity and the innocent
wonder of discovery, is dangerously simplistic. The work of most scientists
is largely determined by social factors. They need to justify their research
to the businesses, governments or grant bodies which fund it. All scientists
carry with them personal and professional values which influence what
they do.

So scientific work is directed by social forces, and the products of this
work, from cloning to nuclear reprocessing, can have implications for
everybody. Society as a whole has a right and a duty to help direct how science is conducted and applied. Nowhere is this more important than when
science impinges on the environment, with the potential for massive
impacts affecting living things for generations to come.

As the power and prestige of science grows, so does our appreciation of
its limits. As science helps to diminish some risks, such as those from infec-
tious diseases, so it reveals and contributes to new ones. But usually
the scale of these risks, especially when they are environmental risks, is

uncertain or even unknown. We are worried about global warming, biodiversity loss and marine pollution because science has allowed us to detect these dangers. But science cannot tell us just how worried we should be, because there is no scientific consensus on how certain, or how serious, these and other risks are. Coping with them requires skills, vision and commitment which cannot come from science. At a fundamental level, decisions on how we deal with environmental risk depend on our values, and science cannot tell us what to value.

Uncertainty in the face of risk, and the primary importance of values (rather than of technological information) in making decisions, are the threads which tie this book together. It has been written by scientists and social scientists working in diverse areas of environmental risk. Since there is no such thing as zero risk, the level that occurs in these different areas will depend on what is seen as 'acceptable'. This book shows how science is just one of the resources that can help determine 'acceptability'.

Chapters 1–3 introduce our main themes, starting with 'pure' science, 'uncontaminated' by social influences, and introducing increasing layers of complexity. Chapters 4–10 show how these themes are relevant in case studies drawn from a range of problems in applied environmental science. Whilst chapters 4–10 have some themes in common, the topics they discuss have been chosen because they each illustrate one of these themes particularly well.

Chapter 1 considers what is meant by a 'scientific' explanation, and looks at the logic of testing ideas in science. Chapter 2 looks at some of the absolute limits of scientific explanation. It shows how value judgements, both conscious and unconscious, invevitably influence scientific work, and questions whether the 'fact/value' divide can be maintained, even in principle. Chapter 3 expands on this by considering the sociology of science; the ways in which commercial and political influences affect how science is actually executed and used, in real-world situations where subjectivities and values must inevitably operate. It discusses the precautionary principle, a good illustration of how decision makers deal with scientific uncertainty.

Chapter 4 looks at the controversy over the use of genetically modified organisms in agriculture. This issue shows how huge commercial interests can direct scientific research. Chapter 5 considers the threat of global climate change. As this is one of the biggest, most uncertain and most difficult environmental risks to face us, debates over global warming provide a crucial test case for how the precautionary principle is interpreted internationally. Chapter 6 explores the arguments for conserving biodiversity, in the face of mass extinctions brought about by humanity. It demonstrates the primary importance of values, rather than of science, in the conservation case. Chapter 7 discusses the roots of the crisis in the world's fisheries. It shows how simple management rules, supported by science, are often better in real-life applications than complex scientific models. Chapter 8 looks at recent decisions about dumping wastes at sea, as an illustration of how purely 'scientific' risk assessments cannot deal with some of the most important considerations. Chapter 9 looks at how scientific models are used in practice; in this case in making decisions about eutrophication. It shows how research models and policy tools can, and often should, be very different. Finally, chapter 10 discusses the science and policies behind assessing the risks of low-level radiation. This case study shows how value judgements can be incorporated even into the measurement of 'objective' scientific units, and why low power in scientific studies can make it impossible to eliminate uncertainty.

Our purpose in writing this book is to provide an overview of the problems and challenges – philosophical, statistical, social and political – in using science to answer pressing environmental questions. Our intended audience is students of ecology, environmental sciences and geography, but we hope the book will prove useful to anyone with an interest in how science works, and in how it can, and cannot, help in coping with environmental risk. Because we are able to provide only an introduction to these important issues, we include suggestions for further reading and references with each chapter; if the reader is stimulated to pursue these, then our job will have been a success.

Foreword

Science is under fire. This is not new. Science has always been a cause of both wonder and suspicion. Mark Huxham and David Sumner seek to put science in its place. The traditions of honest enquiry set in rules of strict observation, verification, falsification and independent replication have stood science well since the Enlightenment. Much of what we rely on today, from the concept of time itself to electricity to motion power could not occur without this rich intellectual heritage.

Nowadays, however, there is challenge to the hegemony of science that is persistent and growing. Some of this critique rests fairly at the feet of science. Errors of judgement have been made both as to the use of peer review, and the mismanagement of public relations. The Pusztai affair, in which a scientist looking at the possible health effects of genetic modification techniques claimed to have discovered an unusual jolt to the immune system of rats, was one such case (see Box 4.4 in the Chapter by Sue Mayer). The scientist concerned 'went public' before full peer review was completed, and then suffered the indignity of censure and adverse commentary from blue riband panels of scientists who had all the appearance of trying to 'get him'. The text in this book shows how the science was handled by perfectly conventional approaches. The public relations aspects of his sacking and subsequent partial reinstatement did nobody any good. From then on, the genetic modification debate came alive, as Sue Mayer reveals in her chapter.

Images and symbols are important to the media. Pusztai was portrayed as a martyr of the conventional scientific establishment, anxious to retain its political and grant raising credentials. Scenes of Greenpeace activists damaging crops in a legal GM-related field experiment placed the farmer concerned as the villain, when he had trespass rights as well as the experimental integrity on his side, while the Greenpeace activists had their populist day in court. In many ways this was a tragic incident. The farmers were dangerously out of control and damaged much of Greenpeace property. Whatever the rights and wrongs, wilful damage and grievous bodily harm to trespassers are unacceptable criminal behaviour. The Greenpeace activists will use their public sympathy to defend a technically illegal act, deliberately seeking to destroy the kind of field trial on which science relies to make progress.

This text exposes once and for all, just how politicised science has now become. Climate change, waste disposal, toxic chemical analysis, genetic modification, gene therapy – all of these zones of science extend to the make of social acceptance and public ethics. These are political realms, as these are the very themes that are the stuff of political debate and public accountability.

More to the point, much of this kind of 'civic science' depends on the responses of the public for its social value. Take the essence of climate change, discussed by Mick Kelly in the text that follows. If the world's scientists are correct, then all climates from now on are technically 'non-natural'. Their rhythms are unavoidably interfered with by human use in the form of emitted 'greenhouse gases'. As societies come to terms with these climate futures, they will realise that the future of climate is not a 'given' natural event. It is shaped by the very politics that determine just how people assess the consequences of reducing greenhouse gas emissions. So the climate of the future is the outcome of an interrelated process, a coupled relationship, between science prediction, story telling, and scenario generation all of which are socially constructed and will influence the nature of social response. This response cannot be taken for granted. It depends on social networks, degrees of choice in livelihoods, personal efficacy in making complex decisions, and the ways in which climate futures are presented. It appears therefore that science is no longer an independent agent (if it ever was). It is an inescapable part of social change and political learning.

Where may science go next? In many directions, it seems. There is now a happily increasing drift to interdisciplinarity, and not before time. This will only survive if young scientists are allowed time and freedom to publish jointly and show mutual learning across disciplines. Interdisciplinarity still has to earn its spurs, however. This means being credible both to scientists and to the business and policy interests.

There is also the emergence of intuitive methodology. This involves the combination of qualitative measurement with various subtle ways of gaining confidence about recording and reporting feelings and outlooks. To do this will involve trust and close contact between research and researched, and ways of communicating that build in faith in the reliability of the answers. Such a methodology will be a complement to conventional social science research approaches, not a substitute. The key to this approach lies in the empathy and in the level of enjoyment between the researchers and the researched. We hear a lot of the term 'social capital' these days. This elusive concept involves building trust and connectedness between individuals, their households, their neighbourhoods and their wider communities. It is still an idea that lacks theoretical comprehension and methodological rigour. It is dependent on a sense of feeling and bonding, as well as empowerment and emancipation. Such ideas lie at the heart of sustainability and the new enlightenment that should form the basis of an extended, participatory science for the new millennium. This important and comprehensive text acts as a midwife for its birth.

Tim O'Riordan
February 2000

Acknowledgements

Many people have helped with the often frustrating but ultimately rewarding task of writing this book. We would like to thank Sarah Madden, Peter Pollard, Mark Young, Dave Raffaelli, Iain Fairlie, Teresa Fernandes, Peter Gilmour, Peter Darmady, John Doharty, Chris Richmond and Sarah Bury for helpful comments and guidance on individual chapters. The text was inspired and improved by the input and enthusiasm of many students at Napier University. Tim O'Riordan provided advice on earlier drafts, and helped improve the editorial introductions. Alex Seabrook at Pearsons maintained her enthusiasm for the project throughout, and was an excellent guide through the editorial labyrinth.

To Sarah, Jill and Eva – thanks for everything.

List of Contributors

Dr Mark Huxham teaches ecology and environmental biology at Napier University, Edinburgh. His main research interests are food web theory – looking for patterns in how organisms interact with each other – and how ecological science integrates with policy.
Email: m.huxham@napier.ac.uk

Dr David Sumner was educated at Imperial College, London and the Nuclear Physics Department, University of Oxford. From 1971 to 1990 he was based at the Department of Nuclear Medicine, Stobhill General Hospital, Glasgow. He is now an Associate Lecturer with the Open University and an independent consultant on radiation issues.
Email: dsumner@globalnet.co.uk

Dr Quentin Merritt trained as a physicist before becoming a sociologist. He was formerly Senior Lecturer in Environmental Policy at the University of Greenwich. Dr Peter Jones is Principal Lecturer in Environmental Studies at the University of Greenwich.
Email: p.c.jones@greenwich.ac.uk

Dr Sue Mayer is director of GeneWatch UK, an independent policy research group. She has practiced as a veterinary surgeon and has lectured in veterinary medicine. She is a former director of science at Greenpeace UK.
Email: gene.watch@dial.pipex.com

Dr Mick Kelly is an atmospheric scientist with the Climatic Research Unit in the School of Environmental Sciences at the University of East Anglia and director of the MSc in Climate Change. Concerned that all aspects of society have access to reliable scientific information, he is a frequent contributor to television and radio programmes on the climate issue as well as to the broader climate debate.
Email: m.kelly@uea.ac.uk

Dr Callum Roberts is a marine conservation biologist based at York University, who has spent most of his career documenting the decline of marine biodiversity and seeking ways to reverse it. Currently his research focuses on improving the design and performance of marine reserves as conservation and fishery management tools.
Email: cr10@york.ac.uk

Gillian Glegg obtained her PhD in marine chemistry in 1988 and went on to work at Greenpeace UK on scientific aspects of the marine pollution campaigns. She currently lectures and researches issues in marine science, pollution and policy at the University of Plymouth.
Email: G.Glegg@plymouth.ac.uk

Paul Tett (MA Cambridge, PhD Glasgow) is Professor of Aquatic Environmental Biology at Napier University, Edinburgh. He is a biological oceanographer who currently co-ordinates a European Union study of eutrophication in fjords and other semi-enclosed coastal waters.
Email: p.tett@napier.ac.uk

Chapter 1

Science and the search for truth

Mark Huxham

1.1 Introduction

What do we mean by a scientific explanation? In a recent doorstep discussion, a visitor explained his belief that God created the universe, the world and all life approximately 6000 years ago. I challenged this idea on the basis that it was not logical; a number of arguments suggest that the world is much older. For example, I said, we know what the speed of light is (299 792 458 metres per second), and how far away many of our neighbouring stars are. Six thousand years is not enough time to allow the light from many of these stars to reach us, so if the universe really was that young, the night sky would be darker than it is, and we would occasionally see new stars, blinking on as their light arrived on earth. After a brief pause, he responded that if God can make all the stars and planets, he can also simultaneously create the light between them, so that all the currently observable stars would have been glittering in the sky from day one.

My accusation that my visitor's belief was illogical turned out to be wrong. His response showed how it was possible to construct perfectly logical arguments in defence of his position, given that one believed in an all-powerful, creative God. The current scientific consensus is that the universe was created around 15 billion years ago in the 'big bang', with the earth forming from gas approximately 4.6 billion years ago and life evolving gradually through natural selection. If it is not logic, then what is it that makes this second explanation more scientific than the first?

This chapter aims to answer this question by looking at some of the distinctive features of scientific thought. I begin with a discussion of four common ways of defining science. Science is full of unusual terms and jargon, so I include a 'taxonomy of terms', looking at what is meant by theory, law, model and hypothesis in science. Scientists need to distinguish good theories from bad; some criteria for doing this are suggested. Finally, theories need to be tested, so the logic of some common ways of doing this is explored.

1.2 Ideas about science

1.2.1 Science as common sense

Science is nothing but trained and organised common sense. T. Huxley

One view of science sees it as a rigorous form of organised common sense; a no-nonsense, plain-speaking system for people without time for fancy indulgences. Consider the case of the Loch Ness monster. Common sense suggests that it does not exist (because we do not encounter many mythical beasts in our daily lives). But who really knows? Perhaps there is a large and lonely reptile in the waters of Invernesshire. Science supports common sense in showing how unlikely this is (see Lawton 1996). The annual production of fish in the loch could support a maximum population of ten 1.5 tonne monsters, which must have survived for at least 12 000 years (since this was the last time the loch was connected to the sea by a river large enough to accommodate a monster). Much ecological and genetic theory shows that such a small population is very unlikely to survive for this long (Caughley and Gunn 1996). So scientific explanations sometimes sound like sophisticated common sense. But this is misleading, for two reasons (Wolpert 1992). First, many of the scientifically revealed facts which we take as common sense today (such as the fact of the earth orbiting the sun) came as profound shocks to those who first heard them, and many years had to pass before they were commonly accepted knowledge. Second, much of present-day scientific thinking is entirely counter-intuitive. For example, dwindling populations of fish (see Chapter 7) have led fishers to call for culls of the natural predators that compete with humans for the fish. But ecological science shows that killing the seals which prey on cod could lead to a decrease in the numbers of these fish (Yodzis 1998). So common sense is not a useful description of how science works.

1.2.2 Science as collecting facts

In 1937, three British sociologists launched an extraordinary project, called Mass Observation. They intended to gather as many observations and facts as possible about the lives of ordinary people, with the aim of 'presenting, classifying and analysing the immediate human world'. To achieve this, over a thousand people throughout Britain were recruited to keep detailed records of everything they did on selected days; their breakfasts, visits to aunts, the colour of their new hats, all were lovingly recorded. The thousands of published words (along with photographs and newspaper clippings) that this produced make fascinating reading for historians, but the sociologists' ambitions went beyond embellishing posterity: their purpose was, at least partially, scientific. They hoped that by somehow analysing all the facts, a 'unity' would emerge. Mass Observation is a particularly extreme example of the view that science works by simply collecting as many facts as possible, and then looking for patterns within the data. It also stands as a good illustration of why this view is wrong. Perhaps we could discover from the exercise that 32% of participants drank beer before supper. But why choose to focus on this? There are an infinite number of facts which could be collected at any moment (none of the reports include accounts of the number of hairs on the respondents' heads that morning, or more interestingly, explicit details of their sex lives). So facts are only useful if we have a question we want answered (such as 'what percentage of the population of Britain drank beer in the 1930s?'). And if we do have such a question, then collecting the facts to answer it is a much more complicated task than simply asking a few people (see section 1.5).

1.2.3 Science as proving things

In order to convict a person of murder in Britain or the USA, it must be shown 'beyond a reasonable doubt' that they are guilty. Given the dire consequences of this conviction (certainly many years behind bars, and possibly death), why are the courts not required to *prove* that the defendant is guilty (after all, what is 'reasonable doubt'? A one in a thousand chance that they are innocent? Or a one in a million?). The legal system does not require proof, because if it did conviction rates would tumble, and justice would not be done; absolute proof in criminal cases is as rare as absolute honesty in politics. Science is often described as a procedure for proving things. Yet proof in science is at least as difficult as it is in law (many would argue that it is impossible). It is useful to distinguish two ways in which we might try to prove something, deduction and induction.

Logical deduction

Logic is that branch of knowledge designed to provide proofs, through a process known as deduction. Although the language used in logical deduction might be ordinary words or mathematical symbols, the process is always essentially the same, and was originally developed by the ancient Greeks in the form of **syllogisms**. A syllogism starts with a proposition ('all species of reptile lay eggs'), follows with an observation ('a crocodile is a reptile'), and concludes with a deduction ('therefore, crocodiles lay eggs'). Given the truth of the proposition and observation, the deduction *must* be true; it is proved. So logical deduction can provide absolute proof. But the usefulness of deduction is limited in two ways. First, syllogisms only work because of the way in which the symbols (words or numbers) used within them are defined. Mathematical deduction can prove that two multiplied by two equals four, but this is because the number 4 is defined as 2×2 within mathematics. The statement merely says the same thing twice, in different ways; it is a **tautology**.

Second, the truth of the deduction depends absolutely on the truth of the proposition and the observation. How do we know these are true? Can we find a syllogism to prove the proposition contained in our syllogism? If so, can we find a syllogism to prove the proposition contained in this second syllogism? An infinite regress becomes necessary; we must keep digging to find the foundations upon which our foundations rest. In practice, the digging has to stop somewhere. The bedrock which eventually turns the logician's spade is called the **axiom**. This is the proposition, upon which the whole system sits, which is itself accepted as true without proof. An example of an axiom that most people accept in their daily lives is that the world is real, and not just a dream (how could you prove this axiom?). If the founding axiom(s) or subsequent proposition or observation are wrong, then our conclusion could be wrong. Crocodiles do lay eggs, but there are reptiles that give birth to live young. The syllogism above would mislead us because the proposition is incorrect.

Because sensory experiences can mislead us (think of how the world looks when you are drunk) some philosophers have believed that we must strive to understand absolute realities using just our reason, without any aid from the senses, a philosophical position known as **rationalism**. But as the conversation with my visitor, described at the start of this chapter, showed, the conclusions we reach using logic depend on our assumptions. Like a sycophantic celebrity photographer, rationality alone shows us only what we want to see. For cellulite-and-all reality, we need to consult sensory experience.

Induction and cause and effect

Deductive reasoning, as described above, starts from general propositions (all reptiles are cold blooded) and moves to specifics (*this* animal is cold blooded). **Inductive reasoning** reverses this. It uses sensory experience to make a specific observation (providing **empirical evidence**), and then tries to generalise. For example, based on the observation that a moving object (like a car) needs force to keep it moving (like the expansion of hot gases following the combustion of petrol), you might generalise that all objects will be still unless there is a force moving them.

Rather than just state this as an axiom, you go out and test it against experience. All the moving objects – bullets, balls, cars, marathon runners – that you observe do indeed come to rest if there is no force moving them, so it seems that there is considerable evidence to support your generalisation. After all, attempts to invent a perpetual motion machine have always failed.

So perhaps the evidence of our senses can lead us to proof? But a problem arises, first described by the philosopher Hume (see Box 1.1). Just how many moving objects do you have to observe before you conclude that your generalisation is proved? The more observations you have confirming your generalisation, the more confident you might be, but the possibility still exists that one day, somewhere, someone will make an observation that doesn't fit in. In the current example, if you stayed on the planet, years of observations could support your generalisation, but a single trip into space could quickly disillusion you. A football kicked in outer space will continue moving, at a constant speed and in a constant direction, potentially forever. On earth, forces such as friction and air resistance act against movement. In the absence of these forces, moving bodies go on moving. This is Isaac Newton's first Law of Motion, and it is the reason the sun rises in the morning; there is no force pushing the earth around its star. So inductive reasoning, based on the association between two things (such as movement and force) detected by sensory experience, can also lead us astray. Proof remains elusive.

1.2.4 Science as disproving things

Hume dealt a killer blow to claims that inductive logic can lead to proof. Billions of observations confirming a suggestion cannot prove that suggestion. All of science (and most of everyday life) relies on an unprovable belief that things tomorrow will follow the same natural laws as they did yesterday.

If we cannot prove things, how can knowledge progress? The answer to this that currently enjoys the most popularity within science was given by the Austrian philosopher Karl Popper in 1934. Popper recognised that proving a theory was impossible, and so argued that science could progress through the exact opposite; disproving theories. Consider that favourite scientific whodunnit, the riddle of the dinosaurs' demise. Why did such successful animals disappear so suddenly? One hypothesis is that their sudden extinction was caused by a vast asteroid colliding with the earth. If this is true, a number of predictions follow. For example, the collision must have created a crater, so we might expect to find evidence

Box 1.1 David Hume, the merry sceptic

On Edinburgh's Royal Mile a statue of a rather portly gentleman, confusingly dressed in an off-the-shoulder toga, watches the tourists with an expression of good humoured bemusement. Although the clothing is inappropriate for Scotland, the sculptor has got the personality just right; David Hume, an eighteenth century Scottish philosopher, saw the world as a pleasing but deeply mysterious place. Hume was fascinated by the question 'what is knowledge?' He recognised the power of logical deduction, describing how one type of knowledge (to do with what he called 'relations of ideas') could be demonstrated 'by the mere operation of thought, without dependence on what is anywhere existent in the universe'. Such knowledge could be sought in arithmetic and geometry. However, Hume was no rationalist; he knew that inductive reasoning, based on experience, was essential. But he also identified induction's major problems.

Stick your hand in a flame, and it will get burnt. If you are unfortunate enough to repeat this experiment a number of times, you are likely to confirm your original experience, and conclude that the flame causes the burn. Hume said this was because of a **constant conjunction** – the two things always seem to go together. But he identified two problems with this. First, just because two things always go together, we cannot conclude that one is the cause of the other; night follows day, but isn't caused by it. Second, even if one event has always followed (and been caused by) another in the past, we have no logical grounds for supposing that it will always do so in the future. We assume nature will remain the same, but can't prove it. Tomorrow, flames might not burn hands (if the hands belong to a mystic, who can happily walk on burning coals?). Following this line of reasoning, Hume develops a profound scepticism about the power of reason to justify any of our beliefs. He realises this presents him with a dilemma: he has used reason to reject reason; what can he do to dispel the confusion this creates? In the end 'I dine, I play a game of backgammon, I converse and am merry with my friends.' Hume did not think sceptics needed to be miserable.

of this. It would have thrown up clouds of dust, leaving a mark in the geological record, and so on. We could confirm these predictions without proving the hypothesis, for the reasons discussed above. However, suppose a stratum of rock was discovered dated five million years after the proposed impact, which contained dinosaur fossils. This would show that one prediction of the impact hypothesis, that the extinction must have happened very suddenly, was false. This single observation would disprove the hypothesis. Popper realised that whilst proof might be impossible, disproof (or **falsification**) was often straightforward – a single observation might be enough.

The question that started this chapter was: why were the views of my religious visitor less scientific than my own? I have already suggested one answer. His arguments were tautological; they referred back to their own internal logic, with no need to look outside at the evidence. Popper provides us with another, and more powerful, way to discriminate scientific from non-scientific views. He suggests that scientific theories must be open to falsification. They must make predictions which are open to disproof. Scientific theories are like mountaineers. The more improbably ambitious, original and risky the route they take, the better they are. Consider three economic hypotheses: 1. Free-market capitalism is the best way to global happiness and security. 2. Shares will increase in value next year. 3. Shares in Walt Disney will increase by 40% in value in the next two months. According to Popper, hypothesis 1 could never be considered scientific – it would be impossible to disprove. Hypothesis 2 is scientific, in that it could be falsified, but it does not take many risks; shares somewhere are likely to go up in value at some time next year, so it is not much use. Hypothesis 3 is much more daring. It makes a specific prediction which could easily be disproved, and because of this it is the best of the three hypotheses in terms of its scientific content.

1.3 A taxonomy of terms

We have too many things, and not enough forms. G. Flaubert

I have been discussing hypotheses, theories and ideas as if they were interchangeable, but these words mean different things. Figure 1.1 shows a simplified description of the relationships between these central terms in science. Different authors use these words in different ways; the distinctions between a law and a theory, and a hypothesis and a model are particularly hazy. However, most scientists would agree with the relative positions of the terms shown in Figure 1.1.

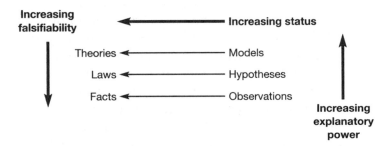

Figure 1.1 A simplified description of the relationships between six key terms in science.

1.3.1 Facts – was Descartes' head a glass pumpkin?

The intellectual cul-de-sac into which rationality alone can lead us means that science must be based on observations of the real world. These observations are, we hope, factual. But a simple observation might not be true. For example, I can observe the book about the great seventeenth century French philosopher René Descartes sitting on my bookshelf; I take it as a fact that it is there. But it was Descartes, above all, who pointed out reasons to be suspicious. As he argued, he was certain that 'these hands and body are mine' except that he could think of people who thought they were kings, or that their heads were glass pumpkins. Such people were mad, but clearly their sensory impressions were letting them down; maybe his were too? In some sense, all observations are interpretations. To describe a poppy as red is to make an interpretation of the world which will be shared with most people (although not those who are colour blind) but not with bees, who would interpret the poppy quite differently as they observe it through compound eyes sensitive to ultraviolet light. When we are using instruments, such as thermometers or microscopes, for observation, then the possibility arises that they also 'interpret' the world, possibly in misleading ways. For example, the temperature of the open ocean was traditionally measured in water collected in canvas buckets. The readings were consistently lower than expected – the fact of the temperature contradicted the expectations of global warming models (see Chapter 5). Eventually it was realised that evaporation from the sides of the buckets was lowering the temperature; the 'fact' was rejected. So scientists need to be suspicious of observations, and not too quick to give them the title of facts.

1.3.2 Laws

> The laws of gravity are very, very strict, and you're just bending them for your own benefit. B. Bragg

In Egypt, smoking cannabis is tolerated, but drinking alcohol is deviant. Cross the border to Israel, and the laws change; alcohol is accepted, cannabis forbidden. Laws created by humans are specific to particular cultures, and can be broken. Scientific laws cannot be broken (they cannot even be bent), and if they are true they apply universally, or at least wherever the conditions covered by the law apply. They cannot be more or less strict, only true or false (although they can be more or less *precise*; all laws are approximations at some level). This is a heavy burden of responsibility to bear, so the scientific community only confers the title 'law' to an idea or generalisation for which there is a great deal of evidence. New or poorly tested ideas are usually called **hypotheses** – these are 'apprentice laws'. Nearly all scientific advances, at whatever level, begin by conjecturing new hypotheses.

Scientific laws predict and explain facts, usually by linking two or more variables together using mathematics. Isaac Newton's Laws of Motion provide the classic example; they predict the movements of the planets – and all other objects – when acted on by some force. They explain the fact that a motorbike is harder to push from standing than a bicycle, by mathematically relating acceleration (getting the thing going) to the force required and the mass involved (acceleration = force divided by mass; bicycles are much lighter than motorbikes). Although even Newton's laws are only approximately correct under some conditions (particularly for subatomic particles moving at very high speeds), they deserve to be called laws, rather than hypotheses, because they have been successfully tested so many times.

Whilst it is easy to find examples of laws in physics and chemistry, the same cannot be said for the environmental sciences, where most hypotheses are yet to graduate to the level of laws.

1.3.3 Theories

Theories destroy facts. P. Medawar

Before attempting to push either a motorbike or a bicycle, it is best to inflate the tyres. To do this, you need to increase the air pressure in the pump by decreasing the volume available for that air. One of the first physical laws to be described predicts the relationship between pressure and volume in your pump. If you halve the volume, you will double the pressure. This is Boyle's Law (discovered by the seventeenth century English chemist Robert Boyle), and can be simply stated as:

pressure × volume = a constant value (at any given temperature)

This law predicts an infinite number of possible observations on the pressure and volume of gases, and explains any given volume in terms of the pressure on a gas, but does not explain *why* gases should behave like this. For the next level of explanation, we need to look to theories.

While laws predict and explain facts, theories predict and explain laws. The theory of molecular motion explains Boyle's Law by describing molecules as tiny particles, whizzing about and colliding with each other. If you reduce the area available for movement, there will be more collisions, leading to a higher pressure. Theories are more general than laws. Whilst the theory of molecular motion can explain Boyle's Law, it also explains many other observations. For example, temperature also affects the pressure of a gas; this is explained by relating temperature to the average speed of the molecules. As it gets colder, they slow down, so the pressure they exert by colliding into the walls of a container (such as the main vessel of a bicycle pump) is reduced, because there are fewer collisions per unit time.

Are theories in the environmental sciences 'weak'?

Once again, it is easier to find 'strong' theories (those that have been carefully tested, and are yet to be falsified) in physics and chemistry textbooks than in environmental science literature. This is probably due to three things:

- **Maturity.** Many of the disciplines that form an important part of environmental science, such as ecology and meteorology, are relatively new sciences and are still developing rapidly (see Box 1.2).
- **Complexity.** The systems that physicists and chemists study are relatively simple. If a chemist is interested in understanding a chlorine atom, she can be pretty confident that what she knows about one atom will apply to another (under the same conditions); the atoms of most elements come in only one (or a very few) types. But living things are different, because all the individuals within a species are different from each other – you can't assume one chimpanzee will behave like another. Not only is there infinite variety at any one time, there is also change through time because living things evolve and learn. So any sciences dealing with living things must cope with much more variability, which makes prediction harder.
- **Sample size.** All scientific theories deal with **probabilities** and can thus be described as **probabilistic** (see section 1.5). Another way of putting this is to say that they look for average properties of things, and are therefore vulnerable to small sample sizes. As an example, consider the biological theory that explains why girls and boys are born with (roughly) equal probability (i.e. there is a 50% chance of a mother having either a girl or a boy). If you found that 100% of the eight births this year in the village where you live were girls, would there be reasons to suspect the theory (or to look for something in the water?). Maybe, but the probability of this happening by chance is quite high – 1 in 256 (see Figure 1.2). In contrast, if you lived in a town, and found that all the 800 births this year in the maternity ward there were girls, you might want to drink only bottled water. The probability of this arising by chance is 1 in a quadrillion (1 with 24 noughts) – so small that it is for all practical purposes the same as being impossible.

  So having large sample sizes allows us to test for average properties easily, without the problems of finding strange results just by chance. Physicists and chemists usually have enormous sample sizes. Although

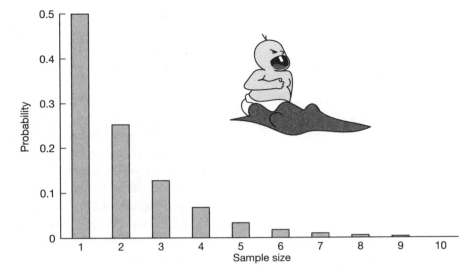

Figure 1.2 It's a girl! But the chances of all the babies in a random group being girls decline rapidly with sample size, as this plot of probability against sample size shows. If there really is a 50% chance of any baby being a girl, the probability of having 100% girls in any randomly chosen group of 10 babies is less than 1 in 1000

Boyle's Law only deals with the average properties of gas molecules, the sample sizes available mean that it is reliable – there are approximately six hundred trillion (6 with 20 noughts) molecules of gas in a bicycle pump. When I push the handle, I know that the average behaviour of the molecules will provide a very good description of how the pressure will change. In contrast, the environmental sciences often have small sample sizes (perhaps only a few individuals of a rare species), making conclusions more susceptible to chance events.

So in the environmental sciences many of the theories are tentative and deserve to be treated with considerable suspicion. These areas of science are still in the condition referred to by Flaubert – there are many facts, with few secure theories in which to house them. The often ramshackle and temporary shelters which have to do are better described as models.

1.3.4 Models

Sometimes models in science might be similar to human models on a catwalk; they are physical objects which have characteristics useful for the modeller. For example, researchers in the neurosciences talk about using the giant nerve or axon of squid as a model for the investigation of all axons, because these nerve cells happen to be particularly large and easy to manipulate in squid. In such cases, the models are used as exemplars of the system of interest. Usually, however, models are intellectual constructs

11

which may be on the way to being theories (they are 'apprentice theories'), or may be too specific to be considered theories – dealing, for example, with the effects of pollution at one particular site, rather than with pollution effects in general (see section 1.7 and Chapter 9). A central purpose of models and theories is to simplify reality; a good model of a Boeing 747 does not have to fly – it just has to emphasise and illustrate the particular features of interest. Similarly, simple scientific models might be better than complex ones, because they are easier to understand and they emphasise what is important. If they are designed for practical applications, then they will also be easier to apply in practice (see Chapter 7).

By simplifying reality, theories and models 'destroy facts', as Peter Medawar put it. For example, there has been a reduction of approximately 8% in ice cover in the northern hemisphere in the last 25 years. There are increasing frequencies of pest outbreaks in Alaskan forests. Global atmospheric concentrations of CO_2 have increased by 26% in the last 300 years. The current decade has included five of the warmest years on record. What could link all these facts? The theory of global climate change (see Chapter 5). If the current models that attempt to describe climate change evolve to become powerful predictive tools, there will be no need to catalogue the immense number of facts related to the phenomenon – the important outcomes will be predicted by the models.

1.3.5 What makes a good model or good theory?

If a theory, model or hypothesis is non-tautological, it must rely on empirical evidence. But there are an infinite number of ways in which any data set could be interpreted. Remember the different hypotheses put forward to

---

Box 1.2 A simplified description of how a scientific field develops

- **Stage 1**. People take interest in certain phenomena and realise that they are related.
- **Stage 2**. A taxonomy of terms and shared definitions emerges.
- **Stage 3**. Careful observations begin to show how the phenomena are related.
- **Stage 4**. Experiments manipulate variables, and help establish causal mechanisms for the observed relationships.
- **Stage 5**. Laws are discovered which form the foundations for general theories, which are further tested by experiments.
- **Stage 6**. An established body of theory can be used to resolve problems, and suggest new hypotheses.

Adapted from Cohen and Manion 1994.

explain the visibility of stars at the start of this chapter. So we need criteria by which to judge scientific theories, models and hypotheses. Many such criteria have been proposed for use within the environmental sciences (see for example Peters (1991) and Schrader-Frechette and McCoy (1993)). Here, I summarise four of the most important:

Prediction

Many scientists consider predictive power as the essential criterion dividing science from non-science. Following Popper (see section 1.2.4), scientific theories should make falsifiable predictions. This provides the ultimate 'reality-check'. The more precise and specific those predictions are, the easier it will be to determine whether they have been falsified.

Explanation

Not all sciences are equally predictive. Physics has attained a high degree of predictive power, whilst sciences such as ecology and economics are only capable of fairly weak, vague predictions. This does not imply that the latter subjects are not sciences at all; their weakness in relation to the 'traditional' sciences of physics and chemistry might arise for many reasons (see section 1.3.3).

An alternative goal for such sciences might be explanatory power. One of the best examples of how predictive and explanatory power do not always coincide is the theory of evolution by natural selection. Few, if any, specific and falsifiable predictions can be made based on this theory (see Peters 1991, p. 60). However, it convincingly explains an enormous range of disparate facts; in particular, it provides the best explanation for the majority of cases of adaptation in the natural world. The danger with explanation as a criterion for science is that it is possible to take the same facts and explain them in very different ways – witness the different interpretations of astronomical evidence at the start of this chapter. This is why specific predictions are useful. However, the theory of evolution by natural selection explains not only physical adaptations, but is also consistent with evidence from geology, palaeontology, astronomy, psychology, ethology, genetics, molecular biology and other disciplines. It is this convergence of evidence that makes this explanation so convincing. Compare that to a non-scientific subject that also seeks explanation, such as history. Many historians have argued that an important explanation for the Second World War was the policy of appeasement pursued by other European states towards Nazi Germany. Yet no historian would expect to find that all wars are caused by appeasement, or that appeasement always leads to war. Such historical explanations tend to be for unique events.

Generality

Theories that predict and explain over a wide range of conditions are preferable to those that are limited in scope, since they 'kill more facts'. There are over 100 000 different chemicals in use in the European Union, making comprehensive toxicological testing of all of them an impossibility (see Chapter 8). A theory that can predict the toxicology of many different types of chemical (based, for example, on how they concentrate rising up food chains) is clearly preferable to a theory that deals with just one chemical. An additional advantage of a general theory is that, because it predicts over a wider range of circumstances, it allows more opportunities for falsification.

Simplicity

> Seek simplicity, but distrust it. A.N.Whitehead.

Simple theories are preferable to complex ones, all else being equal. This is mainly a matter of convenience; a simple theory will be better understood and easier to use than a complex one. Again, simple theories are often easier to falsify than complex ones; if the testing of a theory, model or hypothesis requires measurement of many different variables, errors are more likely to occur, making the theory more difficult to falsify.

1.4 So what is a scientific theory?

This chapter opened with the question 'what do we mean by a scientific explanation?' A summary of our approach to answering this is provided below (for further reading, see Richards 1987):

- Deduction is a route to knowledge that relies on logic alone – it is not dependent on sensory experience. Although it can provide logical proofs, these are open to the dangers of tautology and may rest on erroneous axioms.
- In contrast, induction uses empirical evidence to draw conclusions; it is therefore central to scientific reasoning. However, Hume demonstrated how induction could never lead to absolute certainty.
- Recognising the problems inherent in finding proof, Popper proposed that scientists should instead attempt to disprove (or falsify) hypotheses.
- Following Popper, most scientists believe that an essential definition of scientific theories and hypotheses is that they should make predictions that can be falsified. They should also be as general and simple as possible.

Science, then, is based on ideas that can be, or have been, tested against reality, in ways that can be repeated and scrutinised by others. The next part of this chapter looks at some of the main approaches to testing ideas used in the environmental sciences.

1.5 The probabilistic nature of science

The sign of a truly civilised person is to be deeply moved by statistics.
                                                                    G.B. Shaw

'Smoking Causes Cancer' is one slogan decorating cigarette boxes in Britain. As a statement of fact, it has impeccable scientific credentials, backed by years of research. But my grandmother Jill enjoyed her first unfiltered, tar-rich inhalation as a teenager, and continued smoking until the age of 86 when she died of heart failure. So smoking did not cause cancer in her case. Clearly, the truth of a statement like this is different from that of a logical tautology (as we have seen) but also from that of an observation relying on 'Humean causality' (a 'constant conjunction' of cause and effect, like Hume's example of fire and heat). Although there is no constant conjunction between smoking and cancer (because smoking does not always lead to cancer) there is nevertheless a strong **statistical association**. Most of the theories of interest to environmental science rely on this second kind of causality, because the causes of the phenomena of interest might be multiple, complex and operating at a distance – in time or space – from their effects. To deal with this complicated situation, scientists rely on the methods of statistics.

1.5.1 How to test hypotheses

Statistical techniques are applied to the results of investigations that attempt to test in some way the hypothesis of interest. An idealised description of what happens during hypothesis testing is given in Figure 1.3. First of all, there is a worldview or perspective which means that certain observations are made. In this case, people are sufficiently interested in frogs and other amphibians (for whatever reasons) to notice that they seem to be declining worldwide. Models are proposed to account for this decline, and hypotheses made based on these models. For example, some people believe that depletion of stratospheric ozone has led to increased levels of ultraviolet (UV) radiation at ground level, and that this may be responsible for the decline. A possible hypothesis arising from this model is that raised levels of UV are reducing the number of eggs that hatch successfully. Before we can test this hypothesis, a philosophical problem arises. As Popper showed, it is impossible to prove a hypothesis. To

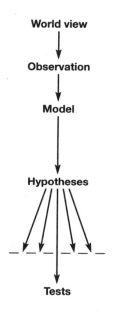

World view   An interest in amphibians, for many possible reasons

Observation   An apparent worldwide decline in amphibian populations

Model   An intellectual construct, involving a few or many factors, which attemps to explain the decline. For example, the speculation that thinning stratospheric ozone is the ultimate cause for the decline

Hypotheses   Testable predictions arising from the model, such as exposing amphibian eggs to raised levels of ultraviolet radiation will reduce hatching success

Tests   The hypotheses are put through the 'filter' of a formal test. If a 5% significance level is used, there is only a 1 in 20 chance of the hypothesis surviving the test – that is, of it not being rejected – when in fact it is wrong

Figure 1.3 A highly simplified illustration of the origins and testing of scientific hypothesis; the example in this case is the worldwide decline in amphibians.

side-step this issue, scientists define the logical opposite of the hypothesis of interest (called the **null hypothesis**), and attempt to *disprove* this. Here, the null hypothesis is that the relevant levels of UV have no effect on hatching rates, and the opposing hypothesis is simply that UV does affect hatching success. If the null hypothesis can be disproved, then the hypothesis of interest might be true. After testing the null hypothesis, the information gained can be used to further refine the models, and thus generate new hypotheses.

1.5.2 Labelling errors – the logic of statistical testing

To err is human. To demonstrate at least associate membership of the human race, statisticians also make errors, although formally only of two kinds (and not to be confused with mistakes). In statistics, a **Type I error** is when you accept a hypothesis that is untrue (i.e. you reject a null hypothesis that is true). A **Type II error** is the opposite: rejecting a true hypothesis. The more cautious you are about the first, the more likely you are to commit the second. The central task of statistics is that of attaching probabilities to the two types of error. Deciding on the best balance between the two is a matter of judgement, not of science, and should depend on the consequences of making each type of error (see Box 1.3 and Chapter 2).

Box 1.3 Blaise bets on salvation

When the brilliant seventeenth century French scientist Blaise Pascal was not busy laying the foundations of probability theory or hydrodynamics, he searched for truths through biblical study and mysticism. For him, there was no contradiction between science and religion. But there were already plenty of sceptics who disagreed, so Pascal looked for a rational argument to demonstrate the importance of faith. He found inspiration in his pioneering work on the statistics of gambling, and developed his famous theological argument: Pascal's Wager. His logic was simple: why not bet our lives on the hypothesis that God exists? If it is false, we lose little by living a life of piety. If it's true, we gain eternal bliss.

The Wager is a warning against Type II error. Pascal believed that the consequences of erroneously rejecting the hypothesis that God exists are much greater than those of erroneously accepting the hypothesis, so we should prefer Type II to Type I error in this case. Given Pascal's founding interest in Type II error, it is ironic that most modern statistical routines are designed to measure Type I error only (see Chapter 2).

By tradition, the results of statistical tests are termed 'significant' if the chance of Type I error is no more than 5% (the 'alpha level' of the test is set at 0.05). This arbitrary cut-off point was first proposed by the inventor of many of the most important modern statistical tests, R. Fisher:

If one in twenty does not seem high enough odds, we may ... draw the line at one in fifty (the 2% point) or one in a hundred (the 1% point). Personally, the writer prefers to set a low standard of significance at the 5% point, and ignore entirely all results which fail to reach that level.

This has important implications for the 'truth' of scientific investigations that use statistics. Suppose a series of experiments were run to test the hypothesis 'being called Jill protects you against cancer'. If our Type I error level was set at 5% (as is normally the case) we would expect 1 out of 20 (or 2 out of 40, etc.) investigations designed to test this hypothesis to suggest that the name Jill provided statistically significant protection from cancer, *simply by chance* (provided, of course, that being called Jill does *not* actually affect a person's chance of suffering from cancer). This is one reason why most hypotheses are not accepted on the basis of just one or a few experiments.

The rest of this section deals with some common designs used to test null hypotheses and to explore patterns in nature. Analysing environmental data can be complex and describing particular approaches is beyond this book (see Pentecost (1999) for an introduction). However, the underlying logic of the approach is more important than the particular techniques being used. No amount of advanced statistics will save a logically flawed study (although statistics may be used to disguise the flaw). So

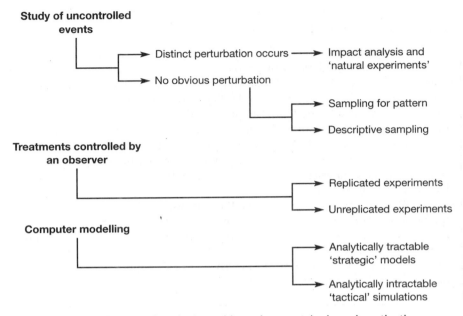

Figure 1.4 A classification of methods used in environmental science investigations.
Adapted from Eberhardt and Thomas 1991.

logical design is the most important aspect of any scientific study. Methods can be placed in one of three categories (Figure 1.4).

1.5.3 Sampling and correlation

Descriptive sampling is often the first part of any study. For example, a first step in studying the ecology of the common cockle (*Cerastoderma edule*, a bivalve mollusc that lives buried in intertidal sediments) may be to discover how common or rare it is at the field site. Since it is impossible simply to go out and count all the individuals at the site, a sampling procedure must be devised. Unless the underlying distribution is known, a high number of randomly taken samples is the best approach (Figure 1.5). While descriptive sampling such as this can give a more or less accurate estimate of a variable, such as density per m², it cannot explain anything about that variable – how and why it changes with time or space, for example.

To investigate what causes patterns in nature, at least two variables must be recorded. If these variables are associated in a reliable fashion, we can say they are **correlated**. The techniques of correlation (and related statistics) allow the testing of hypotheses. For example, during the descriptive work above, the ecologist might have noticed that the density of the cockles varied dramatically from place to place, and seemed to be higher in

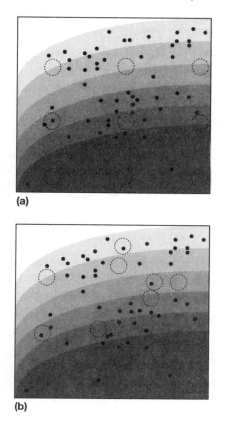

(a)

(b)

Figure 1.5 Cockles (the black dots) live buried in the sand. How many are there? This figure illustrates two approaches to finding out: (a) regular sampling, (b) random sampling. Because the cockles themselves are not randomly distributed (they tend to avoid the dark, muddier sand), regular sampling gives an inaccurate estimate because the sample sites (dashed circles) happen to coincide with areas of low density. The possibility of such unknown, underlying patterns makes random sampling (b) a better option.

areas where she did not sink so far into the sediment. This might generate a hypothesis: that cockles prefer to live in sandy, firm sediment rather than in muddy, 'sinky' sediment. This hypothesis could be tested by taking random samples of cockles along with samples of the sediment in which they are living, and plotting the number of individuals found against the average grain size of the sediment (Figure 1.6).

Figure 1.6 shows a statistically significant, positive correlation between density and grain size. That is, there is less than a 5% chance that the relationship shown occurred purely by chance. The hypothesis has not been falsified – it might be true! Note the importance of sample size. A small sample of data which is highly scattered, like this, can give a false impression.

19

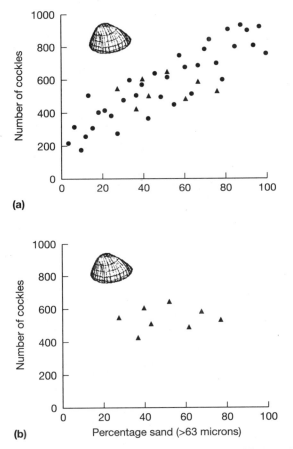

(a)

(b)

Percentage sand (>63 microns)

Figure 1.6 Cockles prefer sandier sediments, as the highly significant relationship in (a) shows. However, there is considerable scatter (or variability) in the data – individual data points often lie far away from the average value. This means that if we took a smaller sample size of the same data – as in (b) – the true relationship might not be apparent.

TV saves lives?

A global correlation of average number of hours of TV watched per day against average life expectancy gives a positive correlation. But this does not imply that watching TV makes you healthier. Instead, there is a **confounding variable** (poverty), a variable which correlates with both the other factors and which is the true causal agent of the apparent link (identifying these confounding variables can be very difficult – see Chapter 10 for some examples). Most people in the world are too poor to afford a television, and have nowhere to plug it in even if they had one; their relatively low life expectancy is caused by their poverty, not by their lack of TVs. So correlation in itself can never demonstrate cause (as Hume realised). Cockles actually live happily in muddy sediment, but so do crabs (*Carcinus maenus*), one of their most important predators. The correlation shown in

Figure 1.6 arises because crabs are not so successful in sandy sediments. The cause of this pattern is not sediment grain size itself, but the behaviour of crabs, which is related to grain size. Some sciences, such as astronomy, rely entirely on searching for patterns (such as correlations between two variables) in nature. Most sciences, however, can take a step further; they can conduct experiments to manipulate one or more variables of interest.

1.6 Experiments

Experiments provide the most important means by which scientists can test the predictions of theories and hypotheses. Although the word experiment is sometimes used to describe sampling investigations, it is best kept for cases where some intervention has occurred, i.e. one or more variables have been manipulated. Experiments may be replicated or unreplicated (Figure 1.4).

1.6.1 Replicated experiments

40% of children will use drugs. Scotland Against Drugs

Large amounts of money are spent on health education programmes every year. But do these campaigns actually work? The best way to find out is to adopt an experimental approach, using the same logic as any scientific experiment. Suppose you were asked to determine if a new way of teaching teenagers about the dangers of drug abuse led to a change in attitude to drugs. You could set up an experiment as follows: 1. Record the attitudes (perhaps using a questionnaire) of a class of teenagers towards drug use. 2. Expose the class to the drugs education pack. 3. Record the teenagers' attitudes again, and see if they have changed. Consider how you might interpret the possible outcomes of this experiment (Table 1.1).

So the experiment cannot tell you anything useful, because there are many possible interpretations other than 1 and 5. Interpretation 3 is possible if there are doubts about the chosen methods for measuring attitudes; such doubts are present in all scientific experiments. It is always possible that the instruments used (whether they are questionnaires or telescopes) give false readings (see section 1.3.1). Experimenters must use their judgement to choose the most reliable instruments to reduce this element of doubt. The other ambiguities in interpretation arise because of failings in experimental design. Ideally, only the variable(s) of interest, in this case the exposure of students to the drugs education, should change during the course of an experiment. However, this is generally impossible, for two reasons. First, the act of running the experiment itself will cause some changes. These are called **artefacts**, and could result in very erroneous conclusions (see interpretation 4). Even the act of observing something can cause

21

Table 1.1 Interpreting the results of an experiment to measure the success of a drug education programme

Result	Interpretation
Students become more critical of drug use	1. The education programme has worked.
	2. Some unrelated factor (one of the teenagers in the group was arrested for drug use?) has changed attitudes.
	3. Attitudes have not changed at all: students are simply telling you what they think you want to hear.
	4. Attitudes have changed because of the experimental procedure, not because of the education. For example, if the students were asked to complete a questionnaire about their beliefs concerning drugs, this may have caused them to reflect closely on drug use, leading them to change their beliefs.
Students become less critical of drug use	5. The education programme has failed.
	6. Without the education programme, the students would have been even less critical of drug use, because some other factor (a pop song praising drugs?) has changed their attitudes.

artefacts – consider your behaviour when you are alone, compared with when you think you are being observed. Second, as with correlations (section 1.5.3) **confounding factors**, extrinsic to the experiment and beyond the control of the experimenter (such as the release of a pop song), may also change during the course of the experiment. Experiments invalidated by these are said to be **confounded** (see Chapter 6). To deal with these problems, experiments need the design features discussed below: controls, replication and independence.

Controls

The design should include a control as well as a treatment group. That is, there should be a group that is not exposed to the drugs education, but which is exposed to all the other relevant variables, both artefactual and extrinsic. In this case, the control group should be as closely matched (in age, gender, economic and social background, etc.) as possible to the treatment group, which is the best way of ensuring they will be influenced in the same way as the treatment group by extrinsic factors (such as pop songs). The control group should also be exposed to the same experimental procedure (filling in questionnaires at the same times as the treatment group), thus introducing the same artefacts to them. Using controls allows comparisons to be made at the end of the experiment between the control and treatment groups, rather than relying on a before/after comparison of the single treatment group.

Replication

Introducing a control allows comparisons to be made, but it is possible that the control or treatment group may be unusual in some way. For example, if the treatment group happened to have a charismatic teacher, attitudes in this group might change compared with the control group because of this, and not because of the particular educational technique of interest. However, if we had ten treatment and control groups, chosen randomly (see Figure 1.5), it is most unlikely that the treatment groups will all happen to have particularly charismatic teachers, and the control groups particularly poor ones. So this would be a much better design. The results could be analysed by comparing mean differences between the control and treatment groups.

Independence

A good experimental design will ensure that the replicates (of treatments and controls) are independent. Consider running the experiment in a single large school, with five classes as treatments and five as controls. It is likely that students in the control groups will have sisters, brothers and friends in the treatment groups, and will therefore hear from them details of the education that the treatment groups are receiving. This could affect the behaviour of students in the control groups, making the experiment invalid (for example, if the control group students reduced their drug use because what they heard from their friends was so effective, the experimental results would suggest that the education was *not* effective, since there would be no, or little, difference between control and treatment groups). Similarly, if students in the treatment groups have friends in other treatment groups, they are likely to talk about the scheme to each other. Something unique to one group may 'contaminate' the others. For example, there may be a poor teacher in one group who exaggerates the dangers of drugs ('smoking cannabis leads to madness and death'). This could make the students in that group cynical, and they could communicate their cynicism to the other groups. In this case, the treatment groups are not true replicates (they are '**pseudoreplicates**').

To achieve independence, the best replicates may be classes from different schools, in different cities. A fundamental problem arises here for experimenters. The further apart the replicates are, the more likely they are to be independent, but the less likely they are to share the same characteristics (the same social and economic backgrounds, for example). This does have the advantage that it increases the scope (or **statistical domain**) of the experiment. If the treatment works in an experiment involving boys and girls, rich and poor, black and white, then it is an effective treatment. If the experiment was restricted to, for example, private boys' schools, then it would not be legitimate to assume that the results were relevant to other

23

types of school. In statistical language, replicates should be a random, representative sub-sample of the sample population. If you want to test whether a treatment works in all types of school, then you need to include all types within your replicate treatments and controls. However, increasing the diversity of background conditions is likely to increase the diversity of responses to the treatment (perhaps rich students will react more strongly than poor ones?), leading to increased variability in the experimental results. Increasing variability leads to an increase in the chances of Type II error (see Figure 1.6 and Box 1.4). The best way of reducing the chance of this is to increase the number of replicates (and therefore the time and cash needed for the experiment), because this will reduce the probability of making erroneous conclusions based on chance effects. See Table 1.2 for a summary of these factors.

1.6.2 Unreplicated experiments

The units of interest to environmental scientists are often large and difficult or impossible to replicate. For example, studying how the populations of fish on a coral reef recover once fishing on the reef is abolished may help to manage ocean fisheries (see Chapter 7). Because it is the whole ecosystem that is of interest here, the ideal is to run any experiments at this scale. Conducting experiments at smaller scales (for example in containers holding a representative sub-sample of the species found in the reef) will involve many artefacts (perhaps the behaviour of fish in tanks is very different from those in the wild?). But keeping fishers from an entire reef is a very expensive and politically difficult task. Doing the same with four or five replicate reefs, and monitoring four or five controls, is likely to be impossible for most researchers. Practical considerations like this may mean that experiments have only a single treatment and a single control. Sometimes, even controls are impossible. Suppose you wanted to study

Table 1.2 Checklist of the basic ingredients of a good scientific experiment

- Are there controls?
- Are there replicates of both treatments and controls?
- Are all the replicates genuinely independent of each other? If not, then they are not true replicates.
- Are the replicates chosen randomly from the sample population of interest? If the experiment is designed to test hypotheses about a large sample population (e.g. all types of secondary school) then the replicates must be selected from this population, not from a smaller, and probably cheaper, sub-population.
- What is the power of the experiment? If it fails to find an effect, is this because there really is not one, or is it because of Type II error arising from insufficient power?

Box 1.4 Is the experiment worth doing?

The chance of an experiment or survey detecting a real effect of a given size at a given level of statistical significance depends on the **power** of the experiment. Power analysis is a statistical procedure which determines this power in any given case (in other words, it determines the chances of Type II error), and can tell us whether an experiment is worth running at all. In general, the power of any experiment will decrease with:

- decreasing size of experimental effects (i.e. decreasing differences between treatments and controls)
- decreasing numbers of replicates
- increasing variability in the results
- increasing number of experimental variables (factors of interest)

For example, consider the suggestion that weak electromagnetic fields, such as those produced by power lines, can cause cancer. Usually, testing such hypotheses involves experiments on animals or epidemiological studies (see Chapter 10). But both of these have problems. If we did not care about costs and ethics, we could use human beings as our guinea pigs. Imagine that a cruel dictator with an interest in medical science decides to test the hypothesis that long-term exposure to electromagnetic fields increases the risk of cancer in humans by 1% per year. He designs an experiment which involves exposing replicate treatment groups of 1000 people to electromagnetic fields (perhaps by building houses for them under pylon lines), and comparing the mean rate of cancer in these groups with that found in replicate control groups, kept in villages without electricity, after leaving both groups for ten years to allow the cancers time to develop. How many replicates will he have to use? The information he needs is (figures based on cancer rates in Scotland 1995):

- The mean background rate of deaths per year from cancer in the population – approximately 2.9 deaths per 1000 people.
- The variance associated with this mean – 1.95. (Although the average number of deaths per 1000 people might be 2.9, if you selected any given group of 1000 people the actual number of deaths is likely to be different from this. The variance provides a measure of this 'scatter' around the mean.)
- The effect level – in this case, an increased risk of 1%, so if the hypothesis is true, average rates in the treatment groups will be 2.929%.

A 'rule of thumb' for experimental power is that there should be at least an 80% chance of detecting a significant difference if one really exists. To achieve this level of power, the dictator would need 4200 groups of 1000 people – over 4 million people! And even then there would be a 20% chance of making a Type II error. There are many more powerful and realistic experiments the dictator could spend his gold on.

the diving behaviour of a whale species. If you were very determined and lucky, you might be able to find a whale and attach a radio transmitter to it, so that you could track its movements. Of course, it is possible that carrying a transmitter will change the normal behaviour of the animal (an experimental artefact). Only by tracking control animals, without transmitters, could you tell for sure, but of course it would be impossible to do so.

Such constraints mean that some experiments cannot be controlled or replicated. This does not invalidate their results; they may be more valuable than properly replicated experiments that are conducted at inappropriate scales. However, it does mean that the results of such experiments need to be treated with caution. Without replication, it is difficult to know whether the system being studied is representative or unique.

1.6.3 Impact analysis and 'natural' experiments

Much of environmental science is concerned with identifying human impacts on nature. Often, manipulative experiments such as those described above are impossible because the impacts are not controlled by the scientist (see Chapter 8 for examples). Consider the following example. A new factory begins discharging chemicals into a river. Does this discharge have a harmful effect on mayfly larvae living in the river? It is not possible (or desirable) to create more replicate pollution sources in other rivers, so there is no replication of the 'treatment' here. The following approaches might be adopted (see Underwood 1996, 1997 for more details):

1. Uncontrolled before/after design (Figure 1.7a)

If samples were taken from the river before the factory opened, the average abundances of mayflies can be compared before and after the discharges began. A decline in abundance could indicate an impact by the discharge. The problem with this design is that it is uncontrolled. Mayfly populations might have declined anyway, so the results of this study would be inconclusive.

2. Controlled before/after design (Figure 1.7b)

The solution to the problem in 1. is to use control sites. Although there are no replicates available for the treatment sites, every effort should be made to replicate control sites. Note that control sites do not have to be identical to the treatment site (after all, no two sites are ever exactly the same). All that is required is that they are representative of the variables of interest; in this case, that they all contain similar populations of the mayfly. Samples taken at the same time before the factory was opened should be compared

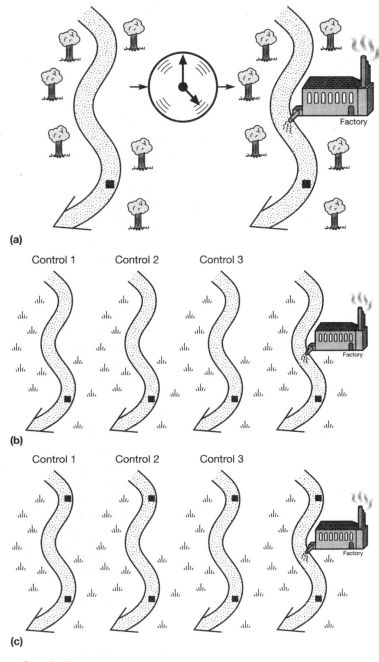

(a)

Control 1   Control 2   Control 3

(b)

Control 1   Control 2   Control 3

(c)

■ Sample sites

Figure 1.7 Three approaches to measuring the impact of a discharge on a river. (a) shows a simple before/after design, with no replication or controls. Designs comparing control rivers with the affected one are better (b), but could be improved by using an above/below design with replicated controls (c).

with samples taken simultaneously after opening. If there is a significant difference between the way in which the population in the treatment site responds, compared with the populations in the control sites, then there is strong evidence of an impact.

3. Upstream/downstream design

The sample designs described in 1. and 2. are not always possible. If the chemical discharge occurred as an accident, rather than a planned waste disposal, there would be no prior warning. Samples of mayfly populations from before the accident might not be available, so no comparison with the present populations would be possible. It may also be impossible to find a control site (perhaps the mayflies are very rare, and restricted to this one stream?). An alternative approach is to use an upstream/downstream design. A site above the discharge is selected to act as a control for the site below. A significant decrease in mean abundances between the two sites is evidence of an impact.

4. Replicated upstream/downstream design (Figure 1.7c)

The design in 3. suffers from the usual problems of no replication – how much would we expect the mayfly population to change between two sites on the same river, regardless of any impacts? If it is possible to find control sites, then these could provide comparisons; upstream/downstream sites, separated by similar distances to that between the sites in the treatment river, could be sampled. But another problem arises with upstream/downstream designs. Since there will be drift of animals down the current, it is possible that the upstream and downstream sites are not independent. Large populations of mayflies above the accident spot or discharge could result in large samples being taken below it, because animals are being washed down by the current, leading to the conclusion of no effect even if there is one (i.e. Type II error). So care needs to be taken to avoid non-independence. Statistical tests that allow for this could be used. Alternatively, all the control rivers could be divided into two groups, and upstream data taken from one with downstream data from the other.

These examples are not specific to rivers – designs 1. and 2. could be used in any habitat, whilst designs 3. and 4. are appropriate whenever there is an 'upstream/downstream' situation (for example, strong ocean currents, prevailing winds and hillsides). Although the event being investigated is beyond the scientist's control, and no replicates of it are available, there are many ways in which sampling can be designed to improve confidence in the results.

1.7 Computer models and simulations

Everything that is complex is useless; everything that is simple is false.

P. Valery

How will the earth's climate respond to increasing concentrations of CO_2 (Chapter 5)? What is likely to happen to the ecosystem of the North Sea under increased nutrient loads (Chapter 9)? If high level nuclear waste is to be stored underground, how deep, and in what location, should the hole be (Chapter 10)? These and many other pressing environmental issues share several important characteristics: they are too big and complex for direct experimentation, or for intuition, or for past experience to provide a reliable guide for action. The most successful and powerful solution to this problem has come through the use of computer models. There are many different kinds of computer model, but a useful distinction can be made between 'strategic' models and 'tactical' simulations.

Strategic **models** are those that are open to mathematical analysis. That is, they are simple enough to allow standard mathematical procedures to analyse their behaviour. Examples include the original Maximum Sustainable Yield models used to calculate how many fish can be safely taken from a population (see Chapter 7, p. 174). They were developed before modern computing, and their predictions can be calculated using a pen and paper, but by using a computer this process is made much easier (especially if the size of the populations after many generations is required). Because such models are simple, they are relatively easy to understand; changes in the value of one variable can be traced back to the variable that caused those changes. The disadvantage is that they are often unrealistic. Like a good caricature, a simple model captures the essence of one part of a system. But when the system is complex, understanding one part of it is often not enough.

Computer **simulations** are attempts to recreate, within a computer, realistic representations of actual systems. They may be extremely complex. For example, the European Regional Seas Ecosystem Model (ERSEM) was developed 'to provide a generalised model of the cycling of carbon and the associated (re)cycling of the macronutrients nitrogen, phosphorus and silicon' for the whole of the North Sea (Baretta et al. 1995). To achieve this ambitious objective, the modellers divided the ecosystem into thirteen different modules, linked together with flows of nutrients and involving 70 state variables (the essential physical and biological components of the model, such as nitrogen concentration and mass of photosynthetic plankton) (Figure 2.2, p. 47).

Such simulations are often designed to provide predictions about specific habitats or ecosystems. They do not claim to provide universal or general predictions; in this sense they are quite different from the more general scientific models discussed earlier. Because of their complexity, they cannot be mathematically analysed. Instead, researchers explore the properties of large simulations **numerically**. This means that the values of one or more input variables are systematically altered, and the values of one or more output variables sytematically recorded. The relationships between the variables can therefore be explored as if they were recorded from the field. Researchers can construct hypotheses about how the simulation performs, and conduct experiments to test these hypotheses entirely within the 'computer world' of the simulation itself. So in the ERSEM model mentioned above, a researcher might suppose that doubling the amount of carbon fixed by photosynthesis will cause a doubling of the biomass of small fish in the North Sea – this could be tested by running a series of simulations with doubled primary productivity and a range of values for other important variables. These could be regarded as replicate 'treatments'. Control simulations without increased primary productivity could be run to provide a comparison using identical logic to that of manipulative experiments.

Two challenges facing all those designing and using such simulations are first, how should they be tested, and second, how should they be understood?

Testing simulations

The essential feature of a worthwhile simulation is the same as in any branch of science – it makes predictions that can be tested. But this is often particularly difficult for large simulations. They may make predictions about events far into the future (such as global climate in 50 years time – see Chapter 5) or involving summary statistics which are difficult to collect in the field, or about many different variables simultaneously. In practice, many simulations are tested against the previous behaviour of a system; if the fit between the recorded history of a system and what the simulation says that history should be is a good one, then the simulation is taken to be accurate. But a danger of tautology arises. Data from the past are usually used in creating the simulation, so there might be no surprise if the model predicts what it already contains. Judgements must be made over how good the fit needs to be, and, if more than one variable is predicted, how many of the predictions should be correct for the simulation to be considered successful (see Chapter 9, p 229). In ERSEM, for example, the fit between the predicted and observed values for some variables (e.g. phosphate) is quite good, the fit for others (e.g. phytoplankton biomass) is poor, and the fit for many (e.g. benthic biomass) is unknown, since the field data are unavailable (Baretta et al. 1995). So deciding whether the model should be accepted or rejected is difficult.

Understanding simulations

The second problem arises because simulations may be so complex that the causal mechanisms involved in producing predictions are obscure; the model might make the right prediction for the wrong reasons (or at least, for reasons that are not understood). This is one reason why simple models are preferable, if they can provide sufficient predictive power. Another is that the more **free parameters** (variables that need to be specified each time the model is run) in a model, the harder it is to obtain good estimates of them all from field data. So modellers will make guesses, which could lead to errors. In general, the art of modelling in environmental sciences involves choosing the simplest level of detail that will provide the information that is needed, and may involve deliberately incorporating 'margins of error' (Chapter 9).

1.8 Testing hypotheses in science – a summary

The second part of this chapter has considered the most important methods used in the environmental sciences to test hypotheses. To summarise our main conclusions:

- Because the causes of phenomena are often obscure and probabilistic (they only cause things to happen 'on average') scientists usually need to use statistics when looking for patterns and differences in nature.
- As the amount of variability (or 'scatter') in a data set increases, it becomes more difficult to find statistically significant patterns – larger sample sizes are needed to attain sufficient power.
- The central task of statistics is to tell us how likely we are to have committed one of two errors – either accepting, or rejecting, the null hypothesis erroneously.
- Scientific hypotheses can be tested by looking for patterns in nature, by conducting manipulative experiments and through computer modelling and simulation.
- All these methods are valuable, but are only worth pursuing if well designed and logically conducted. Often, perfect design is not possible (where there are no replicates of large scale events, for example). This does not invalidate the study, but it does mean that we should be more cautious in interpreting the results.

Further reading

Chalmers, A. (1988) *What is this Thing called Science?* Open University Press, Milton Keynes. An accessible introduction to philosophy of science.

Pentecost, A. (1999) *Analysing Environmental Data*, Pearson Education, Harlow. Provides a good overview of the basic quantitative techniques, including multivariate approaches.

Underwood, A.J. (1997) *Experiments in Ecology: Their Logical Design and Interpretation Using Analysis of Variance*, Cambridge University Press, Cambridge. A more advanced look at the logic of experimental design.

References

Baretta, J.W., Ebenhow, W. and Ruardij, P. (1995) The European Regional Seas Ecosystem Model, a complex marine ecosystem model. *Netherlands Journal of Sea Research*, **33**, 233–246.

Caughley, G. and Gunn, A. (1996) *Conservation Biology in Theory and Practice*, Blackwell Science, USA.

Cohen, L. and Manion, L. (1994) *Research Methods in Education*, Routledge, London.

Eberhardt, L.L. and Thomas, J.M. (1991) Designing environmental field studies. *Ecological Monographs*, **61**, 53–73.

Lawton, J. (1996) *Nessiteras rhombopteryx. Oikos*, 77, 378–380.

Pentecost, A. (1999) *Analysing Environmental Data*, Pearson Education, Harlow.

Peters, R.H. (1991) *A Critique for Ecology*, Cambridge University Press, Cambridge.

Richards, S. (1987) *Philosophy and Sociology of Science,* 2nd Edition, Basil Blackwell, Oxford.

Schrader-Frechette, K.S. and McCoy, E.D. (1993) *Method in Ecology: Strategies for Conservation*, Cambridge University Press, Cambridge.

Underwood, A.J. (1996) Spatial and temporal problems with monitoring. In G. Petts and P. Calow (eds) *River Restoration*, Blackwell Science, Oxford.

Underwood, A.J. (1997) *Experiments in Ecology: Their Logical Design and Interpretation Using Analysis of Variance*, Cambridge University Press, Cambridge.

Wolpert, L. (1992) *The Unnatural Nature of Science*, Faber and Faber, London.

Yodzis, P. (1998) Local trophodynamics and the interaction of marine mammals and fisheries in the Benguela ecosystem. *Journal of Animal Ecology*, **67**, 635–658.

Chapter 2

The limits and assumptions of science

David Sumner

2.1 Introduction

> Mr Bosher, upon being appealed to for his opinion, explained that science
> was alright in its way, but unreliable: the things scientists said yesterday they
> contradicted today, and what they said today they would probably repudiate
> tomorrow. It was necessary to be very cautious before accepting any of
> their assertions.
>
> Robert Tressell, *The Ragged Trousered Philanthropists*

The fictional Mr Bosher, voicing his opinion in Edwardian England, would
be even more cautious today. Anyone reading the newspapers regularly or
watching TV programmes is bombarded by a plethora of statements and
(often conflicting) advice, appealing to scientific authority either explicitly
or implicitly. Sometimes scientists are quoted on opposite sides of an issue.
What are the dangers of producing and eating genetically modified foods?
Can we go on eating as many fish as we want? Should we discharge
radioactive waste into the sea, or dump redundant oil installations in it?

Mr Bosher and his present day counterparts might wonder how all this
is to be squared with the frequently heard assertion that science is one of
the most successful of human enterprises. In this chapter we try to separate scientific knowledge from the value judgements that are inevitably
entangled with it. We begin by using an analogy between scientists and
map makers to illustrate the uncertainties that are inherent in the practice
of science. Then we look at some of the more fundamental limits to science: philosophical, observational, logical and ethical. The existence of
ethical limits highlights the fact that science in itself can say nothing about
values, although values can influence the interpretation of scientific results.
Policy makers and politicians must deal with a mix of scientific facts and
value judgements (including values of their own, of course); faced with
this, there is a temptation to opt for what appear to be 'objective' methods
such as cost–benefit analysis.

2.2 The scientist as map maker

The truth is rarely pure, and never simple. Oscar Wilde

Truth is a Difficult Concept. British Civil Servant, Scott Inquiry

Truth is hard to come by. Karl Popper

Most if not all scientists would describe themselves as seekers after truth, trying to understand the material world as deeply and as comprehensively as they can. They devise theories to explain that world, in ways we have described in Chapter 1. It is tempting to envisage scientists as miners, cutting through soil and rock to reveal, slowly and painstakingly, rich seams of buried truth. Once revealed, everyone recognises the reality of gold and values it accordingly. But this is not an analogy that either Mr Bosher or a present day onlooker would find at all helpful. A more fruitful analogy is one suggested by the physicist John Polkinghorne – to think of scientists as map makers, exploring new territory and learning as much about it as they possibly can. Both analogies assume, of course, that there is real, objective truth 'out there' to be discovered, a real territory to be mapped or real gold to be mined.

This latter assumption is one that most scientists would make, a position usually called **realism**. In contrast, there are some who reject the possibility of wholly objective knowledge, and claim that *all* knowledge (including scientific knowledge) reflects the specific historical and cultural conditions under which it is produced. This position – usually called **constructivism** – will be discussed later in the chapter (see section 2.6). For the time being, we will assume that, even though the maps that scientists make may have lots of imperfections, there *is* a real world to be mapped, and we can get closer and closer approximations to it.

Some parts of the material world are so well mapped that everybody feels confident about what is there. However, much contemporary scientific activity is exploring new, previously uncharted territory – areas that we cannot usually explore directly by teams of surveyors with theodolites and clip boards. The question of exactly what areas are explored, and the available resources for exploring them, will be a result of decisions made by politicians as well as (or perhaps instead of) scientists. When the scientists do get to work on map making, their exploration may be at a distance, perhaps by taking the equivalent of satellite photographs which may be open to differing interpretations; sometimes we will see what we want to see. They may also be working at the limits of their available techniques – what they are trying to detect may be comparable with the uncertainty of their measurements, in other words there may be a high 'signal to noise' ratio.

When a part of the world is very well mapped, scientists are usually very reluctant to change their minds about what is there, and confronted with possible evidence that contradicts their previous secure knowledge will look for ways in which the new findings are the result of experimental error or artefacts. For example, in physics the laws of conservation of energy and momentum are regarded as well nigh impregnable, so when a problem arose in beta decay the existence of a new particle (which remained undetected for more than 20 years) was proposed rather than abandon the conservation laws (see Box 2.1).

Einstein's Theory of Relativity is now almost as solid as the laws of conservation of energy and momentum, and it would require a very convincing experiment, reproduced several times over by different groups of scientists, for it to be shaken. There was a time, however, when the Theory did not have such strong experimental support, and some of the evidence that was cited as supporting the theory does not look quite so good in retrospect. We return to this point later (Box 2.3). A more frivolous example is the case of the Loch Ness Monster; as we saw in Chapter 1 (p. 2), on biological grounds its existence is very unlikely. Scientists are usually of a cautious and sceptical turn of mind, and when confronted with a rather doubtful photograph purporting to be a Loch Ness Monster, will generally favour the possibility that there is an alternative explanation, or even a deliberate hoax. This example illustrates an ever-present pitfall when we come to interpret any data – the danger of seeing just what we want to see. It also raises the possibility that what we are seeing may be a complete fraud. We will return to these points later in the chapter.

Box 2.1 The problem of beta decay

Soon after the discovery of radioactivity by Becquerel in 1896, Rutherford showed that two distinct kinds of particle could be emitted in radioactive decays: alpha particles and beta particles. Alpha particles were subsequently shown to be helium nuclei, and beta particles electrons.

In 1914 it was shown that the energy of a beta particle emitted by a given nucleus could take any value from almost zero up to a definite maximum value. According to the principles of conservation of energy and momentum, this was impossible; if a fixed amount of energy is shared between two bodies (the beta particle and the nucleus) the energy and momentum of both must have a single, invariable value. Could it be that these principles actually didn't apply in the atomic nucleus?

In 1930 Pauli proposed a solution to this problem: another (undetected) particle was emitted along with the beta particle. The available energy could then be shared between the particles in an infinite number of ways, giving rise to the observed continuous range of energies. The missing particle – named the **neutrino** – was not detected until 1956. The great conservation principles were saved.

2.3 Absolute limits to science

In the previous section we saw that, when new territory is being explored, there are many possibilities of misinterpretation. But before looking in more detail at different sorts of bias and uncertainty in science, we need to say something about the areas of knowledge that are inaccessible to science – sticking with our map analogy, are there territories that science won't be able to explore? There may be technological limits, and probably also economic ones – we simply may not be able to afford to acquire as much knowledge as we would like to. But are there limits that are more fundamental, areas of the map that we will never to be able to describe? We now consider various kinds of such limits.

2.3.1 Kant and the nature of reality

We saw in Chapter 1 (p. 8) that the philosopher Descartes observed that our senses could sometimes deceive us. A century and a half later, Immanuel Kant (1724–1804) made a careful distinction between how we experience the world through our senses and how it really is. He argued that our understanding of the world is always conditioned by the concepts that our brain provides, and there is therefore always a gap between the real world and the world as we experience it. The basic form of scientific laws is imposed by us on the nature that we perceive through our senses, and although we can bring those laws closer and closer to nature, we can never fill in all the details. The effect of these insights on Western thought has been very profound: as Paul Guyer says, 'after [Kant] wrote, no one could ever again think of either science or morality as a matter of the passive reception of entirely external truth or reality.' Just how big the gap is between reality itself and our perception of it, and how important it is, remain contentious to this day; we will return to this topic later in the chapter (section 2.6).

2.3.2 Metaphysics

> The fact that the utterances of the metaphysician are nonsensical does not follow simply from the fact that they are devoid of factual content.
>
> A.J. Ayer, *Language, Truth and Logic*

It follows from Kant's insight that science cannot address questions of what is often called **metaphysics** (from the Greek, literally 'beyond physics'). Metaphysical statements are concerned with the nature of existence and reality beyond the realms of immediate experience, and it doesn't make sense to ask whether they can be experimentally confirmed or not. This limitation was recognised by one of the founding spirits of scientific investigation, the philosopher Francis Bacon (1561–1626), who said that we should not 'presume by the contemplations of nature to attain the mysteries of God'.

Metaphysics fell into temporary disrepute, at least in philosophical circles, in the 1920s and 1930s. A movement called logical positivism claimed that statements could only be of two kinds: 1. statements of which the truth was self-evident, effectively contained within the sentence itself (e.g. this man is my son, so I am his father); or 2. statements that could be empirically verified (e.g. my hair is grey). This distinction was essentially the same as that established by Hume, two centuries before (see Chapter 1). Statements that did not belong in either category (e.g. 'I believe in God') were dismissed as nonsense and devoid of meaning. Essentially, according to the logical positivists, there was just science and nonsense. It is generally agreed that this position has now been discredited, due in large measure to the work of the philosopher Karl Popper (1902–1994). In Chapter 1 we saw that Popper had shown, building on the work of David Hume, that scientific propositions could *not* be verified. The foundation stone of logical positivism – the verification principle – turned out to be made of sand. As a workable alternative Popper showed that a distinction between science and non-science was that propositions in science could (in principle, at least) be *falsified*. This was not, however, just a mirror image of the verification principle; Popper did not take the view that a principle of falsifiability should be a criterion of meaning – he thought that 'metaphysics need not be meaningless even though it is not science.'

In any case, whatever philosophers may think, many people obviously feel that metaphysical questions such as 'what is the meaning of life?' do make sense, and that science by itself cannot provide answers.

2.3.3 Limits of observation

[Heisenberg's] uncertainty principle … says that if I know where an electron is I have no idea of what it is doing and, conversely, if I know what it is doing I do not know where it is. The existence of such elusive objects clearly modifies our notion of reality. John Polkinghorne

Another type of limit in science may arise directly from within science. In Chapter 1 we discussed some of the 'laws of nature'. By the end of the nineteenth century physics had built up an impressive list of laws – Newton's laws of motion and gravitation, the laws of thermodynamics, etc. – and physicists were inclined to think that the universe was completely governed by deterministic laws (that is, mathematical laws which in principle can describe exactly the future condition of a system). In the words of the French mathematician Pierre Laplace (1749–1827) 'we may regard the present state of the universe as the effect of its past and the cause of its future.' However, the development of quantum mechanics, to explain phenomena such as atomic spectra and black body radiation, led to the rejection of determinism. Quantum theory says that nothing can be measured or observed without disturbing it, so the role of the observer is crucial. Heisenberg's uncertainty principle puts a fundamental limit on the precision of any simultaneous measurement of two physical quantities, such as the position and momentum of an electron. Some physicists (notably Einstein, whose famous comment was 'God does not play dice') have been extremely reluctant to accept this, and have clung to the idea that there may be a deeper level of determinism underpinning quantum mechanics. Contrary to the impression that you might get from some popular literature, quantum mechanics does not have any startling implications in the macroscopic world. Nevertheless it does seem to set fundamental limits on what can be observed at the subatomic level.

2.3.4 Logical limits

Even mathematics has important limitations of its own. The Austrian logician Kurt Gödel (1906–1978) showed that in a formal arithmetical system there will be propositions that cannot be *proved* to be true (or false) even though we can 'see' that they are true (or false). In other words, Gödel's theorem proves that some things can never be proved! In 1952 the American logician John Myhill extended Gödel's theorem in a very interesting way. He showed that there are properties that could not be completely described by any collection of rules – beauty and ugliness, for example. This confirms what we often feel – that scientific knowledge by itself is not adequate to account for many of life's important experiences. John Barrow expresses it thus: 'No *non-poetic* account of reality can be complete' [emphasis added] (Barrow 1998).

2.3.5 Ethical limits

There is some knowledge that scientists could only obtain by doing experiments that would not be ethically permissible. For example, information about the effect of toxic agents such as ionising radiation on humans could be obtained by exposing large numbers of humans to fixed doses of radiation and then monitoring their health for years afterwards. Knowing as we now do that there would inevitably be some cancers caused, such an experiment could never be sanctioned.

Because experiments with humans are ruled out, much information has been, and continues to be, obtained from animal experiments (2.5 million in 1997 Britain alone, nearly half in medical research). But here too our ethical norms are changing and animal experimentation is becoming much less acceptable.

The use of animals in experiments is a complex issue which we cannot deal with in detail here. For many people the suffering of animals may be offset by the benefits of the experiment, such as the development of new drugs for the relief of human suffering. When the benefits are much less clear, such as in the testing of cosmetics, the suffering of animals may not be justified. But others believe that there should be no trade-off between risks and benefits at all, that animals have rights, and that there should be no animal experimentation of any kind. We will return to these points later in the chapter, when we come to consider the question of whether decisions can ever be made objectively.

2.3.6 Science and value

The discussion of animal experiments in the previous section raises a fundamental question about science which forms a major theme of this book: namely, is scientific knowledge itself totally unconcerned with questions of value? Is it true that, as Lewis Wolpert says, 'reliable scientific knowledge has no moral or ethical value ... science tells us how the world is ... '? (Wolpert 1999.)

The question of whether Wolpert's basic claim is true will be postponed to later in the chapter (see section 2.6). At this point we should note the key word 'reliable', an adjective capable of a range of meanings. So first we need to digress and look in rather more detail at the meaning of 'reliability' in a scientific context. We can then return to a consideration of the role of values in the acquisition and applications of scientific knowledge, and re-examine Wolpert's claim.

2.4 Confidence and uncertainty

We now return to the areas that science can legitimately explore, and focus in more detail on uncertainties.

Every measurement we make will have some experimental error or uncertainty. In some cases we are measuring a variable which only has one 'true' value – for example, the half-life of a radioisotope or the concentration of carbon dioxide at a particular location. But usually the situation is much more complicated than this; we are often measuring a variable in a sample of plants, animals or humans. For example, we might be measuring the concentration of a particular pollutant in a sample of fish. In cases like this there will be two kinds of experimental error or uncertainty. Every *measurement* will have some uncertainty (which will depend partly on the technique being used), and there will also be a *sampling variation* – all animals (and certainly all humans) are individuals. If our samples are small and the variability is large, we may have difficulty in distinguishing the 'signal' we are looking for from the surrounding 'noise' (see Figure 1.6, p. 20).

2.4.1 Confidence intervals

Suppose we are investigating differences in cancer rates between two populations with different exposures to a particular pollutant. Our null hypothesis will be that there is in fact no difference. If the observed difference is unlikely to have arisen by chance (the convention is to take the level of 'unlikely' as a probability of less than 5%) then the null hypothesis is rejected.

We saw in Chapter 1 (p. 16) that two kinds of error are possible, Type I and Type II. A Type I error is when we reject the null hypothesis but should not have done (a false positive), a Type II error is when we don't reject the null hypothesis and should have done (a false negative). From the Type II error is derived the concept of **power** – the probability of detecting a given size of effect (Box 1.4).

We want now to introduce a related and very useful concept, the **confidence interval** (Box 2.2). Confidence intervals are generally more useful than p values, as they can alert us to the possibility of a Type II error in studies that are not statistically significant ($p < 0.05$). Consider the follow-

---

Box 2.2 What is a confidence interval ?

Suppose we have a sack containing a large number of white balls and black balls. Let us also suppose that someone has already ensured that one in five of the balls are black, that is to say, 20% of the balls are black and 80% are white. If we now select a sample of 100 balls from the sack without looking, how many black balls will we get? Obviously we won't always get 20 black balls and 80 white ones – there will be quite large variations either side of an 'expected' value of 20 black balls. It can be shown theoretically that in 95% of samples the number of black balls will be between 12 and 28. Another way of expressing this is that the expected number of black balls is 20 ± 8. The range of ± 8 is determined by the size of the sample; a larger sample will reduce the range of uncertainty, a smaller sample will increase it. Usually, of course, we don't know what the 'true' value is, but we can estimate the range of uncertainty from the size of the sample. In the example we have here, we know that it is very likely that the true value will be within ± 8 of the value that we find. This interval is called a 95% confidence interval – in 95% of samples, the 'true' value will lie within the interval.

Now suppose we have another sack in which someone has ensured that 22% of the balls are black and 78% are white. The 95% confidence interval in this case is from 14 to 30. As you can see, there is quite a large overlap between the confidence intervals; if we had only a small sample we should not be able to tell that the two sacks contained different proportions of black balls. Normally of course, we don't know what the true difference is, so quoting a confidence interval is useful because it gives *a range of values with which our data are compatible*.

ing example. Levels of a pollutant, say mercury, have been measured in two groups of mussels from different locations. We could carry out a test to see if the difference between the mercury levels in the two groups was statistically significant. In this case, however, it would be more useful to calculate the confidence interval of the difference. There is a simple relationship between the confidence interval and the p value: if the 95% confidence interval includes zero, the difference is not statistically significant ($p > 0.05$); if the interval doesn't include zero, then the difference is statistically significant ($p < 0.05$). However, the confidence interval is more informative than the p value. For example, a wide confidence interval, even if it includes zero, means that the difference is compatible with a range of values. This is illustrated in Figure 2.1. In Figure 2.1a, studies 1 and 2 both show differences which are 'statistically significant', but the results of study 2 are compatible with a much larger possible difference than study 1. Figure 2.1b shows two further studies, 3 and 4, in which the difference is not statistically significant, but the conclusions are certainly not the same. The difference in study 4 could have been quite large, unlike study 3 where it appears to have been relatively small. Broadly speaking, studies of low power tend to produce wide confidence intervals (because of large variability and/or small sample size). So study 4 is likely to have

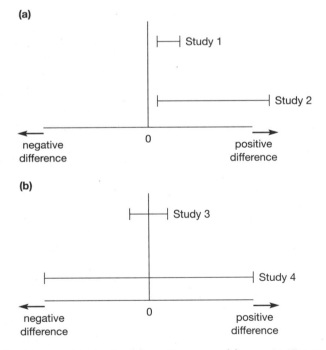

Figure 2.1 Confidence intervals: the (a) significant and (b) non-significant differences of the means of two groups. Horizontal scale is arbitrary.

been of low power, with the strong possibility of a Type II error. The result of studies such as study 4 are sometimes expressed in words such as 'there is no evidence for a difference between ... [whatever it is]'. The figure shows that this statement is very misleading. Altman and Bland (1995) point out that 'absence of evidence is not evidence of absence':

> Statements about the absence of evidence are common – for example, in relation to the possible link between violent behaviour and exposure to violence on television and video, the possible harmful effects of pesticide residues in drinking water, the possible link between electromagnetic fields and leukaemia, and the possible transmission of bovine spongiform encephalopathy from cows. Can we be comfortable that the absence of clear evidence in such cases means that there is no risk or only a negligible one?

A final and very important point can be made about Figure 2.1. Assuming all four studies are using comparable methods, we see that, p values notwithstanding, studies 1 and 2 do not contradict the findings of 3 and 4. All four studies are in fact consistent with a small positive difference.

It is easy to see how confidence intervals can be used when a single quantity is being measured in two groups. However, in a great deal of current science, especially environmental science, we rarely have such a simple situation. We have to use models, perhaps very complicated models.

2.4.2 Uncertainty in complex models

In Chapter 1 (p. 11) we saw that the term 'model' can have a range of meanings. The everyday use of the word is to mean a physical object that has some correspondence with the reality it represents: for example, some maps can be built as three-dimensional scale models of a landscape. Such a model will necessarily be a simplification, as it cannot show every house and every tree, let alone every leaf on every tree, and almost certainly will contain mistakes – some things may be in the wrong place, some dimensions may be incorrect, and so on. Nevertheless the model may well be useful for giving us an idea of what the landscape is like.

A model doesn't have to be a scaled down representation of a real object (like a model landscape, or a model car). It can be something which has certain characteristics of use to the modeller – for example, the model could be an animal bred or treated in a certain way which makes it suitable for the study of a human disease process, or it could be an isolated muscle used for testing in toxicology.

Models don't even have to be real physical objects; they can be intellectual constructs (called 'apprentice theories' in Chapter 1), formulae, or equations. For example, consider the famous series of experiments carried out by the Austrian monk Gregor Mendel, published in 1865. Mendel worked with varieties of the garden pea which had different characteristics such as round/wrinkled, tall/short, purple/white and so on. When he cross-fertilised round-seeded plants with wrinkled-seeded ones, he found that the first generation were all round-seeded, but when these were cross-fertilised the next generation was found to contain about three-quarters round-seeded and one-quarter wrinkle-seeded, that is, a ratio of three to one. (When the experiment is actually performed the ratio is never *exactly* three to one, a topic we will return to later in this chapter!)

Mendel himself didn't know *why* the ratio should be three to one. It wasn't until the discovery of DNA almost a century later that the secrets of inheritance were finally revealed. But even without knowledge of the actual mechanism of inheritance, we can model it as a mathematical process and predict the consequences of a particular cross-fertilisation from the laws of probability.

Whatever the kind of model, it is always a *simplification* of reality. The renowned statistician George Box put it rather well when he said: 'All models are wrong, and some are useful.' In saying this, Box is stressing that while no model gives a perfect representation of something, some models usefully represent aspects of it.

The complex nature of many mathematical models usually means that a computer is necessary; the model is then formulated as a set of instructions to the computer – a computer program. Known data, or experimental observations, serve as input to the program. The computer may then give, as its output, predictions that *can be tested*. For example, we might want to predict global temperatures over the next century (Chapter 5); estimate allowable fish catches using assumptions about the influences of environmental fluctuations on replenishment of fish stocks (Chapter 7); predict the occurrence of eutrophication in waters that receive sewage (Chapter 9); or predict radiation doses to a group of people living near a reprocessing plant (Chapter 10). Such models have many uncertainties, which we can classify as follows, using examples from the case studies in this book.

Measurement uncertainty

Models have to be based on experimental data, and all measurements have associated uncertainties. Under this heading we can distinguish four broad categories of uncertainty. These categories are not completely separate and clear-cut, as many measurements will have several kinds of uncertainty.

Our first category could be dubbed the problem of obtaining *representative* values – for example, taking an average of a set of measurements. As we saw earlier, if our measurements are on a number of individual people, animals, plants, etc., there will inevitably be variation. So when we talk of an average of a sample, we are assuming that the sample is representative of the whole population, but it may not be. If we wanted to obtain the average height of the inhabitants of a certain town, we would not obtain a very accurate value by measuring members of the local rugby team.

All sorts of additional problems arise when we try to combine measurements over a long period of time, or from many different sources. Consider the example of measuring average global temperature (Box 5.2, p. 126). Today, surface observations are available for nearly all areas of the world, but this was certainly not so in the nineteenth century. Satellite data now provide global coverage, although the data cover a relatively short time – the last 20 years or so. Combining many measurements to estimate an average means that all sorts of errors and biases have to be allowed for – changes in instruments and techniques, changes in the environment of the recording stations (particularly urbanisation), and so on.

Under this heading we must also mention the uncertainties associated with the values of parameters used in models. In Chapter 9, a decision has to made about the yield of chlorophyll from dissolved nitrogen. Estimates of the yield from 60 sets of chlorophyll and nitrate concentrations gave values ranging over more than an order of magnitude (Box 9.5, p. 234). Which value should be used? The median? Or the maximum, to be on the safe side?

The second category of uncertainties arises from inadequacies in the measurement technology itself. Measurements of many environmental pollutants are difficult and expensive, and may be at the limits of a particular technique. For example, wastes dumped at sea may contain synthetic organic compounds, many of which are toxic, persistent and liable to bioaccumulate. However, their concentrations and toxicity thresholds are both often very low and their analysis very difficult and expensive (see section 8.2.2 p. 202). Some of the liquid waste discharged from nuclear reprocessing plants contains very long-lived radionuclides, such as iodine-129 and technetium-99, which are difficult to measure, especially at low concentrations. Lack of good data can seriously compromise model building.

Thirdly, measurements are made and collected by human beings, who introduce all sorts of biases of their own. We will be looking in more detail at the subject of bias later in this chapter (see section 2.5). A good example of human bias having an important influence on data quality is included in Chapter 7 (p. 181). Poor data quality is a general problem for fishery managers, as fishers do not land all that they catch, and do not declare all that they land.

Lastly, we sometimes cannot measure what we really want to, because it's just too difficult. We have to use a **surrogate**, something that substitutes for the thing we're really interested in. In Chapter 8, for example, we will see that a complete assessment of industrial wastes is not possible because some effluents contain over a hundred individual chemicals and the composition of the effluent can change from day to day. Only a few selected properties such as pH and Biological Oxygen Demand (BOD) can be measured. BOD may act as an approximate surrogate for overall pollution, but may give a very inaccurate idea of the concentrations of some pollutants.

Choice of model

As we have said, a model is always a simplification of reality. A number of different models might be consistent with the data available, especially as the data themselves are uncertain and may be limited. When this is the case we say that the model is **underdetermined** by the data. So usually a choice has to be made between different possible models.

Chapter 1 included the example of a possible relationship between the cockle population of a sediment and the amount of sand in that sediment. When the sample size is small, there is no obvious relationship (Figure 1.6, p. 20) and we have to say that the model is underdetermined by the data. When the sample is larger, the relationship becomes more obvious.

In Chapter 10 we will see that data on excess cancer incidence following exposure to ionising radiation can be fitted by a number of models, the simplest of which is a linear relationship between dose and risk that goes right down to zero dose (Figure 10.2, p. 246). The reason that several models are possible is that the confidence intervals on the risk for each group are quite large, as the sample size is relatively small.

In Chapter 7, it is of considerable interest to predict the numbers of fish vulnerable to capture from the size of the spawning stock. If this relationship is known, it should be possible to predict future catches of fish from present stock sizes. Unfortunately, real data show a lot of variability and it is usually impossible to discriminate between different underlying relationships (Figure 7.3, p. 180).

Chapter 9 looks at different models for predicting eutrophication – one fairly simple one, and some more sophisticated ones. The more complicated models may be a more faithful approximation of the underlying science, but in practical decision making the simple model is preferred because of its more precautionary approach.

Sometimes technology is a limiting factor in the choice of model: for example, sophisticated models of the climate have only become possible in the last two or three decades, with the development of more and more powerful computers (see Chapter 5). Recently the National Research Council complained that the USA had fallen behind other countries in modelling climate change because US researchers are prevented from buying powerful supercomputers from Japan.

Extrapolation

It often happens that we have a set of data points and a model which allows us to fit a line (straight or curved) through them. If we then extend this line beyond the reach of the data (at either the high or low end) we are said to be indulging in **extrapolation**. We mentioned an example of extrapolation in the previous section – estimating the cancer risk from low levels of ionising radiation. This example is dealt with in more detail in Chapter 10.

In modelling, extrapolation can mean extending the domain (p. 23) of the model beyond the time period over which data have been gathered. It often happens that, for example, experimental data have been gathered over a certain time span (say ten years) but the model is being used to make predictions over a much longer time period. Monitoring of foodstuffs for radioactivity originating from discharges of radioactive waste has been carried out for several decades; however, the radioactivity may remain in the environment for many hundreds or thousands of years. Predictions of the behaviour of these radioactive substances over time periods very much longer than the available data will inevitably have some uncertainties (Chapter 10).

In some systems there may be fundamental limitations to forecasting over long time periods, because the way in which the system develops over time is very sensitive to the initial conditions. This is a feature of 'chaotic systems'; a familiar example is weather forecasting, which cannot be done reliably over a period of more than a few days.

Representation of the model

Just as in our mapping analogy we cannot represent every detail in the map of an area of countryside, so we cannot represent every aspect of reality in a set of equations or a computer program, however long and sophisticated it is. Inevitably there are simplifying assumptions; often equations must be solved numerically rather than analytically (that is, they cannot be solved exactly, using algebraic methods, but must be explored by substituting numbers into the equations).

In Chapter 1 (p. 29) we met the European Regional Seas Ecosystem Model (ERSEM) which was developed to model the cycling of carbon and the associated (re)cycling of nitrogen, phosphorus and silicon in the North Sea. To simplify an immensely complex ecosystem, the modellers divided the ecosystem into thirteen different modules (Figure 2.2). But why choose these particular modules? Figure 2.2 shows a box entitled 'zoobenthos', with five categories in it. These categories include hundreds of thousands if not millions of species – should the modellers have tried to represent more of these? Species such as seals and seabirds are entirely ignored in the

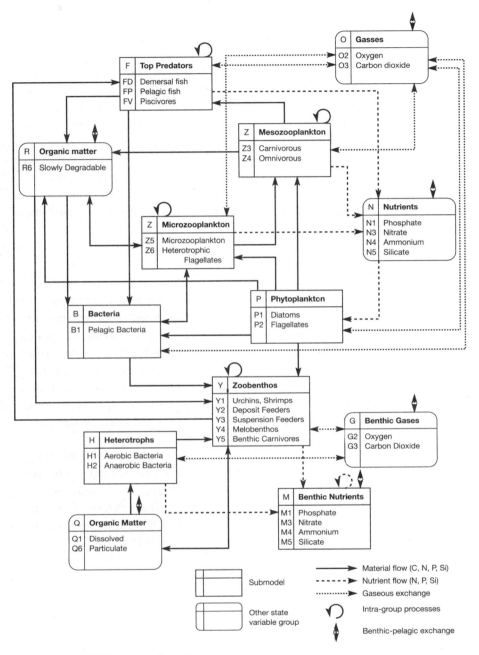

Figure 2.2 ERSEM process flow diagram.

Redrawn from Baretta et al. 1995 (see Chapter 1 for reference).

model. Clearly the modellers have had to make many decisions about what should be represented in their model, and it is possible that they have entirely ignored some very important components of the ecosystem.

The dispersion of radionuclides discharged into northern European waters has been estimated using a model which divides the oceans and seas north of 30° latitude into 34 regional compartments. To make the model tractable it is assumed that there is instantaneous and uniform mixing within each compartment. Since some of the compartments are very large (one extends from the Canaries to beyond the Arctic Circle) the assumption seems obviously untrue; nevertheless, the predictions of the model may be adequate for radiation protection purposes.

Models of the climate, however sophisticated, cannot have an unlimited resolution in space and time: in other words, they can only have a limited number of latitude and longitude bands, and have to chop the timescale up into suitable intervals, from minutes to years depending on the problem under investigation (Box 5.3, p. 128).

Ignorance

Obviously, the model cannot include processes of which we are ignorant. The history of science and technology contains many examples of surprises. Chlorofluorocarbons (CFCs) became popular as refrigerants and propellants in aerosol spray cans because they were cheap to produce, non-toxic, and (it was thought) relatively inert. Unfortunately, once released to the atmosphere, they are slowly transported up into the stratosphere and broken up by sunlight. Chlorine is released, which through a series of chemical reactions destroys stratospheric ozone. This process was not predicted, because we were ignorant of the pathways involved.

In Chapter 10 we will see that the cause, or causes, of childhood leukaemia around the Sellafield nuclear facility in northern England remain unclear. The estimated radiation doses, obtained from complicated models, are too low to account for the excess leukaemias. But perhaps there are pathways that have not been included, pathways of which (at present) we are completely ignorant. An example of this occurred in early 1998, when feral pigeons contaminated with radioactive material were discovered in the village of Seascale, near the Sellafield reprocessing plant. The pigeons were congregating in large numbers at a small bird sanctuary in a private dwelling. Levels of manmade radionuclides measured across the garden at the bird sanctuary were up to 800 times the typical concentrations for the region, and the radiation dose to residents of the bird sanctuary more than ten times higher than the dose from manmade radionuclides to average inhabitants of the village (COMARE/RWMAC 1999).

There may be some important pathways missing from climate models. Despite considerable progress in understanding the carbon cycle, some of the carbon released as a result of human activities cannot be accounted for.

There are several possible explanations for this, but considerable uncertainty about which (if any) are correct, and this undoubtedly reduces confidence in the models (see p.125).

From the above, it is clear that working out confidence intervals on quantities which are predicted by complex models is not straightforward. If the model has many parameters, each with some uncertainty attached to it (and for some parameters we may not even know what the uncertainty is!), estimating the uncertainty of the final prediction may be next to impossible.

2.5 Bias and fraud

The account of uncertainties in the previous section should provide some insight into the many ways in which a given set of data can be interpreted. Not only are measurements themselves subject to uncertainty, we have to make so many choices: what measurements should we make? What model should we choose? What are the model parameters? For various reasons we might have a prior inclination to measure one particular item, to choose one particular model, or prefer one particular explanation. We can group all such 'prior inclinations' under the heading of **bias**.

That bias might creep in to all these choices would seem almost inevitable, and even the best of scientists may, like the Loch Ness monster hunters, see what they want to see. An important prediction of Einstein's General Theory of Relativity – the bending of light by the sun's gravitational field – appeared to be confirmed by measurements taken during the solar eclipse of 1919. But in retrospect the evidence does not seem to be as clear cut as was claimed at the time (see Box 2.3).

A fairly common practice (even though it does cause some heart searching) is the rejection or removal of **outliers**, data which look as if they might have been rogue measurements, mistakes or artefacts. Some of us at school fiddled our data points so that they all lay on a straight line (if that's what they were supposed to do!) only to be caught out and told that our data were 'too good to be true' (see Figure 2.3). Babbage, in his book *Reflections on the Decline of Science in England* (published in 1830) classified manoeuvres of this kind into 'trimming' (smoothing irregularities to make the data look accurate and precise) and 'cooking' (the scientist retains only those results that fit the theory and discards other results).

Trimming and cooking have an even longer and more distinguished history than Box 2.3 would suggest. A famous nineteenth century culprit was Mendel, the discoverer of the laws of heredity. The famous statistician R.A. Fisher pointed out that the ratios Mendel obtained for his different

Box 2.3 How the general theory of relativity was proved – or was it?

Einstein's General Theory of Relativity (published in 1915–16) predicted that light would be bent in gravitational fields. The earth's gravitational field is not big enough to show a detectable effect, but the sun's is, and an eclipse of the sun provides an opportunity for measuring the effect. Stars close to the sun should be displaced from their usual position because the light from them will be bent as it passes through the sun's gravitational field.

However, the expected deflection of a light ray grazing the sun would be very small, only about 5 ten-thousandths of a degree. Comparisons had to be made on photographic plates between the apparent positions of a star at the solar eclipse and six months later. Eddington's observations made in the solar eclipse of 1919 (at two locations – Sobral, in Brazil, and Principe, an island off the coast of West Africa) had large uncertainties and there was considerable ambiguity in the conclusion (see table below).

Deflection of starlight (in seconds of arc)

Sobral SD	Mean – 1.5 SD	Mean	Mean + 1.5
8 good plates	1.713	1.98	2.247
18 poor plates	0.140	0.86	1.580
Principe			
2 poor plates	0.944	1.62	2.276

Einstein's prediction for the deflection was 1.7 arc seconds, whereas Newtonian theory predicted 0.84 seconds. Eddington took the results of the eight good plates at Sobral as the main finding, supported by the two poor plates at Principe, and effectively ignored the other 18 plates at Sobral. The results were hailed as confirming the General Theory of Relativity (Collins and Pinch 1998).

After the Second World War new techniques of radar and radioastronomy allowed more rigorous tests of the General Theory to be made, and the bending of light rays by gravitation was indeed found to be in accordance with the predictions of Einstein's Theory. According to Weinberg (1993) 'the astronomers of the 1919 expedition had been carried away with enthusiasm for general relativity in analysing their data ... I believe that the general acceptance of general relativity was due in large part to the attractions of the theory itself – in short, to its beauty.'

varieties of pea were too good to be true, given the small size of samples he was using. A plausible explanation seems to be that Mendel's gardeners had a good idea of the ratio he was expecting, and did a little extra work with the hoe to ensure he got the results he wanted (Medawar 1982).

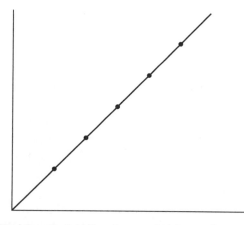

Figure 2.3 Data fitted to a straight line: too good to be true?

The rejection of outliers, as practised by Mendel and Eddington, can be said to constitute bias. Where does bias end and deliberate deception, or outright fraud, begin? In terms of our mapping analogy, fraud would amount to complete fabrication of aerial photographs, or a map with non-existent towns on it. Genuine fraud in science seems to be mercifully rare (indeed, Weinberg claims that there has never been an 'important case of outright falsification of data in physics'), so much so that when a case is uncovered it receives a great deal of publicity. One notorious case is that of Sir Cyril Burt (Box 2.4). In discussing the cases of Burt and Mendel, Medawar draws attention to the crucial difference between them: Mendel was right. Scientific investigation will eventually uncover the truth, even if it gets diverted on the way by deceptions and frauds. Sometimes the deception takes a while to uncover. The 'Piltdown man', a fossil skull discovered in 1913 at Piltdown in Sussex, and believed to be the earliest known human remains in Europe, was finally proved to be a hoax 40 years later. In the long run, outright falsification is likely to be exposed.

Box 2.4 Sir Cyril Burt

Identical twins who have been separated and brought up separately provide a way of testing the relative importance of 'nature' and 'nurture'. One of the most famous, indeed notorious investigators in this field was Sir Cyril Burt, Professor of psychology at University College, London, who published a series of papers in the 1950s purporting to show that heredity, as opposed to upbringing, was by far the major influence on IQ. Investigations in the 1970s by a team of investigative journalists on the *Sunday Times* showed that the data had been invented or manipulated. The *Sunday Times* also claimed that Burt had even invented two colleagues – Miss Howard and Miss Conway – whose names appeared on papers published between 1952 and 1959.

Why are scientists tempted to commit fraud? In some cases it may be the allure of a theory; in the case of General Relativity, a theory that was just too beautiful to be wrong. Ambition is often a potent factor too, as of course it is for men and women in all professions. John Polkinghorne, a Minister of the Church of England as well as a theoretical physicist, has admitted that his ambition to become an FRS (Fellow of the Royal Society) was so 'potent and disturbing' that 'if you had put to me some curious scheme by which my election would have been assisted by the murder of my grandmother, I would certainly have declined, but there would have been a perceptible pause for mental struggle before I did so' (Polkinghorne 1996).

More potent reasons for fraud now are the increasing competition for research funds and the constant pressure to publish. Because of these pressures there have been claims that fraud is increasing. A recent review stated that, although the number of reported cases of misconduct is relatively small compared with the total volume of scientific publications each year, 'the few surveys carried out suggest that the level of misconduct may be significantly higher than reported.' (Abbott 1999.)

There have been some long and very expensive cases of scientific fraud in the USA. Recently a neuroscientist was found to have fraudulently falsified data in published articles and grant applications, after a court case probably costing more than two million dollars (Box 2.5).

Box 2.5 Five steps to deception

What the panel found here was not honest error, not disputes in interpretation of data, not preliminary results that later proved overly optimistic, not even carelessness, but rather intentional and conscious fraud.

Report of a US Federal Appeal Panel on the conduct of Kimon J. Angelides, a neuroscientist formerly working at Baylor College of Medicine, Houston, Texas. Reported in *Nature*, **397**, 549 (18 February 1999).

2.6 Types of knowledge

It is common in philosophy to divide knowledge into two apparently discrete categories, namely **positive** and **normative** knowledge. Positive knowledge concerns the nature, properties, state, etc. of an entity (e.g. activity, thing, process, system) in the past, present or future. This may be essentially empirical knowledge – that is, based on measurements or observations (e.g. concerning the atmospheric concentration of carbon dioxide);

or theoretical knowledge – that is, based on models (e.g. concerning the causes of global warming). Positive knowledge in general is claimed to be 'objective' (i.e. it is concerned with facts), and is clearly the stuff of which science is purportedly made.

By contrast, normative knowledge pertains to the importance, morality or value of an entity in the past, present or future. This includes statements of good and bad, right and wrong, better and worse, as well as statements about how an entity should be or ought to be (e.g. concerning the importance of protecting biodiversity, or the ethics of animal experimentation). In contrast with positive knowledge, normative knowledge expresses human judgements: it is, therefore, 'subjective' knowledge.

The difference between these two categories of knowledge is, at its simplest level, the distinction between **facts** and **values**. On the face of it, there is a simple enough distinction between a statement of fact ('this is a book') and a statement of value ('this is a very good book'). But if we look back at some of the examples used so far in this chapter, we can see that things are rarely straightforward. Is it a statement of fact to say that 'the General Theory of Relativity was confirmed by observations made in the solar eclipse of 1919'? Value judgements of various kinds are inextricably entwined with the process of scientific investigation; we have to consider the possibility that scientific knowledge itself is not truly objective.

If we take a **realist** approach to knowledge (as most scientists do), we do allow for the possibility of purely objective knowledge: that is, knowledge of external reality which is independent of the knowing subject and her/his subjective judgements. Such knowledge must, necessarily, be valid in an absolute or universal sense.

However, anti-realists argue that all knowledge – including scientific knowledge – inescapably reflects the specific historical and cultural conditions under which it is produced. This view (which we referred to earlier) is called **constructivist**, and for a great deal of knowledge does seem to accord with common sense. After all, it is fairly well known that what people believe about the world varies both within and between cultures, and changes with the passage of time (see, for example, Berger and Luckmann's seminal *The Social Construction of Reality* (1966)). However, the idea that scientific knowledge is socially constructed contradicts the widely held view of its objectivity.

In the most extreme form of constructivism, it is claimed that all knowledge – including scientific knowledge (see, for example, Woolgar 1988) – is entirely determined by social processes and, hence, that such knowledge tells us nothing whatsoever about external reality. This is sometimes referred to as **strong constructivism**. (Strong constructivists sometimes claim that it is meaningless to talk about 'external reality' at all, because we cannot know anything about it – or even that there is any such thing as 'external reality'.) In a more moderate version, knowledge is seen as reflecting both social processes and external reality. This is sometimes called weak constructivism or, to use Woodgate and Redclift's (1998) less value-laden term, **mediated constructivism**. This kind of constructivism allows for greater and lesser degrees of subjectivity in knowledge claims, including scientific knowledge claims, but does not admit the possibility that subjectivity can be eliminated altogether.

In one form or another, constructivism is now widely accepted in the fields of science studies and the sociology of scientific knowledge (Murphy 1994). However, realism is still alive and well in the philosophy of science, where ever-more sophisticated accounts – sometimes referred to as **critical realism** – have been produced in response to the constructivist challenge. (For an introduction to critical realism, see Bhaskar et al. 1998.) In this view, science should be seen as a process in which subjectivity is progressively reduced 'through successive refinements and elaborations' – and thereby 'achieves a more adequate theoretical grasp of the phenomena it seeks to describe or explain' (Norris 1997:19)

In their general features, critical realism and mediated constructivism appear to be saying more or less the same thing. Both seem to accept that scientific knowledge necessarily contains both objective and subjective elements; and that while the degree of subjectivity can be progressively reduced, it can never be eliminated entirely. Note that we are not all that far here from Kant's insight which we discussed briefly in section 2.3.1. There must be a gap between our subjective knowledge of reality, and reality 'in itself'. So we cannot make a simplistic division between facts and values, especially in environmental science; our philosophical position has to be some form of critical realism or mediated constructivism. Chapter 3 expands on this point, and shows how, in real situations, many subjectivities influence even 'scientific' environmental decisions.

Some scientists feel that these debates are irrelevant – science 'works' (we can predict eclipses, put a man on the moon, fly aeroplanes, engineer DNA, and so on) and whether it really describes the nature of an external objective reality doesn't seem to matter. However, there are other scientists – for example, elementary particle physicists who are trying to understand the structure of matter at its deepest level – who are provoked by the anti-realists into a more trenchant response. If there really is no good reason to prefer one social construction to another, can there be any notion of progress in science? What is the point of research into elementary particle physics if it isn't bringing us any closer to the 'truth' about nature?

Such questions are probably unanswerable, certainly within the scope of this chapter. But the topic raises another very interesting question: how can science justify itself? Why do science (of any kind) at all? There may be many good reasons, such as the quest for truth for its own sake, curiosity about the natural world, the good of the human race (Hinshelwood 1991); or less laudable reasons such as the desire for power over nature, commercial gain or personal ambition.

The point here is that scientists themselves would admit that these motives cannot arise from within science itself. So, although realists may argue with constructivists about what science can do, what should now be clearer is what science *cannot* do. Returning to Wolpert's assertion (p. 39), we can't be sure about the second part of his claim ('science tells us how the world is'), but there does seem to be agreement about the first part ('scientific knowledge has no moral or ethical value'). In Weinberg's words: 'Science may be able to tell us how to explain or to get what we value, but it can never tell us what we *ought to value.*' (Weinberg 1995; my emphasis.)

2.7 Values

We can now attempt a more systematic classification of the values that influence scientific knowledge. Shrader-Frechette (1991) divides values into three types:

- methodological values
- bias values
- contextual values

Rather than thinking of these as three separate categories, it is probably more instructive (as the subsequent discussion will demonstrate) to think of them as overlapping concentric shapes (Figure 2.4).

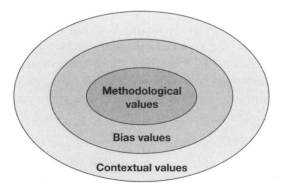

Figure 2.4 Methodological, bias and contextual values.

2.7.1 Methodological values

Methodological values are all the judgements and choices that we have to make as we collect, analyse and interpret our data. We have seen earlier in this chapter (section 2.4.2) that we usually have a very wide range of choice as to what we measure. Having collected our data we have to decide how to treat them. Can we ignore the outliers? What averages should we take? Having carried out this first stage of processing, we will probably want to use the data to test a hypothesis. What model should we use? What have we ignored? Even a decision like setting a threshold for statistical significance ($p = 0.05$ is usually, but not invariably chosen) is a value judgement. Despite all the possibilities of choice, there are general values which all scientists would espouse: for example, that methods should be consistent, reproducible by other workers, and subject to peer review. Research carried out which respects these generally held values will, scientists believe, gradually yield value-free knowledge. Sometimes, however, this can take a while, if evidence that does not conform with currently accepted theories is ignored or explained away as being the result of experimental errors or artefacts. A 'mindset' can grow up, not totally unlike the position of the doorstep visitor described at the beginning of Chapter 1. A more formal way of examining this issue – **discourse analysis** – is discussed in Chapter 3.

2.7.2 Bias values

A 'mindset' can give rise to bias values which can influence methodological value judgements (hence our depiction of them as concentric shapes). Attachment to a particular explanation or theory may influence our rejection of outliers, choice of model and so on. Eddington wanted Einstein's General Theory of Relativity to be true, and chose to put more weight on the measurements that supported it.

Barrow has pointed out a more subtle form of bias which may be growing as a result of the 'information age'. Communication between scientists around the world is now faster and more widespread than ever before. This may well have the result of moving scientific progress along certain tracks: 'it might dictate the types of question that get asked and the sort of answers that are found' (Barrow 1998). Wittgenstein expressed a similar concern, albeit more graphically: 'Science lays down railway tracks. And for scientists it is important that their work should move along these tracks.'

2.7.3 Contextual values

Surrounding bias values are contextual values, which may well create bias and in turn affect methodology. The term 'contextual values' (as used by Shrader-Frechette) includes a wide range of influences – personal, cultural, and social. In modern capitalist societies, financial considerations obviously represent an important class of contextual values; the source of funding for research may not influence the results that are obtained but it can be an important influence on the *direction* of the research, on the territories that we can explore. Science may not be socially *constructed*, as the 'strong programme' sociologists claim, but it can certainly be socially *influenced* (Polkinghorne 1996).

There are important connections here too with Type I and Type II errors (see p. 16, 40). If there are vested political or commercial interests in an effect not being present, Type II errors will tend to be ignored. In general, industry will be more anxious to avoid a Type I error but the public will want to avoid a Type II error. But this is by no means clear-cut. A new factory may discharge a pollutant into the environment, posing a hypothetical health risk to those living nearby. On the other hand, it may bring jobs to an area of previously high unemployment. The association between unemployment and ill health is now well established, and it may be that the local inhabitants will be prepared to risk a Type II error in return for greater economic security.

Pressures of this kind operate on a much larger, even global, scale. Chapter 4 deals with the topic of GM crops and foodstuffs. Here the scientific assessment of possible consequences is at a very preliminary stage, and the long-term risks are not known. But the pressure from the manufacturers to test and market the crops is very strong, as biotechnology is an important growth area for modern capitalism. Indeed it has been described as the 'engine of capitalism' for the twenty-first century, much as cars and computers have been for the twentieth. A recent suggestion by a law professor that 'science will need to wait and help ethics to catch up' (Somerville 1999) provoked the comment that 'we would be better served if bioethicists were willing and able to work within the realm of the modern, market-oriented world to come up with practical solutions to bioethical problems' (Silver 1999).

Chapter 6, which discusses species conservation, provides examples of all three types of value (methodological, bias and contextual) operating in the same situation. If we study a biological community then we make judgements about what organisms to study. These might be based on practicalities (we study vertebrates rather than bacteria because we can see them and collect them and systematise them more easily) – these are methodological values. We might choose to study the plants, because of a bias value that ecosystems are controlled by 'bottom-up' processes (rather than by their predators). We might choose to study the grizzly bears rather than the fungi because of contextual values that these are more attractive and more likely to get funding. Contextual values are discussed further in Chapter 3.

2.7.4 The incompatibility of values

Our policy makers or politicians will therefore be faced with a complex and confusing mix of scientific facts entangled with all shapes and sizes of value judgement. They will of course bring their own values and those of their governments or employers to the surrounding context as well. There may be many things that they feel they ought to value: the profits and economic well-being of industry, providing employment, protecting public health, preserving biodiversity and so on. Making a decision usually involves a difficult compromise between many conflicting values. If we restrict fishing in the interests of conservation, what about the jobs of fishermen? Even those who accord the environment a very high priority may find as individuals that they have to decide between competing values. Can we get enough vegetables from our garden without killing at least some pests?

From the beginning of literature, writers have described dreams of utopia, in which men and women live together in harmony with themselves and with nature. The writings of many environmentalists imply that we can, with sufficient will and ingenuity, create a sustainable society built on principles of respect for nature. However, the twentieth century has not been kind to utopian ideas, partly due to the unprecedented horrors of this century but also because of the growing realisation that many of the values that we deem to be important – freedom and justice, for example, are not fully compatible, even in principle. Isaiah Berlin has persuasively argued that civilisations are incompatible because of irreconcilable values:

> [Values] can be incompatible between cultures, or groups in the same culture, or between you and me ... we can discuss each other's point of view, we can try to reach common ground, but in the end what you pursue may not be reconcilable with the ends to which I find that I have dedicated my life. Values may easily clash within the breast of a single individual; and it does not follow that, if they do, some must be true and others false ... total liberty for wolves is death to the lambs.
>
> (Berlin 1990).

In a democracy of course, we will have many conflicting voices trying to make themselves heard. The recent growth of the Internet is turning this chorus into a worldwide Babel. In the words of a current activist: 'It allows us to say what we want to say ... that's democracy.' (Vidal 1999.)

If there is no objective and rational way to balance the requirements of different competing values, we should at least ensure that the debate makes it clear which values are being invoked and that scientific knowledge is presented in as 'value-free' a way as possible.

Before leaving the topic of values, something must be said about emotion and feeling. In debates about environmental issues, these terms are often used in a pejorative way. Shell UK said of the Greenpeace Brent Spar campaign (see Chapter 8) that it was 'an emotive campaign … [which gave the Brent Spar] … a symbolic significance beyond any rational, scientific calculation of its impact' (Shell UK 1995). Here 'rational' and 'scientific' are being opposed to 'emotive', where 'emotive' implies an appeal to feeling without *reasons* of any kind, something like 'I don't *like* this' or 'I *feel* this is wrong'. Feelings can only be expressed, not discussed or argued about (Buruma 1999). It would be preferable to say that 'I feel this is wrong *because* it endangers the environment, sets a precedent, etc. …' However, this does not remove the problem (if there is one), because we are then down to setting one value against another, something we have already said cannot be decided in any 'objective' way. It may be that when someone describes a particular view or campaign as 'emotive', they are simply saying that it is based on values that they do not share.

2.8 'Objective' decision making

Faced with a barrage of conflicting and competing voices, many policy makers are tempted to take refuge in decision making procedures that appear to be objective. These methods are sometimes even dubbed 'scientific'. One method in common use is cost–benefit analysis, in which financial values are attached to all the supposed benefits and detriments of a particular development. If we have a choice of several different options, the one that has the biggest positive difference between benefits and detriments would be the preferred one.

Cost–benefit analysis is rooted in a system of moral philosophy called utilitarianism, first developed in a systematic way by the English philosopher Jeremy Bentham (1748–1832). In utilitarianism, it is the consequences of actions that are important; an action is right if it maximises the happiness or well-being of those likely to be affected by the action, famously condensed into a slogan by Bentham as the 'greatest happiness of the greatest number'.

There are a number of problems with utilitarianism (and hence with cost–benefit analysis): the difficulty of reducing everything to a 'scale' of happiness, the impossibility of knowing all the consequences of an action, and the counter-intuitive nature of some of the conclusions that can be drawn from utilitarianism. For example, killing people might be perfectly permissible if the end result were an increase in total happiness. Adams (1995) has written very trenchantly about the problems of cost–benefit analysis, and the impossibility of assigning monetary values to environmental amenities. Nevertheless utilitarianism remains an attractive system for decision makers, as it gives the appearance of being scientific and objective, and attempts to collapse all the difficult value judgements we have discussed into a single scale of benefit (on the positive side) or detriment (on the negative). It should be noted, incidentally, that utilitarianism does not necessarily exclude such concepts as animal rights. The utilitarian philosopher Peter Singer has extended the moral community to all animals that are capable of experiencing suffering (see p. 159).

Even though cost–benefit analysis or something similar may not be used explicitly, many professional decision makers will take it for granted that some kind of **consequentialist** approach is suitable; that is, nothing is right or wrong *in itself* – risks and other potential problems can nearly always be outweighed if the expected benefits are great enough (Clark 1994). Utilitarianism is one type of consequentialist approach. In practice, most people would regard at least some acts as wrong *in themselves* – for example, the killing of innocent people – even if they might conceivably have some beneficial consequences. Ethical theories of this kind are called **deontological** theories. Many contentious moral issues (abortion, for example) are essentially conflicts between utilitarian and deontological points of view.

Similar tensions, albeit less conspicuous, can also arise in environmental decision making. For example, suppose we are discharging something into the environment for which there is no threshold of harm. (Discharges of radioactive waste, discussed in Chapter 10, are a good illustration of this.) Then any level of discharge could result in one or more fatalities, even though the identity of those affected may never be known. It would be very expensive to operate with no discharges at all, so cost–benefit analysis is sometimes applied to decide what level of protection is justified, an analysis which amounts to deciding how much a life is worth. Similar considerations are sometimes applied in other areas, such as transport. Trading lives against economic gains is acceptable from the point of view of a utilitarian, but clearly not for a deontologist who takes the view that the killing of innocent people is always wrong. It would be incorrect to say that either party is 'irrational'; rather, they could be said to have 'competing rationalities'. The topic of different rationalities will be explored in more depth in the next chapter.

2.9 Summary

- Scientists can be thought of as map makers of the material world. Some areas are very well mapped, others are much less certain.
- Some areas are permanently closed to scientific exploration: metaphysics, and worlds beyond our experience. Quantum theory sets limits to what can be observed at the subatomic level. Some experimental work in science is ruled out on ethical grounds.

- Confidence intervals are a useful way of indicating the range of values with which our data are compatible. Studies with large confidence intervals will have low power and hence a higher chance of Type II errors.
- Models have many uncertainties, and it may be difficult to obtain confidence intervals on the predictions that they produce.
- Because of all the uncertainties in data collection, measurement, modelling, etc., there are many opportunities for bias. Bias may become deliberate deception, although this seems relatively rare.
- The distinction between positive and normative knowledge (facts and values) is not clear-cut. This calls into question the supposed objectivity of scientific knowledge.
- Traditional realism and strong constructivism represent two opposing theories of knowledge. Between these two extremes, mediated constructivism and critical realism both broadly accept that knowledge – including scientific knowledge – necessarily contains both objective and subjective elements.
- The value judgements involved in the interpretation and use of scientific results can be classified into three types: methodological, bias and contextual. Financial considerations form an important type of contextual value.
- Different values may not be compatible, even in principle. Decision making in a democracy is usually a difficult compromise between competing values.
- Cost–benefit analysis appears to offer an 'objective' way of making decisions, but has many flaws.

Further reading

Gardner, M.J. and Altman, D.G. (1989) *Statistics with Confidence*, British Medical Journal, London. A useful introduction to confidence limits.

Guyer, P. (ed) (1992) *The Cambridge Companion to Kant*, Cambridge University Press, Cambridge. For those who want to explore Kant's thought, and deontological philosophy in particular.

Kuhn, T. (1962) *The Structure of Scientific Revolutions*, University of Chicago Press, Chicago. This presents the classic case for the social construction of science.

Magee, B. (1987) *The Great Philosophers: An Introduction to Western Philosophy*, BBC Books, London. A good general introduction.

References

Abbott, A. (1999) Science comes to terms with the lessons of fraud. *Nature*, **398**, 13–17.

Adams, J. (1995) *Cost-Benefit Analysis: Part of the Problem, Not the Solution*, Green College Centre for Environmental Policy and Understanding, Oxford.

Altman, D.G. and Bland, J.M. (1995) Absence of evidence is not evidence of absence. *British Medical Journal*, **311**, 485.

Barrow, J. (1998) *Impossibility*, Oxford University Press, Oxford.

Berger, P. and Luckmann, T. (1966) *The Social Construction of Reality*, Penguin.

Berlin, I. (1990) The pursuit of the ideal. In: Hardy, H. (ed) *The Crooked Timber of Humanity*, Fontana, London.

Bhaskar, R. et al. (eds) (1998) *Critical Realism: Essential Readings*, Routledge, London.

Buruma, I. (1999) The joys and perils of victimhood. *New York Review of Books*, 8 April, 4–9.

Clark, S.R.L. (1994) Genetic and other engineering. *Journal of Applied Philosophy*, 233–237.

Collins, H. and Pinch, T. (1998) *The Golem: What you Should Know About Science*, Cambridge University Press, Cambridge.

COMARE/RWMAC (1999) *Radioactive Contamination at a Property in Seascale, Cumbria*, NRPB Information Office, Chilton, Didcot, Oxon OX1 0RQ.

Hinshelwood, R. (1991) Social cybernetics: an enlightenment contradiction. *Medicine and War*, 7, 218–221.

Medawar, P. (1982) *Pluto's Republic*, Oxford University Press, Oxford.

Murphy, R. (1994) The sociological construction of science without nature. *Sociology*, **28**(4), 957–974.

Norris, C. (1997) *Against Relativism. Philosophy of Science, Deconstruction and Critical Theory*, Basil Blackwell Publishers, Oxford.

Polkinghorne, J. (1996) *Beyond Science: The Wider Human Context*, Cambridge University Press, Cambridge.

Shell UK Ltd (1995) Brent Spar. *Shell Magazine*.

Shrader-Frechette, K.S. (1991) *Risk and Rationality*, University of California Press, Berkeley.

Silver, L.M. (1999) Bioethicists must come down to Earth. *Nature*, **399**, 728.

Somerville, M.A. (1999) Reported in *Nature*, **399**, 12.

Vidal, J. (1999) Warfare across the Web. *Guardian Weekly*, 7 February 1999.

Weinberg, S. (1993) *Dreams of a Final Theory*, Hutchinson Radius, London.

Weinberg, S. (1995) Reductionism redux. *The New York Review of Books*, October 5, 39–42.

Wolpert, L. (1999) Is science dangerous? *Nature*, **398**, 281–2.

Woodgate, G. and Redclift, M. (1998) From a 'sociology of nature' to environmental sociology: beyond social construction. *Environmental Values*, 7(1), 3–24.

Woolgar, S. (1988) *Science. The Very Idea*, Ellis Horwood and Tavistock Publications, Chichester.

Chapter 3

Science and environmental decision making: the social context

J. Quentin Merritt and Peter C. Jones

3.1 Introduction

As with previous chapters, our central concern here is with scientific knowledge, as developed and deployed in the context of environmental decision making. Most decisions of greatest environmental consequence are made by large and powerful institutions – especially business corporations and governments. Hence, it is on the decision making of *professional* scientists, managers, politicians and other 'experts' that we mainly focus, here as in other chapters. However the costs and benefits associated with such decisions – e.g. whether to license genetically modified crop strains for commercial production (Chapter 4); how to dispose of redundant oil platforms (Chapter 8) – are increasingly perceived as socially, politically, economically, ethically, and hence environmentally, contentious. Not surprisingly perhaps, the context of environmental decision making frequently includes 'opinion-formers' and other 'agents of persuasion' – notably expert communities, interest and pressure groups, the mass media, and 'public opinion' – who variously seek to influence, and/or whose endorsements are sought for, such decisions.

In part, our account of science and environmental decision making develops out of the *philosophical* foundations established in Chapters 1 and 2. Contrary to widely held opinion, we take the view that scientific knowledge cannot easily be equated with 'certainty', 'fact' or 'truth'. This does not mean, of course, that we deny the capacity of science to yield effective or useful knowledge. But the philosophically problematic nature of scientific knowledge does have important implications for environmental decision making, especially under conditions of perceived environmental risk, as we seek to show in this chapter.

Our analysis, however, is principally a *sociological* one. We conceive of scientific knowledge, not simply as a store of codified wisdom (for example, on library shelves or in the heads of experts), which is held in universally high esteem – but rather as a stream of frequently contested 'knowledge *claims*', advanced variously by decision makers and by those agents of persuasion who 'act on' the decision making process itself. (See Box 3.1 for an illustration of this point, with reference to some recent knowledge claims advanced in relation to genetically modified foods.) Many such 'claim makers' enjoy unparalleled access to those resources required for the advancement of credible scientific (and other) knowledge claims – and are able to mobilise their knowledge, along with other forms of power and privilege, in making and/or influencing environmental decisions. However, we argue that the judgements that inform such claims and decisions tend to reflect – in some measure – the perspectives of those 'stakeholder' and 'knowledge' communities (for example, the 'industrial–scientific' community and its influential supporters; the 'green–scientific' community and its influential allies) with whom they most closely identify, or on whom they are most reliant for achievement of their wider goals.

Combining these philosophical and sociological lines of argument, we firstly examine some characteristics of knowledge, including scientific knowledge, and then focus our attention on the intensely contested science of environmental risk. Risk and uncertainty are recurrent themes in the case studies of science and environmental decision making in Chapters 4–10. Hence our overview of the literature and debates that characterise this field is intended to complete the preliminary theoretical framework which these three opening chapters seek to provide.

3.2 Scientific knowledge: some sociological perspectives

What does it mean to speak of the 'knowledge' that individuals and groups in society hold about the environment and their interactions with it? And how can we comprehend the intellectually perplexing and politically charged world of competing environmental knowledge claims – especially those competing 'expert' claims made in the name of science? In this section, we develop some sociological ideas about knowledge in general, and environmental-scientific knowledge in particular.

3.2.1 Knowledges, discourses and rationalities

Much of what individuals and groups claim to 'know' is contentious in nature: it may be contested by others, perhaps for its factual accuracy, or for its logical soundness, or for the legitimacy of its values. But of course what people *think* they 'know' is likely to influence their decisions and actions – at least insofar as they are free to choose between one course of action and another. This point may be illustrated with reference to the

---

Box 3.1 Contested scientific knowledge claims: genetically modified foods

We know, from many years of thorough testing and evaluation, that biotech seeds and plants are safe for human consumption...
Monsanto Corporation (1998) 'Biotechnology and Consumer Issues: Where We Stand' (Monsanto Website: http://www.monsanto.com)

There is no GM food that can be sold in this country without going through a very long regulatory process.
Tony Blair, UK Prime Minister (*The Guardian*, 13 February 1999)

There has been very little research done to assess the health and safety implications to humans from ingesting genetically engineered organisms (GMOs).
Soil Association (no date) 'Genetic Engineering' (Soil Association Website: http://www.soilassociation.org)

One key problem that keeps coming back time and again is that regulation of food is nothing like as strict as regulation for drugs. And when you start tinkering around with the genetic structure of food you have to move towards thinking of food products as pharmaceuticals.
Jonathan Rhodes, Professor of Medicine, University of Liverpool (*The Guardian*, 12 February 1999)

An objective review of the data from these experiments [conducted by Dr Pusztai] leads to the conclusion that consumption of GNA-GM potatoes [modified with snowdrop lectin] in rats has led to significant differences in organ weight and lymphocyte responsiveness.
Vyvyan Howard, Foetal and Infant Toxico-Pathologist, University of Liverpool (*The Guardian*, 12 February 1999)

[W]e cannot yet know whether there are any serious risks to the environment or human health ... Adverse effects are likely to be irreversible; once GM organisms are released into the environment they cannot be subject to control.
British Medical Association (*The Guardian*, 18 May 1999)

We found no convincing evidence of adverse effects from GM potatoes ... Where the data seemed to show slight differences between rats fed predominantly on GM and non-GM potatoes, the differences were uninterpretable because of the technical limitations of the experiments and the incorrect use of statistical tests.
Royal Society scientists' review of Arpad Pusztai's research (*The Guardian*, 19 May 1999)

---

widespread protests in the mid-1990s over the export from Britain to continental Europe of live calves for veal production. The decisions that individuals and groups made – to support or not support those protests – were clearly influenced by what they 'knew' about the nature and extent of suffering experienced by livestock during transportation and subsequently; what they 'knew' about the ethics of suffering; and what they 'knew' about the legitimacy and likely effectiveness of confrontational public protest. 'Normative' and 'positive' knowledge claims (see p. 52) were both involved here, and on each point different people undoubtedly drew very different conclusions.

This case mainly concerns 'lay' or 'non-expert' knowledge, where positive knowledge may be thought especially vulnerable to the distorting effect of individual subjectivities. (However, 'expert' claims were also advanced by, amongst others, Compassion in World Farming, the European Commission, the National Farmers Union, the Road Haulage Association and the RSPCA – including positive, but nonetheless contested, claims about livestock tolerance of long-distance transport.) We maintain that claims to objectivity emanating from 'experts' must be regarded as problematic also. In Chapter 10 it is argued that the unit of radiation dose, the sievert, has value judgements built into it. This is but one instance of a more general tendency for blurring of the distinction between positive and normative knowledge, and for 'experts' to advance knowledge claims whose most fundamental assumptions are routinely concealed, and even denied.

Another example worth mentioning briefly here concerns stratospheric ozone depletion and its potentially harmful effects, associated with increased ultraviolet (specifically UVA) exposure. Ozone depletion was almost unknown until the mid-1980s, though it has clearly been going on for a long time, and researchers are still working through the possible direct and indirect consequences – ranging from the relatively well established risks of skin cancers and threats to food production, to the much more uncertain areas of possible immune suppression and virus activation. Many 'lay' people are also now familiar with the skin cancer risks posed by UVA exposure – though they may have little idea about the *level* of that risk. But many people also 'know' that they like outdoor lifestyles, including sun-bathing.

These different ways of 'knowing' about exposure to sunlight can be thought of in terms of competing 'discourses'. In this context, 'discourse' refers to more or less coherent bodies of ideas, along with their linguistic expression (including the use of characteristic metaphors and images) and associated social practices. Thus for Coupland and Coupland (1997), there is a *recreational* discourse, in which ultraviolet exposure is represented positively as the hedonistic leisure activity of sun-bathing, and an *ascetic body culture* discourse in which it is portrayed as a threat to human health. A complex relationship often exists between lay and expert – and, especially, between scientific and non-scientific – knowledge within discourses. For instance, the ascetic body culture discourse draws heavily on scientific claims concerning the damaging effects of ultraviolet exposure, whilst playing down scientific and non-scientific claims concerning its positive features (notably the production of vitamin D, the prevention of Seasonal Affective Disorder, and the recreational values widely accorded to sun-bathing itself). Scientific claims may play a less central role in the recreational discourse, but are nonetheless prominent in the marketing of skin protection and sun-tanning products. This is but one example of the ways in which 'discourse analysis' can be used to examine the different environmental knowledges held by individuals and groups (see Darrier 1999). So far as environmental decision making is concerned, for example, Litfin (1994), Hajer (1995) and Paterson (1996) have shown how discourse analysis provides a powerful tool in the study of policy making in relation to stratospheric ozone depletion, acid rain and global warming respectively.

However, discourses may themselves be considered to reflect, and be constructed upon, distinctive 'rationalities' – that is, distinctive ways of comprehending, or reasoning about, the world. 'Rationalities' concern, in particular, alternative conceptions of the possible forms which knowledge about the world can take, but whose underlying premises are routinely concealed from – or, at least, taken for granted by – those who draw upon them in constructing their discourses. For present purposes, it is sufficient to distinguish between 'technical' and 'cultural' rationalities, though more complex categorisations are possible (see section 3.3.1).

To proclaim a 'technical rationality' is to assert, explicitly or implicitly, the *superiority* of 'instrumental' knowledge – especially knowledge (for example, of cause–effect relationships) which facilitates the control of physical, biological or other processes. It is, furthermore, to proclaim (again, explicitly or implicitly) the *objectivity* of such knowledge: that is, to assert that it can be meaningfully regarded as existing independently of those who deploy it – for example, independently of any value judgements which pertain to the utility of such knowledge, or to the legitimacy (or otherwise) of using it to exercise control over physical, biological or other processes. To proclaim a 'cultural rationality', by contrast, is to assert that knowledge necessarily contains a subjective component: that human values, motives, interests and intentions are reflected in *all* knowledge claims. It is, then, to proclaim the *connectedness* of instrumental and non-instrumental knowledge – for example, to assert that the quest for knowledge that facilitates control of physical, biological or other processes at least implies a positive judgement as to the legitimacy of that knowledge. Technical rationality most obviously applies to natural scientific knowledge, but it can apply to any circumstances in which values, intentions and other subjectivities are excluded from attempts to understand a situation. For example, in assessing the risks associated with GM crops, only some of the possible sources of harm are characteristically taken into account (see Chapter 4).

Donald Schön (1983, 1992) has argued that professionals in numerous fields – including education and health, as well as environmental management – often erroneously conceptualise their decision making in relation to a 'technical–rational' view of knowledge: that is, on the premise that problems can be addressed through unmediated application of instrumental knowledge (e.g. 'codified' or 'text-book' science). From this perspective:

> **Rigorous professional practice is conceived as essentially technical. Its rigor depends on the use of describable, testable, replicable techniques derived from scientific research, based on knowledge that is objective, consensual, cumulative, and convergent.** Schön 1992: 52

In contrast, for Schön, professional decision making can be more appropriately understood as requiring a case-by-case, and *'reflective'* response to 'messy, indeterminate, problematic situations' (*op cit*: 53). Such an approach depends in part – but only in part – on codified, technical, knowledge. Crucially, it also involves the deployment of 'tacitly-held' knowledge – that is, of a kind which practitioners might associate most readily with 'experience, trial and error, intuition or muddling through' (*op cit*: 55). The danger of 'non-reflective' practice – that is, of operating with a 'technical–rational' view of knowledge – is that decision making strategies are ill-equipped for dealing with uncertainty and novelty of the kind to which many environmental problems give rise:

> **In the early minutes and hours of the 'accident' at the Three-Mile Island nuclear power plant, for example, operators and managers found themselves confronted with combinations of signals they could only regard as 'weird', unprecedented, unlike anything they had ever seen before ... Yet they persisted in attempting to assimilate these strange and perplexing signals to a situation of normalcy – 'not wanting to believe', as one manager put it, that the nuclear core had been uncovered and damaged. Only after twelve hours of fruitless attempts to construe the situation as a minor problem – a breach in a steam line, a build-up of steam in the primary circulation system – did one anonymous key manager insist, against the wishes of others in the plant, that 'future actions be based on the assumption that the core has been uncovered, the fuel severely damaged'.** *op cit*: 61.

3.2.2 Science and subjectivity

Critical realists and constructivists share a belief that scientific knowledge is socially 'mediated' – that is, influenced to some extent by the social context in which it is produced (see Chapter 2). But why do they believe this, and how do they think it comes about? The first question can be answered most simply by reflecting on the history of science. On the 'common-sense' view of science (see e.g. Chalmers 1988: 1), new 'facts' and theories are simply added to the existing body of scientific knowledge. It may be possible, therefore, to believe in the certainty, 'truth' and objectivity of both the existing and the new knowledge. However, there are occasions when existing knowledge is radically altered by scientific advance. Such changes may not occur very frequently; but we must, nevertheless, admit the possibility that some and perhaps most (or even all!) of current scientific knowledge will, at some point in the future, be dismissed as 'false' – and replaced with new scientific 'truths'.

Let us return now to the question of *how* subjectivity enters into scientific knowledge. One approach to this question involves investigating the potential influence of 'vested interests' on the production of knowledge. This may operate at the level of individual scientists, whose work might, for example, be influenced (consciously or unconsciously) by a desire to gain acceptance or establish a reputation. Additionally, however, we should look for subjectivity at the institutional level, where work might, for example, be influenced by competition with other institutions for funding and prestige, or by the possibility of commercial gain. We should particularly note, in this respect, that a considerable amount of contemporary scientific research is commercially funded – that is, undertaken by universities and research institutes operating under contract to large corporations, or by research scientists working directly for such corporations (see Box 3.2). Influences such as these may have an effect on the ways in which data are produced (for example, in terms of measurement and classification decisions) and/or interpreted (particularly given the frequency with which theoretical accounts are 'under-determined' by empirical evidence or may be manifest in decisions about which research to fund – and which not to fund (see Chapter 2). The latter are essentially *social* decisions which reflect the interplay of competing interests and values of key stakeholders (e.g. academic, business, governmental, media and non-governmental organisations, along with public opinion). For example, a decision to increase public expenditure on research into renewable energy sources, at the expense of nuclear power, might reveal a shift in governmental priorities – driven, at least in part, by a changing climate of opinion concerning the relative costs and benefits (economic, social and environmental) of different energy supply systems.

The 'interest-based' approaches described above tend to emphasise the importance of purposeful human (individual or collective) decisions in the production of knowledge. That is, they draw attention to choices

---

Box 3.2 Funding of UK research

According to the UK Government's Office of Science and Technology:

- total expenditure on research and development (R&D) in the UK in 1997 was £14 656 million
- expenditure on R&D came from the private sector (50%), government (31%), private non-profit organisations (4%), higher education (1%) and various overseas sources (15%)
- private sector expenditure on R&D increased (in real terms) by nearly 20% between 1981 and 1997, whilst government expenditure decreased by nearly 20%
- 86% of total expenditure was in civil R&D, and 14% in defence-related activities
- R&D performed in private sector organisations was concentrated in pharmaceuticals (23%), services (23%), electrical machinery (12%), and transport equipment (11%)

Source: Figures extracted from *SET Statistics*, the UK Office of Science and Technology's annual handbook of key science, engineering and technology (SET) statistics, available on-line at http://www.lowpay.gov.uk/ost/setstats (accessed on 29/9/99).

made by individuals acting in pursuit of their own self-interest or the interests of institutions. Somewhat in contrast, 'cultural' approaches focus less on individual choices, and more on the influence of 'cultural context', within which individuals – and institutions – operate. Such influences (examples of which are discussed in Chapter 2) are less widely recognised and more deeply seated than those associated with 'vested interest'. In relation to science, cultural context might be that of an academic discipline (e.g. chemistry), or scientifically trained profession (e.g. environmental health), or wider 'knowledge' community (e.g. the industrial–scientific community). A feature of these cultures and communities is that their members characteristically share a set of beliefs concerning, for example, the nature of 'reality' and ways in which knowledge can be produced and validated; concerning the validity of certain theoretical and 'factual' knowledge; concerning the choice of objects for scholarly and professional attention; and concerning the education and training required for full membership of such a community. Importantly, many of these beliefs are tacitly held and taken for granted – and are not, therefore, routinely subjected to systematic and critical analysis. (For a useful overview of 'disciplinary cultures', see Becher and Huber 1990.)

The various scientific knowledge cultures and communities described above do not, of course, exist in isolation from one another. Rather, they have many features in common which can, in part, be appreciated by considering the historical context within which they have developed. There is insufficient space here to provide a lengthy account of the European scientific revolution (but see, for example, Hamilton 1992, and Pepper 1996). It may, nonetheless, be instructive to identify some essential differences between scientific and non-scientific cultural perspectives, or 'worldviews' – especially in relation to Sheldrake's (1990: 27) characterisation of science as embodying 'a vast inflation of the ambition to dominate nature, a way of treating the natural world as if it had no inherent value or life of its own, and an overthrow of traditional restraints on human knowledge and power.'

Almost without exception, non-scientific ways of 'knowing' the world have viewed nature as fundamentally 'alive', or 'animated', in the sense of being imbued with spiritual properties and significance – as, for example, in the sacred plants and animals of many religions and non-scientific cultures. Furthermore, non-scientific worldviews frequently ascribe properties of 'intrinsic' value and purpose to nature – that is, value and purpose which are *independent* of their significance for humans (see Chapter 6). Clearly science, as a way of 'knowing' the world, does not deal in such matters – and to the extent that scientific ways of 'knowing' have come to pervade modern thinking, these non-scientific ideas are widely regarded as irrational, subjective and intellectually inferior to the knowledge generated by science itself.

The European scientific revolution's legacy, then, is a body of thought whose social and environmental significance is difficult to exaggerate; and a body of thought which is *just that* – namely products of the human intellect which, however, are clearly not the only possible set of ideas on which intellectual engagement with the natural world could conceivably be founded. Contemporary science affords a very distinctive and selective way of knowing the world, which excludes a great many potential perspectives and areas of inquiry, either on the grounds that they don't permit objective observation (for example, the beauty of landscapes, or the intrinsic value of plants and animals: see Chapter 2); or because the predominantly reductionist scientific community does not accord them high priority (for example, holistic medicine or eco-science); or because the major commercial and political sponsors of scientific research choose not to fund them (for example, renewable energy generation). A particularly relevant example in the context of this book is taxonomy – the classification of living organisms – which is a declining specialism at the same time as species conservation is an increasingly important issue (Chapter 6).

Most critical realist and constructivist philosophers of science would acknowledge the potential importance of some, if not all, of the contextual values described above. However, many practising scientists (and non-scientists) would claim that the processes by which scientific knowledge is produced and validated are different from those associated with other

71

kinds of knowledge – and, in particular, that they provide for the ultimate elimination of contextual values. These processes include:

- *Scientific methods themselves* the practice of producing knowledge according to established, standardised and controlled methods (see p. 15).
- *Peer review* the practice of subjecting new knowledge claims – and the methods by which they are produced – to critical scrutiny (usually by anonymous and purportedly independent experts) before they can be published in scholarly journals.
- *Replication* the practice of seeking to replicate published findings under a wide variety of circumstances – usually involving different people working at different institutions (again, see Chapter 1).
- *Self-criticism* an ethos of systematically seeking to question new knowledge and the means by which it is produced.

Can these processes eliminate subjectivity from science? They may in general counteract the effects of 'local' contextual values (i.e. those deriving from the circumstances of individual scientists or institutions) – and bring to light cases of scientific bias, fraud or misconduct (see p. 49). But, of course, the challenge to traditional realism is not principally concerned with cases of scientific misconduct. The supposed objectivity of accepted methods can also be questioned: for example, Shrader-Frechette and McCoy (1994) argue that much ecological research is value-laden, as a consequence of the value-laden nature of the theories that underpin methodological choices. More damning still, science's 'checking processes' (peer review, replication and self-criticism) are themselves processes which take place within their own socio-historical contexts: contexts that can be characterised in terms of the particular individuals, institutions, knowledge communities, etc. that participate in those processes. Consequently, these processes must themselves – at least in part – be subjective. Whilst they might provide a means for eliminating or reducing some kinds of contextual influence, they cannot provide any guarantee of total objectivity. It is for these reasons that we would tentatively endorse many 'critical realist' and 'mediated constructivist' accounts of scientific knowledge – at least in preference to those emanating from 'traditional realism' or 'strong constructivism'.

3.2.3 Scientific knowledge claims: the wider social context

How, then, should we characterise the wider social context within which scientific knowledge claims are produced and transmitted, and wherein environmental decisions are made and enacted, especially by large institutions such as governmental bodies and business corporations? It was suggested in section 3.1 that decision making should be seen within a context which recognises both the power of decision makers themselves, and the influences exerted on them – especially by 'opinion-formers' and other 'agents of persuasion' such as expert communities, interest and pressure groups, the mass media, and 'public opinion'.

From this perspective, some individuals and institutions are clearly more *privileged* than others in their access to the resources required for advancing credible knowledge claims. In particular, academics and other 'knowledge workers' (e.g. commercially or politically sponsored researchers, lawyers, and journalists) are typically able to summon up more substantial reserves of credible knowledge than most ordinary citizens. Commercial and political organisations that are able to fund – or otherwise benefit from – research in fields of direct interest to them, will be similarly privileged. And legal cases which involve contested scientific claims will likewise tend to reflect these inequalities of access to knowledge-related skills and resources (a classic – albeit extreme – example of this is the now-notorious 'McLibel' case, involving an attempt by McDonald's Corporation to sue two private individuals who participated in a leafleting campaign against the company's environmental and social practices: see Vidal 1997).

Likewise, some individuals and institutions are more *influential* than others in their capacity to disseminate environmental knowledge – in most cases, disseminate *their* knowledge (that is, their versions of 'reality'). Clearly the mass media, including those who own and/or exercise direct control over the newspapers, TV and radio stations, etc., are an important part of this picture. But we also (and particularly) have in mind those who are able to use the media to promote their message – either by virtue of commercial or political patronage; or because they are recognised as 'accredited authorities' on a subject of media interest; or because of the inherent attractiveness of their arguments or of the 'source material' (such as video footage) they are in a position to provide. Governmental bodies, political parties, interest groups such as large corporations, and of course environmental pressure groups, all fall into one or more of these categories (see Anderson 1997, and Hansen 1993). There are in effect 'hierarchies' of power and influence, which differentiate individuals, groups and organisations in terms of their capacity to produce and disseminate knowledge – in effect, differentiate them in terms of their ability to set the environmental agenda – and hence to influence what *other* individuals, groups and organisations 'know' about the environment (see, for example, Ploughman 1997).

The controversial case of 'Gulf War Syndrome' illustrates many of these points concerning inequalities of privilege and influence in the advancement of scientific knowledge claims – including the power of the mass media to advance or withhold claims, and to endorse or undermine them.

It also reinforces some of our earlier arguments (in section 3.2.2) concerning 'science and subjectivity'. The Gulf War itself began in August 1990, when Iraq invaded the small neighbouring oil state of Kuwait; it ended in February 1991 with the expulsion of Iraqi forces, by a so-called 'Gulf Alliance' of military forces drawn mainly from the USA and Europe. Since the ending of hostilities, an increasing number of veterans – mainly in the UK and the USA – have claimed to be suffering from a range of illnesses that they attribute to their service in the Gulf, and which have become widely known as 'Gulf War Syndrome' (see Bloom et al. 1994).

The symptoms and conditions reported are highly variable, but with chronic fatigue, joint and muscle pains, severe headaches, sleep disorders and depression amongst the most common. The most frequently alleged causes are:

- Exposure to organophosphate insecticides sprayed on tents, equipment and elsewhere. Organophosphate exposure is known to inhibit the enzyme cholinesterase, and hence damage the nervous system.
- Side-effects from the anti-nerve agent NAPS (Nerve Agent Pre-treatment Set), which also damages the nervous system by inhibiting the enzyme cholinesterase.
- Side-effects from the numerous vaccinations given, particularly against biological weapons such as anthrax, botulism and bubonic plague.
- Exposure to chemical warfare agents, including mustard gas and the nerve gas sarin – either as a result of their deployment in the theatre of war, and/or during subsequent disposal operations.
- Radiation exposure from depleted uranium-tipped missiles, used by the Gulf Alliance forces themselves.
- Exposure to smoke containing NO_x, SO_2 and inhalable particulates, from Kuwait's burning oil wells.

Particular attention has been given to the possibility of synergistic effects – though with little consensus over the relative importance of different contributory factors, or concerning the nature and significance of interactions between them. Indeed, there is intense controversy over almost all aspects of these allegations on both sides of the Atlantic. UK and US governments and military leaders alike have consistently denied the existence of 'Gulf War Syndrome' – though all now acknowledge that veterans are disproportionately subject to a range of illnesses which may be connected with their service in the Gulf, either directly or indirectly (e.g. triggered by psychological stress). Conversely, the case *for* 'Gulf War Syndrome' has been advanced principally by veterans themselves – via pressure groups, legal representatives and the mass media, and with support from some members of the political and scientific communities.

The veterans' case involves three key claims, namely:

- The military authorities' actions exposed service personnel to unprecedented medical and environmental hazards. In relation to the administration of vaccines and other prophylactic drugs, for example, representatives of the Gulf War Veterans Association told the UK House of Commons Defence Select Committee that:

  never before have these drugs been administered in such quantities, in such a mixture, over such a condensed period of time, without proper medical supervision, in such confused dosages.
  House of Commons Defence Select Committee 1995: 61

- During and since the conflict, the military authorities have variously failed to generate, record and act on information of relevance to veterans' illnesses; have withheld and destroyed information; have distributed misleading information; and have obstructed inquiries by others. These actions and inactions are allegedly a consequence of incompetence and conspiracy, the latter motivated by fear of recrimination and massive compensation claims; and have (again, allegedly) obstructed veterans' attempts to reveal the 'truth'.

- Diagnosis and treatment of their illnesses have been impeded, in part by the unprecedented nature of their Gulf War experiences and consequent medical conditions, but also by the military authorities' own obstructive behaviour.

How should these competing claims be interpreted? First, the prior value commitments of most veterans would not, seemingly, predispose them to take a stance against the military authorities. Conversely, many now have a financial – and probably a personal/psychological – interest in the debate, as do their legal representatives. Furthermore, the veterans' testimonies are clearly not independent one from another, and may be influenced by the reluctance of 'battle-hardened' soldiers to acknowledge adverse psychological (as opposed to physical) effects – especially stress-related illness – arising from their Gulf experiences.

Second, however, the military authorities' stance is seemingly consistent with *their* core values and interests, including long-standing relationships with armaments manufacturers whose own interests are particularly threatened by allegations of 'self-inflicted' harm. Furthermore, it is notable that the military authorities have gradually shifted their ground in favour of the veterans' position – for example, in belatedly acknowledging organophosphate and possible chemical weapons exposure. However the significance of these changes may to some extent reside in their perceived political expediency, in the face of widespread public and media hostility.

Third, recent scientific research (notably Haley et al. 1997; Ismail et al. 1999; and Unwin et al. 1999) has produced inconsistent conclusions, which offers only partial support for the veterans' case. But, crucially, it is inherent in these allegations that the possibilities for scientific knowledge of 'Gulf War Syndrome' are: 1. constrained by the unprecedented hazards to which service personnel were exposed; and 2. inseparable from the social (and, especially, political) context governing the provision of 'information', including 'disinformation'. It is particularly apparent that, in the absence of heavy pressure from some sections of the mass media, this social context would be still less favourable to the veterans' claims, and that the science that currently offers limited support would be less well endowed with both funding and evidence.

Finally, however, allegations of 'Gulf War Syndrome' are attractive to several sections of the mass media, and for a variety of possible reasons. This applies in particular to the print media, which are not bound by commitments to 'impartiality' of the kind which (in the UK, at least) govern radio and television. Such allegations have obvious appeal, for example, to a politically liberal/left-leaning and 'anti-establishment' (especially anti-*military* establishment) news-paper such as *The Guardian*, particularly given its commitment to reporting politically and scientifically controversial issues of environmental and public health concern. They are attractive also to those mass market newspapers which thrive on stories of 'human interest' – especially to the extent that such stories can be presented in terms that reflect recurrent themes and 'chime' with wider value commitments. Hence *The Mail* newspapers' extensive coverage of 'Gulf War Syndrome' has repeatedly focused on the plight of individual veterans; has consistently denounced the uncaring attitude of 'faceless bureaucrats' and 'cynical politicians'; and has – implicitly, if not explicitly – espoused the virtues of 'military service' and 'patriotic causes'. For example, the article by former RAF Flight Lieutenant John Nichol, who was shot down and imprisoned in Iraq during the War ('Why do they treat our sick and dying Gulf War heroes like beggars? The conspiracy of silence that must end now': *Mail on Sunday*, 29 December 1996) resonates with each one of these archetypal *Mail* newspaper themes and values.

3.2.4 Scientific knowledge and social context: a summary

Let us be very clear about what we are – and are not – claiming to be the implications of this analysis. We are *not* suggesting that science is somehow 'wrong' in any meaningful sense of the word. On the contrary, we would suggest that the knowledge produced by scientific endeavour is utterly astounding for its revelations and achievements in very many fields – travel and power generation, to name but two. On the subject of travel, scientific commentator Richard Dawkins has wryly asked why it is that, when sociologists who claim scientific knowledge to be no more than a social construct go to international conferences, they 'entrust ... [their] air-travel plans to a Boeing rather than a magic carpet' (quoted in Irwin 1994: 17). In other words, so far as he is concerned, science 'works' and is therefore 'fact' – as opposed to non-science, which does not 'work', and which is therefore fantasy. Amusing though Dawkins' rhetorical question may be, it seemingly misses the point that while science indeed frequently *does* 'work' (spectacular failures such as air disasters and nuclear generator meltdowns excepted), it cannot simply be equated with 'fact' or 'truth'. This is so, we have argued, for several reasons:

- Science affords a very partial – or selective – and distinctive way of knowing the world, mainly grounded in the worldview of 'technical rationality'.
- Science that 'works' can nonetheless be falsified by more soundly based accounts of why it works – since all scientific knowledge is characterised by *provisionality*.
- The distinction between facts and values is, in practice, often difficult to maintain.
- The influence of contextual values on scientific knowledge is not as readily eliminated, by processes such as peer review, as many scientists would like to believe.
- The capacity to advance credible scientific argument is related to claims-makers' possession of power, influence and resources.

3.3 Science and environmental decision making in the 'risk society'

According to the *Oxford English Dictionary*, 'risk' refers to 'danger, hazard, exposure to mischance or peril'. Clearly not all contemporary risks are 'environmental' in any obvious sense; but many are – either because they emanate from the natural or human-made environment (e.g. adverse human health effects associated with pollution (see Chapter 10) or other human modifications of nature), and/or because they pose a hazard for non-human nature itself (e.g. marine pollution incidents (Chapter 8) resulting from oil spillages). As recent debates over (for example) genetic modification and global climate change have shown, questions of risk frequently attract enormous attention from the mass media, environmental and consumer pressure groups, academics and politicians; furthermore, of course, many are the object of intense scientific, public and political controversy. It is probably no exaggeration to say that risk and its management now occupy the centre-stage of environmental decision making.

In this section, we seek to develop a critique of 'mainstream' risk assessment and management, which grows out of our preceding sociological and philosophical analyses of science and environmental decision making. In brief, proponents of this 'mainstream' view assert that environmental risks can be most reliably known through 'expert' science, at least in probabilistic terms; that they can be measured by combining the probability and magnitude of adverse events; and that they can be most effectively managed by existing political and other institutions, using a combination of appropriate policies and technologies. By contrast, most 'lay' assessments of risk are considered to be subjective – and often based on 'irrational fears'. A classic exposition of this view is contained in the Royal Society's (1983) *Risk Assessment: A Study Group Report*. Opponents of this account – for example, sociologist Ulrich Beck (1992; 1995) – typically argue that the uncertainties, vested interests and other subjectivities of science *in general* assume a particularly acute form in cases of environmental risk. They reject the idea of a sharp dichotomy between 'objective' (i.e. expert-scientific) and 'subjective' (i.e. non-expert) assessments of risk – along with the assertion of a singular, technical rationality, on which it is founded – pointing instead to a world dominated by near-universal ignorance of environmental risks (even amongst scientists), and to the existence of 'plural rationalities' (Adams 1995). Furthermore – and paradoxically – Beck and others note that many contemporary risks are themselves products of the very 'technological progress' through which advocates of science have sought to provide security from natural environmental threats and uncertainties (e.g. food insecurities, and the vagaries of disease – which have their latter-day counterparts in the risks associated with, for example, chemical residues in food and antibiotic-resistant pathogens, respectively). Beck has characterised the 'Risk Society' as one in which technological hazards are a pervasive and defining feature, socially and politically. (For an accessible summary of this thesis, see chapter 10 of Adams 1995.) Many of these emergent tensions between advocates and critics of the mainstream view are reflected in the Royal Society's second (1992) report on risk.

3.3.1 Science and environmental risk assessment: the 'mainstream' view and its critics

The field of environmental risk, then, deals with threats posed to human health and safety and to ecosystems. In practice, however – at least, until quite recently – the former have been dominant in the academic literature and in professional applications: for example, in the fields of industrial safety and insurance. Similarly, whilst environmental threats are potentially associated with adverse anthropogenic and natural conditions, the former have attracted considerably more attention. Hence the archetypal environmental risk is that posed *to* human health and safety, and *by* 'technological' hazards such as industrial installations or polluted environments. Regulatory and other legal pressures have been a major driving force behind these developments – as, indeed, they have been also in the more recent (and partial) refocusing of risk-related interest on ecological threats, such as loss of biodiversity.

The paramount intellectual influence on studies of environmental risk has been that of technical rationality (see section 3.2.1). From this perspective, science alone is able to provide a reliable basis for assessing risks and technology is seen to hold out the only realistic hope of avoiding – or at least minimising – most such risks. However, proponents of this view acknowledge that the assessment of environmental risk is, by definition, subject to scientific uncertainty. In Chapter 2 we saw that the processes of measurement and modelling have many associated uncertainties. To these we can add the uncertainties surrounding the occurrence of 'singular' events: not knowing – or knowing only in a probabilistic sense (i.e. from aggregate data) – the likely incidence of human error or of an extreme occurrence (such as the Chernobyl accident), or the response of an individual organism to some known risk factor (such as extreme allergic reactions).

Proponents of the mainstream view also acknowledge that lay (especially public and mass media) evaluations of risk frequently do not accord with those emanating from scientific risk assessments. They commonly distinguish between the *subjective* judgements of non-experts (which are considered to be 'distorted' by factors such as novelty, unintelligibility, bureaucratic secrecy, and perceived absence of choice or control associated with a given risk), and the *objective* assessments of scientists themselves – whilst recognising that 'public fears', however irrational, must also be taken into account when policy decisions are made.

Others are more fundamentally sceptical about the reliability of scientific risk assessment. For example, MacGarvin (1994) argues that attempts to establish safe limits for marine pollution are repeatedly undermined by unexpected research findings, even in intensely studied marine areas such as the North Sea (see Chapter 8). Adams (1995), O'Riordan (see in particular O'Riordan 1995; O'Riordan and Cameron 1994; O'Riordan and Jordan 1995), Wynne (see especially Wynne 1992; Wynne and Mayer 1993) and others are, in various ways, equally sceptical about the potential of science to measure risk objectively. For example, Wynne and Mayer claim that, in the context of debates about safe limits for industrial discharges to the marine environment, reductionist science narrows the range of possible cause–effect relationships that are likely to be acknowledged, in such a way as to exclude 'multiple interactions and composite variables such as the health of an organism's immune system, stress and disease, which are intrinsically less precise and reductionist' (1993: 34). In general, they assert, this approach creates a misleading impression of scientific certainty in environmental risk assessment:

> It may be possible to specify the uncertainties within this reduced scientific framework, but the larger uncertainties – even about whether the right terms and parameters have been identified – are buried. (*op cit*: 33.)

Many philosophers and sociologists of science would probably consider these arguments to be consistent with their wider view of the provisionality, selectivity and value-laden tendencies of scientific knowledge in general (see section 3.2). Indeed, according to Yearley (1991) and others (for example, O'Neill 1993 and Wynne 1992), these problems tend to be particularly acute in the case of *environmental* science – for the reasons identified in Chapter 1, and because the politically charged nature of many environmental issues tends to invite heavily value-laden interpretations. In particular, these 'sceptical' and 'optimistic' accounts of scientific uncertainty reflect wider differences of environmental philosophy, which are manifested in:

- Scepticism (or outright pessimism) and optimism, respectively, concerning the ultimate resilience of natural systems, and concerning the capacity of human societies to overcome obstacles to 'progress' (including resource limitations and other environmental impediments). These views, in turn, legitimate more and less recognition of the interests of future generations.
- More and less questioning of values and political programmes which prioritise economic growth and material prosperity.
- More and less recognition of non-instrumental (especially intrinsic) values in nature – which, in the former view, provides an additional rationale for environmental protection.
- More or less adherence to the view that those who degrade the environment should pay their 'ecological debts' – especially if the damage was/is foreseeable in the light of prevailing knowledge.

In a similar vein, Adams (1995: 169) argues that '[t]here are scientists to serve all the established myths of nature'. Drawing on earlier work by (amongst others) Mary Douglas and Aaron Wildavsky, he proposes a fourfold classification of 'culturally constructed rationalities', which is intended to accommodate the diversity of 'expert' and 'lay' perspectives on risk. The four rationalities, which are depicted in Box 3.3, represent distinctive views of nature and of human–nature relationships – including risk-related decision making behaviours under conditions of uncertainty. Of these four, 'hierarchism' most closely corresponds with the technical rationality that we have attributed to mainstream environmental decision makers – but, in this formulation, it is recast as merely one amongst several competing rationalities. Indeed, Adams explicitly rejects the mainstream assumption that people are fundamentally and invariably risk-averse: he argues instead for a theory of 'risk compensation', according to which individuals' propensity to take risks reflects their evaluation of the likely losses and rewards. A crucial feature of this theory is the centrality of 'balancing behaviour', which Adams likens to that of a thermostatically controlled system (see Figure 3.1):

The setting of the thermostat varies from one individual to another, from one group to another, from one culture to another. (*op cit*: 15)

We do not dispute the argument that individuals often willingly take risks, and frequently resort to 'balancing' behaviour. Indeed, this interpretation seems especially apposite in relation to road safety behaviour (for example, driving speeds) – in which Adams takes a particular interest – and

---

Box 3.3 The cultural construction of risk: four rationalities

'*Individualists* tend to view nature as stable, robust and benign ... They are believers in market forces and individual responsibility, and are hostile to the regulators of the "nanny State" ... Where evidence is inconclusive ... they place the onus of proof on those who would interfere. They tend to an optimistic interpretation of history, and are fond of citing evidence of progress in the form of statistics of rising gross domestic product and lengthening life expectancy.'

'*Egalitarians* cling to the view of nature as fragile and precarious. They would have everyone tread lightly on the Earth and in cases of scientific doubt invoke the precautionary principle ... Egalitarians incline to an anxious interpretation of history; they read it as a series of dire warnings and precautionary tales of wars, plagues and famines, and species and civilizations extinguished through human greed or carelessness.'

'*Hierarchists* believe that nature will be good to them, *if* properly managed. They are members of big business, big government, big bureaucracy. They are respecters of authority, both scientific and administrative ... They believe in research to establish "the facts" about both human and physical nature, and in regulation for the collective good ... Hierarchists take a "balanced" view of history; it contains warnings but also holds out the promise of rewards for "correct" behaviour.'

'*Fatalists* ... believe nature to be capricious and unpredictable. They hope for the best and fear the worst; life is a lottery over whose outcome they have no control ... They do not study history.'

Source: Adams 1995: 40–1.

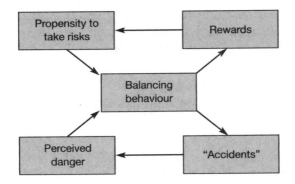

Figure 3.1 The risk 'thermostat'.
Redrawn from Adams 1995.

in other circumstances where risk-related decision making can be 'reduced' to questions of individual 'free will', exercised as an unmediated reflection of the decision maker's 'culturally constructed rationality'. Conversely, it seems rather less illuminating of the many circumstances where individuals are compelled to make decisions – and to act – *against* their 'better judgement'. For example, in the case of poor inner city residents who have little choice but to live with dangerous roads, the 'risk thermostat' may assist in explaining relatively minor aspects of day-to-day decision making – such as whether, when and how to cross such a road – but little else. Equally, and of greater significance for our wider argument in this chapter, the 'risk thermostat' idea may be of limited relevance to understanding corporate (e.g. business and government) environmental behaviour. It seems to us improbable that corporate decision making closely reflects *any one* of the four rationalities – as opposed to, for example, the courting of electoral popularity; the profit motive; and in general the power of large institutions to make, enact and rationalise decisions which are perceived to serve their own interests. More plausibly, then, corporate decision making – at least within the industrial–scientific community and its allies – most closely resembles an eclectic and opportunistic mix of 'individualism' and 'hierarchism': indeed, this seems to be increasingly acknowledged by Adams in his closing chapters.

Finally, Adams' individualistic analysis appears of limited relevance in relation to those large-scale social and technological developments that are tending to foster widespread public scepticism and mistrust towards many public institutions – including governments, business corporations and other decision making bodies, along with the 'institution' of science itself. These developments include the increasingly 'global' nature of economic transactions, information exchange and governance; the unprecedented speed of technological change; the 'fracturing' of contemporary societies (for example, along lines of ethnicity, gender and lifestyle), and associated emergence of 'plural' – as opposed to 'consensual' – value systems; the growing sense of rootlessness and powerlessness that globalisation, techno-logical change and social fracturing may themselves engender; and of course, related to all of the above, heightened awareness of the magnitude and complexity of environmental problems. (See, for example, Hall, Held and McGrew 1992.) We reconsider the significance of these developments for environmental decision making in section 3.4.

3.3.2 Science and environmental risk management: the policy debate

Advocates of (mainstream) scientific risk assessment commonly turn to the 'human sciences' (including philosophy, economics, sociology and psy-chology) for guidance in the fields of environmental risk policy and management. From this perspective, sociology and psychology can assist in revealing and managing public opinion (including 'irrational fears'); eco-nomics offers a basis for weighing the costs and benefits associated with (for example) proposed risk reduction measures; and philosophy can inform judgements about 'fairness' in the social allocation of risk. In this view, however, scientific knowledge *per se* remains effectively 'insulated' from the encroachment of human subjectivities; in large measure, further-more, policy and management tools adopted from the human sciences are precisely that – namely, those (purportedly objective and mainly quantita-tive) approaches which aspire to emulate the natural sciences themselves.

As we have seen, critics of scientific risk assessment reject this 'socially insulated' view of science. They also take issue with the supposed objectiv-ity of cost–benefit analysis (CBA, see Chapter 2), which has formed the cornerstone of conventional approaches to risk management. This is on the grounds that neither the scientific assessment of risk, nor the eco-nomic valuation of costs and benefits associated with alternative management strategies (including choice of a 'discount rate', to reflect the relative valuation of present – *vis-à-vis* future – costs and benefits), are value-free activities. In relation to the risks associated with global climate change (see Chapter 5), for example, O'Riordan and Jordan (1995: 202) argue that:

> Both the likelihood of the global change, and the possible 'costs', are not known for sure. The actual benefits from avoidance action now depend very much on the [proposed] shape of the damage curve 50 to 100 years from now.
>
> Analysts will tend to visualise the significance of such a curve on the basis of how resilient or vulnerable they perceive to be the capacity of the earth's life support systems to adjust. Also critical is the degree to which human society can adjust ... [F]or the 'vulnerability perceivers', cost–benefit analysis is loaded in favour of high costs to reputedly but unproven high benefits,

while for the 'resilience perceivers' the benefits of early avoidance would have to be more clearly justified. Any cost–benefit decision rule therefore is likely to be intensely political, not purely financial.

Hence the critique of CBA combines with that of scientific risk assessment (and with the associated philosophical dispositions noted above) to give an essentially sceptical view of the protection afforded against environmental risks by the mainstream approach. These doubts have led, in turn, to the development of an alternative – so-called 'precautionary' – approach to risk management. The precautionary principle is broadly understood to mean 'erring on the side of caution'. It reflects the view that action to forestall possible environmental harm, or threats to human health and safety, may well be justified, even where conclusive scientific evidence of such adverse consequences cannot be produced – precisely for the reason that such evidence may not be available, particularly within the limited 'window of opportunity' for action to avert ecological disaster or human tragedy.

Advocates of the precautionary principle argue that those wishing to undertake any possibly harmful action should either provide convincing evidence of its harmlessness, or should abstain from that action. The burden should not, in their view, fall on those wishing to protect the environment and/or human health to demonstrate the harmful nature of such an action.

The precautionary principle is now widely recognised by environmental scientists, lobbyists and politicians – though not universally so, as we shall see. Even amongst those who accept the *principle* of precautionary action, however, there is considerable variability of approach, especially in terms of:

- potentially damaging actions to which the precautionary principle should and should not apply
- possible 'targets' for protection (e.g. human health, specified resources or ecosystems, national environments, the global environment) to which it should and should not apply
- the nature and extent of evidence required to trigger action
- possible precautionary measures to be taken
- possible trade-offs or countervailing considerations (e.g. circumstances under which a lower level of environmental protection might be thought preferable)
- on whose shoulders the 'ecological debt' (e.g. costs of remediation) should fall
- whose views should be taken into consideration when decisions concerning the above are taken

These differences of interpretation are systematically documented in Cameron (1994) and Haigh (1994), and are illustrated by the examples in Box 3.4.

Box 3.4 The precautionary principle: some prominent interpretations

... Determined to protect the ozone layer by taking precautionary measures to control equitably total global emissions of substances that deplete it, with the ultimate objective of their elimination on the basis of developments in scientific knowledge, taking into account technical and economic considerations and bearing in mind the developmental needs of developing countries.
Montreal Protocol on Substances That Deplete the Ozone Layer (Preamble, Para.6), as amended in 1990

... AGREES that ... the Contracting Parties shall be guided by a precautionary approach to environmental protection whereby appropriate preventive measures are taken when there is reason to believe that substances or energy introduced in the marine environment are likely to cause harm even when there is no conclusive evidence to prove a causal relation between inputs and their effects.
London Dumping Convention (Resolution LDC 44/14), 1972, as amended in 1991

In order to protect the environment, the precautionary approach shall be widely applied by States according to their capabilities. Where there are threats of serious or irreversible damage, lack of full scientific certainty shall not be used as a reason for postponing cost-effective measures to prevent environmental degradation.
UNCED Declaration (Principle 15), Rio de Janeiro, 1992

The Parties should take precautionary measures to anticipate, prevent or minimise the causes of climate change and mitigate its adverse effects. Where there are threats of serious or irreversible damage, lack of full scientific certainty should not be used as a reason for postponing such measures, taking into account that policies and measures to deal with climate change should be cost effective so as to ensure global benefits at the lowest possible cost.
UN Framework Convention on Climate Change (Article 3 (3)), 1992

Where appropriate (for example, where there is uncertainty combined with the possibility of the irreversible loss of valued resources) actions should be based on the so-called 'precautionary principle' if the likely balance of costs and benefits justifies it. Even then the action taken should be in proportion to the risk.
UK Strategy for Sustainable Development – Department of the Environment Consultation Paper, 1993

A simpler, more flexible and more applicable definition states that 'No wastes should be discharged into the sea unless it can be shown that they are harmless'.
Johnston, P. and Simmonds, M., Precautionary principle (letter). *Marine Pollution Bulletin*, **21**(8), 402

The precautionary principle states that, in the case of marine pollution, no activities should be permitted unless there is a clear understanding of the likely consequences of those activities for the marine environment.
Greenpeace Website: http://www.greenpeace.org

The precautionary principle has become something of a *cause célèbre* amongst its advocates and, equally, a *bête noire* for its opponents, since it embodies many of the wider points of opposition which characterise the highly contested terrain of environmental risk. Amongst opponents, acknowledgement of environmental risk is largely confined to cases of high level (especially accidental) exposure. For example Le Fanu (1995), writing in *Economic Affairs* (journal of the free-market Institute of Economic Affairs), rejects the findings of a Medical Research Council-commissioned report into the threats to male fertility posed by industrially derived xenoe-strogens, for the reason that the amount of naturally occurring oestrogen we consume in food is 4×10^7 higher than that emanating from industrial sources. However, arguments against the precautionary principle are also philosophical in nature. In particular, Milne (1993) has argued that abandoning the 'no cause–effect' presumption of the null hypothesis amounts to a rejection of science itself, in favour of 'moral philosophy'. He has also claimed that '[t]here can be no absolute proof of "safety" or "harmlessness" even if we want there to be one. We have to live with risk' (*op cit*: 36). And Smith (1995: 13) has argued that:

> A wealthier, more technologically progressive society is more resilient and can better ride out whatever adversities are created ... And for that reason, the greatest danger of all is stagnation – the slowing down, the stopping of new technologies.

Most of the *scientific* arguments advanced here are almost certainly not supported by the weight of expert opinion. For example, an important distinction is commonly made – but apparently overlooked by Le Fanu – between naturally occurring oestrogen and industrially produced xenoe-strogens, as the latter are not necessarily broken down or processed by the body. However, the *philosophical* arguments are perhaps less readily dismissed. First, Milne's proposition, that abandoning the 'no cause–effect' presumption of the null hypothesis amounts to a rejection of science itself, has some plausibility – but only insofar as one overlooks those value judgements which underlie the conventional approach itself. Second, while his claim that '[t]here can be no *absolute* proof of "safety" or "harmlessness" even if we want there to be one' (emphasis added) is not widely disputed (since Type II errors can never be eliminated entirely), the criticism applies only to those few advocates of the precautionary principle who are unwilling to accept 'elimination of reasonable doubt' as their criterion for demonstrating harmlessness. Finally Smith's argument, that continuing 'progress' provides the surest basis for responding to environmental threats, goes to the heart of the debate between technological optimists and sceptics/pessimists – and is clearly not the view of an isolated minority.

However, the fundamental objections to this argument, as expressed here, would be:

- In general, its preoccupation with threats posed *by* the natural environment and *to* human well-being; and, conversely, disregard for anthropogenic threats, both to human well-being and to the natural environment itself.
- In particular, its failure to acknowledge that many of the greatest environmental threats are themselves products of the very 'technological progress' on which Smith and others pin their hopes for creating a safer world.

By contrast, as we have seen, it is precisely this paradox which is reflected in recent debates amongst precautionary advocates themselves about the merits of alternative (stronger and weaker) formulations. And it is precisely this paradox also which provided the point of departure for Beck's 'Risk Society' thesis, with which we began the present section.

3.4 Conclusion: from 'exclusionary' to 'inclusionary' environmental decision making

This chapter has explored the social context of science and environmental decision making, focusing mainly on the decisions of large and powerful institutions (such as governmental bodies and business corporations) and, in particular, on the area of environmental risk. We took as our point of departure some of the philosophical foundations pertaining to scientific knowledge, which were established in Chapters 1 and 2. Our own account, however, is primarily sociological in nature.

We have argued that the production of scientific knowledge can usefully be regarded as a process of 'claims making'; and that environmental scientific knowledge claims are characteristically provisional, uncertain, contested by opposing interests (for example, industrialists and environmentalists) and, in some degree, value-laden and subjective. Nevertheless, we have argued also that most environmental decision making is in practice dominated by the perspective of 'technical rationality' (see section 3.2.1) which, mistakenly:

- denies these 'problematic' features of scientific knowledge
- conceives of decision making as requiring the unmediated application of 'codified' or 'text-book' science
- accords priority to 'instrumental' and 'reductionist' forms of science, and hence to knowledge which facilitates the isolation and control of

environmental processes – as opposed to 'ecological' knowledge of multiple interactions, unintended side-effects, etc.
- asserts the superiority of 'expert' science, *vis-à-vis* all other forms of knowledge and all other claims-makers

Not only the validity of 'expert' science, but also the efficacy and legitimacy of conventional decision making bodies themselves, appear to be challenged by recent developments such as those associated with globalisation, rapid technological change and social fracturing (see section 3.3.1). It is no coincidence, therefore, that these developments have coincided with increasing calls for more 'inclusionary' or 'participatory' approaches to decision making in both the private and public sectors (see, for example, Local Government Management Board 1993 and 1994; Quarrie 1992; UK Roundtable on Sustainable Development 1998). Such approaches – of which focus groups, consensus conferences and citizens' juries are three currently popular examples – are intended to allow the interests and values of diverse stakeholders to be represented alongside those of 'experts', and thereby to make decision making more open and democratic. Consensus may well not be reached simply by adopting a more inclusionary process, but decision making *should* be characterised by enhanced communication, mutual understanding and trust, and *legitimacy* of both process and outcome. And, for advocates of inclusionary decision making, process and outcome are inseparable, since:

> **Power lies substantially with those who decide where the boundaries are drawn ... These boundaries not only establish who participates, what participants are allowed to discuss (agenda setting), and who makes what provision for those unable to speak (e.g. Nature, future generations), or the formal practices of engagement, but they also contain the unspoken, but embedded, rules of behaviour and frames of reference which underpin systems of governance.**
>
> Bloomfield et al. 1998: 11

Of course, the idea of public participation in environmental decision making is not a new one: urban and regional planning in the UK, for example, frequently involves public consultation – and, less frequently, public inquiries. However, these 'traditional' forms of participation tend to occur late in the overall process, and to be the preserve of the articulate (*op cit*: 9); they may in some instances be intended principally to generate public support for controversial decisions, such as the siting of nuclear power plants – or as Irwin (1995: 140) puts it, 'to achieve legitimation rather than social dialogue'.

Novel forms of inclusionary decision making may represent a move away from the traditional monopoly of 'experts'. However, they do not typically embrace the 'problematic' view of scientific knowledge that we have sought to develop in this chapter; and they may persist in prioritising expert over lay knowledge and 'establishment' over 'non-establishment' claims. For example, Purdue's (1995) account of the first UK National Consensus Conference of Plant Biotechnology notes that:

Ostensibly, the conference offered scope for environmentalists and others to present their concerns about genetic engineering to the general public and to stimulate wider debate on the issues which could lead to more informed, more democratic decisions. (*op cit*: 170.)

In practice, however, the conference:

ranked people speaking about biotechnology in a distinct pecking order: 'experts', 'counter-experts' and the rest. Any questions that the lower orders asked were presumed to be answerable by those considered to possess expert knowledge ... (*op cit*: 172.)

Purdue concludes that the organisers – namely the British Science Museum, acting on behalf of the Ministry of Agriculture, Fisheries and Food, along with the Biology and Biotechnology Research Council – attempted to use the conference:

to take a quiet first step towards engineering public acceptance of biotechnology in general. (*ibid.*)

Nonetheless, several scholars who have adopted a 'problematised' view of environmental knowledge (for example Hajer 1995 and Irwin 1995) argue that inclusionary decision making has the potential to accommodate the diverse claims that emanate from competing discourses. On their account, then, inclusionary decision making should not pre-suppose the priority of expert over lay, or scientific over non-scientific, knowledges. Rather, it should provide a forum which acknowledges, amongst other things, the provisional, uncertain, value-laden and contestable nature of knowledge; which respects the diverse and sometimes incommensurable discourses voiced by different stakeholders; and which allows for differences to be debated in a spirit of openness and mutual trust. Such an approach would thereby accommodate some of Donald Schön's (1983; 1992) concerns that expert decision makers frequently fail to recognise the subjective and contested nature of their own knowledge claims (see section 3.2.1).

Work is underway to develop practical forms of decision making of this kind. In the academic world, for example, three British universities are currently collaborating with 'user communities' on a project entitled *Deliberative and Inclusionary Processes in Environmental Policy Making*[1] (see also Renn et al. 1995). Similar initiatives can be found in the world of public practice. For example, a report on education and participation in biodiversity conservation commissioned by the Canadian Government (an acknowledged leader in this field: see Fischer 1995 and Local Government Management Board 1994), states:

---

[1] For further information, visit the project web-site at: http://www.geog.ucl.ac.uk/esru/dip/

> People are not simply empty vessels waiting to be filled with new knowledge. Decades of educational research indicate that recipients of scientific information are far from passive, but interact with science, testing it against personal experience, contextualising it by overlaying it with local knowledge, and evaluating its social and institutional implications.
>
> Ham and Kelsey 1998: 5

Widespread adoption of inclusionary decision making processes would clearly represent a major shift in social practice – and a correspondingly significant decentralisation of political power. Consequently, it seems likely that any attempts at a substantial move in this direction will meet with considerable opposition from those individuals and groups whose currently privileged positions and interests are thereby threatened. It remains to be seen, therefore, whether the apparently successful developments in Canada and elsewhere emerge as the new decision making orthodoxy, or turn out to be isolated cases of radical environmental politics in action.

3.5 Summary

- Competing environmental knowledge claims – including those of 'expert' scientists and policy makers, along with members of the 'lay' public – frequently reflect different underlying values, and may be constructed upon competing discourses and rationalities.
- Subjectivities in science are associated variously with vested interests and with the cultural context of scientific knowledge communities. In general, scientific knowledge claims are not impervious to the social context in which they are advanced.
- Given the value-laden nature of scientific knowledge, environmental risks cannot be reliably known through the 'mainstream' approach, which relies exclusively on expert-scientific assessments.
- Doubts about the protection afforded against environmental risks by the 'mainstream' approach, have led to the development of an alternative 'precautionary' approach to risk management.
- Globalisation, rapid technological change and social fracturing are contributing to public mistrust of governments, business corporations and other decision making bodies, along with the 'institution' of science itself.
- There have recently been tentative moves towards more 'inclusionary' approaches to environmental decision making. Some may allow the interests and values of diverse stakeholders to be represented alongside of those of 'experts', and the legitimacy of diverse 'knowledges' to be recognised.

Further reading

Anderson, A. (1997) *Media, Culture and Environment*, UCL Press, London.

Barnes, B. (1985) *About Science*, Blackwell, Oxford.

Barry, J. (1999) *Social Theory and the Environment*, Routledge, London.

Hall, S., Held, D. and McGrew, A. (eds) (1992) *Modernity and its Futures*, Polity Press.

Irwin, A. (1995) *Citizen Science. A Study of People, Expertise and Sustainable Development*, Routledge, London.

O'Riordan, T. (ed) (1999) *Environmental Science for Environmental Management*, 2nd Edition, Prentice Hall, Harlow. This text provides a useful introduction to the policy process itself, as well as developments in 'inclusionary' decision making.

Pepper, D. (1996) *Modern Environmentalism: An Introduction*, Routledge, London.

References

Adams, J. (1995) *Risk*, UCL Press, London.

Anderson, A. (1997) *Media, Culture and Environment*, UCL Press, London.

Becher, T. and Huber, L. (eds) (1990) Disciplinary cultures. *European Journal of Education* (special issue), **25**.

Beck, U. (1992) *Risk Society: Towards a New Modernity*, Sage, London.

Beck, U. (1995) *Ecological Politics in an Age of Risk*, Polity Press, Cambridge.

Bloom, S. et al. (eds) (1994) *Hidden Casualties: The Environmental, Health and Political Consequences of the Persian Gulf War*, Earthscan, London.

Bloomfield, D. et al. (1998) *Deliberative and Inclusionary Processes: Their Contribution to Environmental Governance*. Draft unpublished paper, Environment and Society Research Unit, Department of Geography, University College London.

Cameron, J. (1994) The status of the precautionary principle in international law. In: O'Riordan, T. and Cameron, J. (eds) *Interpreting the Precautionary Principle*, Earthscan, London.

Chalmers, A. (1988) *What is this Thing called Science?* Open University Press, Milton Keynes.

Coupland, N. and Coupland, J. (1997) Bodies, beaches and burn-times: 'environmentalism' and its discursive competitors. *Discourse and Society*, **8**, 7–25.

Darrier, E. (ed) (1999) *Discourses of the Environment*, Blackwell, Oxford.

Fischer, F. (1995) Hazardous waste policy, community movements and the politics of NIMBY: participatory risk assessment in the USA and Canada. In: Fischer, F. and Black, M. (eds) *Greening Environmental Policy: The Politics of a Sustainable Future*, Paul Chapman Publishing, London.

Haigh, N. (1994) The introduction of the precautionary principle into the UK. In: O'Riordan, T. and Cameron, J. (eds) *Interpreting the Precautionary Principle*, Earthscan, London.

Hajer, M. (1995) *The Politics of Environmental Discourses. Ecological Modernization and the Policy Process*, Clarendon Press, Oxford.

Haley, R et al. (1997) Is there a Gulf War syndrome? Searching for syndromes by factor analysis of symptoms. *Journal of the American Medical Association*, **277**, 215–22.

Hall, S., Held, D. and McGrew, A. (eds) (1992) *Modernity and its Futures*, Polity Press.

Ham, L. and Kelsey, E. (1998) *Learning about Biodiversity. A First Look at the Theory and Practice of Biodiversity Education, Awareness and Training in Canada*, Environment Canada, Ottawa, Ontario.

Hamilton, P. (1992) The enlightenment and the birth of social science. In: Hall, S. and Gieben, B. (eds) *Formations of Modernity*, Polity Press.

Hansen, A. (ed) (1993) *The Mass Media and Environmental Issues*, Leicester University Press, Leicester.

House of Commons Defence Select Committee (1995) *Gulf War Syndrome. Report, Together with the Proceedings of the Committee Relating to the Report, Minutes of Evidence and Memoranda*, House of Commons Paper No 197, Session 1995–96.

Irwin, A. (1994) Science's social standing. *Times Higher Education Supplement*, 30 September, 17–19.

Irwin, A. (1995) *Citizen Science. A Study of People, Expertise and Sustainable Development*, Routledge, London.

Ismail, K et al. (1999) Is there a Gulf War syndrome? *The Lancet*, **353**, 179–82.

Le Fanu, J. (1995) Can we determine what level of environmental toxins presents a serious risk? *Economic Affairs*, **16**, 15–18.

Litfin, K.(1994) *Ozone Discourses. Science and Politics in Global Environmental Cooperation*, Columbia University Press, New York.

Local Government Management Board (1993) *Local Agenda 21. The UK's Report to the UN Commission of Sustainable Development*, Local Government Management Board, Luton.

Local Government Management Board (1994) *Canadian Roundtables and Other Mechanisms for Sustainable Development in Canada*, Local Government Management Board, Luton.

MacGarvin, M. (1994) Precaution, science and the sin of hubris. In: O'Riordan, T. and Cameron, J. (eds) *Interpreting the Precautionary Principle*, Earthscan, London.

Milne, A. (1993) The perils of green pessimism. *New Scientist*, 12 June, 31–7.

OECD (1979) *Technology on Trial: Public Participation in Decision-Making Related to Science and Technology*, OECD, Paris.

O'Neill, J. (1993) *Ecology, Policy and Politics*, Routledge, London.

O'Riordan, T. (1995) Environmental science on the move. In: O'Riordan, T. (ed) *Environmental Science for Environmental Management*, Longman, Harlow.

O'Riordan, T. and Cameron, J. (1994) The history and contemporary significance of the precautionary principle. In: O'Riordan, T. and Cameron, J. (eds) *Interpreting the Precautionary Principle*, Earthscan, London.

O'Riordan, T. and Jordan, A. (1995) The precautionary principle in contemporary environmental politics. *Environmental Values*, **4**, 191–212.

Paterson, M. (1996) *Global Warming and Global Politics*, Routledge, London.

Pepper, D. (1996) *Modern Environmentalism: An Introduction*, Routledge, London.

Ploughman, P. (1997) Disasters, the media and social structures: a typology of credibility hierarchy persistence based on newspaper coverage of the Love Canal and six other disasters. *Disasters*, **21**, 118–37.

Purdue, D. (1995) Whose knowledge counts? 'Experts', 'counter-experts' and the 'lay' public (editorial). *The Ecologist*, **25**, 170–72.

Quarrie, J. (ed) (1992) *Earth Summit '92. The United Nations Conference on Sustainable Development*, Regency Press, London.

Renn, O., Webler, T. and Wiedermann, P. (1995) *Fairness and Competence in Citizen Participation*, Kluwer, Dordrecht and Boston.

Royal Society (1983) *Risk Assessment: A Study Group Report*, The Royal Society, London.

Royal Society (1992) *Risk: Analysis, Perception and Management*, The Royal Society, London.

Schön, D. (1983) *The Reflective Practitioner: How Professionals Think in Action*, Basic Books, New York.

Schön, D. (1992) The crisis of professional knowledge and the pursuit of an epistemology of practice. *Journal of Interprofessional Care*, **6**, 49–63.

Sheldrake, R. (1990) *The Rebirth of Science*, Rider, London.

Shrader-Frechette, K. and McCoy, E. (1994) How the tail wags the dog: how value judgements determine ecological science. *Environmental Values*, **3**, 107–20.

Smith, F. (1995) Assessing the political approach to risk management. *Economic Affairs*, **16**, 11–14.

UK Roundtable on Sustainable Development (1998) *A Stakeholder Approach to Sustainable Business*, UK Roundtable on Sustainable Development, London.

Unwin et al. (1999) Health of UK servicemen who served in the Persian Gulf War. *The Lancet*, **353**, 169–78.

Vidal, J. (1997) *McLibel*, Macmillan, Basingstoke.

Wynne, B. (1992) Uncertainty and environmental learning: reconceiving science in the preventive paradigm. *Global Environmental Change*, **2**, 111–27.

Wynne, B. and Mayer, S. (1993) How science fails the environment. *New Scientist*, 5 June, 33–5.

Yearley, S. (1991) *The Green Case*, Routledge, London.

Chapter 4

Genetic engineering in agriculture

Sue Mayer

Editors' introduction

> Scientists should ask some penetrating questions of all 'environmental' research: Does the experiment itself damage the environment? Is it a major commitment (financial, political or both) to a harmful activity? Has society had a say on whether it should go ahead? Is research into alternatives being funded? Is there any mechanism for saying 'no' to expansion of the technology or practice? (Wallace 1999).

A broad coalition of environmental, consumer, development and health groups opposed to the commercialisation of genetically modified (GM) crops is developing worldwide. Whilst some of these groups are calling for a moratorium on commercial planting for five years, to allow public debate and scientific research, others go further and oppose all field trials of GM crops, even for the purposes of scientific study. Opinion polls show that a majority of the public in Europe are suspicious of the technology, and 77% of the British public want a ban on the growing of GM crops until their effects have been more fully assessed. Genetic modification (or genetic engineering) is a cutting-edge technology, developed from fundamental biological science, which holds massive promise for revolutionising agriculture and medicine and has been hailed as the key to solving world hunger. But to the surprise of many scientists, politicians and industrialists, the introduction of this technology has met with fierce resistance. This chapter considers some of the reasons why this has happened.

Greenpeace is one of the groups opposing field trials of GM crops, because it feels these trials fail the tests outlined by Helen Wallace, a Greenpeace scientist, in the quote above. Her first test concerns ethics. In Chapter 2, one of the fundamental limits of science was described as an ethical one; some research is ethically impermissible. For many people, environmental research which itself risks damaging the environment lies beyond this limit, at least if there are not strong compensatory benefits. Greenpeace claims that experimental field trials of GM crops will not have such compensatory benefits, in part because they will be too limited to resolve many of the important areas of scientific uncertainty discussed in this chapter. In essence, it claims that the experiments are statistically unrepresentative and have a statistical domain which is too narrow (see p. 23). For others, the ethical limits on GM research come not from the possible environmental impacts themselves, but from concerns about 'playing God' with nature. Such people disagree with the 'technocentric rationality' described in Chapter 3, viewing nature from a *theocentric* rather than anthropocentric perspective (see p. 144).

Beyond these fundamental ethical concerns, Helen Wallace identifies three issues which concern the social context of research: Is it being pursued by powerful commercial and political interests? Are alternatives being investigated and funded? Who is involved in deciding how the research is conducted and applied? As this chapter makes clear, the answers to these questions are vital in determining how the risks and benefits of scientific developments can be weighed.

Chapter 3 illustrated the growing importance of commercial funding in scientific research and development, and how this can provide the contextual values which underpin the work. The issue of genetic engineering, as described in this chapter, provides an excellent illustration. The need to ensure a financial return directs commercially driven research down narrowly focused channels; although organic agriculture may prove as efficient as biotechnology in meeting food requirements, it receives little financial support because innovations here are unlikely to make large profits. In order to protect their investments, companies and universities involved in biotechnology seek patents on their products, and much of the scientific information they produce is commercially confidential. These factors – a narrow commercial focus combined with secrecy – provide fertile ground for widespread public mistrust. Chapter 3 identified the media and environmental organisations as important agents of persuasion in environmental decision making. In the case of genetic engineering, both of these groups have managed to capitalise on this public mistrust to pursue their agendas. There are similarities here with the case of the Brent Spar, discussed in Chapter 8. However, an additional element is that of the possible direct human health effects of genetically modified organisms. For years, environmental organisations had little success in gaining media coverage for the many issues raised by genetic engineering. Then Dr Pusztai and others, discussed in this chapter, began suggesting that there could be impacts on human health, and this angle was considered attractive enough by the media to justify mass exposure of the genetic engineering story.

In response to the growth of public resistance, the biotechnology industry has launched numerous advertisements and 'education' campaigns. But polling evidence suggests that even though people now know more about the technology, they trust it less than they used to. This may be because 'recipients of scientific information are far from passive, but interact with science ... evaluating its social and institutional implications' (Ham and

Kelsey 1998, quoted on p. 90). Simply 'educating' people does not work. Instead, the genetic engineering debate provides a stark reminder to business and governments of the need to involve a wide range of people in decision making over major scientific and technological issues, perhaps using some of the approaches outlined in chapter 3, 3.4. A first few steps have been taken, but as this chapter makes clear concerns about genetic engineering, whether based on science or wider issues, will not be properly addressed without much broader public debate and involvement.

An important additional element in the GM debate is the role of the food business as a whole. It is certainly the case that the food processing corporations (such as Unilever and Nestlé) had much to lose in adverse consumer reaction had they done nothing about the GM issue. So the recent decisions by some of these corporations not to incorporate GM crops in their food products was perhaps taken more on grounds of protecting their reputations than on any scientific advice or moral considerations. Yet such corporations, and the retailing chains that sell their food products, are also becoming committed to a more consumer-sensitive approach to handling risk. In this sense, therefore, the science becomes incorporated in commercial considerations as well as political issues.

4.1 Introduction

The use of genetic engineering in food and agriculture has become deeply contentious across the world. The possible dangers of eating and growing genetically modified (GM) crops have held the headlines in the UK for weeks at a time. Farmers in India have burnt GM crops to express their anger at the possible introduction of 'Terminator' technology which results in sterile seed.

In an area that seems unequivocally 'scientific' and where there are constant calls for regulation and controls to be science-based, how does science perform? Are critics scaremongering and using the issue for political ends? Can decisions be based upon science alone and what scientific knowledge is needed in the evaluation process? These are some of the questions that this chapter will seek to address.

4.2 Genetic engineering techniques

Genetic engineering is also known as genetic manipulation and genetic modification (see Box 4.1 for a glossary of terms). It involves the transfer of genetic material (DNA) between species. It is used to alter the characteristics of an organism, for example to make a crop resistant to a disease or insect attack. Usually this involves transferring one gene that gives the desired characteristic (often called the 'gene of interest' or GOI) together

---

Box 4.1 Glossary of the main technical terms used in this chapter

Construct: a series of genes joined together which are to be transferred into an organism using genetic engineering.

Gene: a unit of hereditary information that is located on a chromosome and directs the synthesis of proteins.

Gene flow: the movement of genes from one organism to another by natural processes.

Genetic modification: the transfer of DNA between species using laboratory techniques. Also known as genetic engineering, recombinant DNA (r-DNA) technology and genetic manipulation.

Genetic pollution: gene flow from a genetically manipulated organism to a related wild organism, transferring DNA which is not part of the natural gene pool (or stock of genes) of that species.

Plasmid: circular strands of extra-chromosomal DNA carried by bacteria.

Promoter gene: a gene that controls the action of another by activating it.

Suppressor gene: a gene that controls the action of another by ending its period of activation.

Transgene: a gene that has been transferred from one species to another.

Transgenic organism: an organism that contains genes from a different species.

Vector: a bacterium or virus that can act as a vehicle for DNA and allow the DNA to be transferred to another organism.

---

with a promoter gene to activate the gene and another, a suppressor gene, to switch it off. A marker gene, such as an antibiotic resistance gene, is also included to allow the cells that have been genetically modified to be identified. The genes that are transferred are often called 'transgenes' and the GM organism (GMO) produced, 'transgenic' (Figure 4.1).

The group of genes to be transferred are joined together using molecular biological techniques to form what is known as a construct, and this is moved into a cell using one of three methods:

- In broad-leaved plants (such as sugar beet, soybean and oilseed rape), a bacterium, *Agrobacterium tumifaciens* is used to transfer the DNA. This is called a vector. Agrobacterium normally causes crown gall in plants and is able to infect cells and transfer genetic material into the genome of the cell it infects. When used in genetic engineering, the gene construct is included in a plasmid of a disarmed Agrobacterium (which cannot replicate and spread the infection), which also includes genes that facilitate gene transfer.

Genetic engineering in agriculture

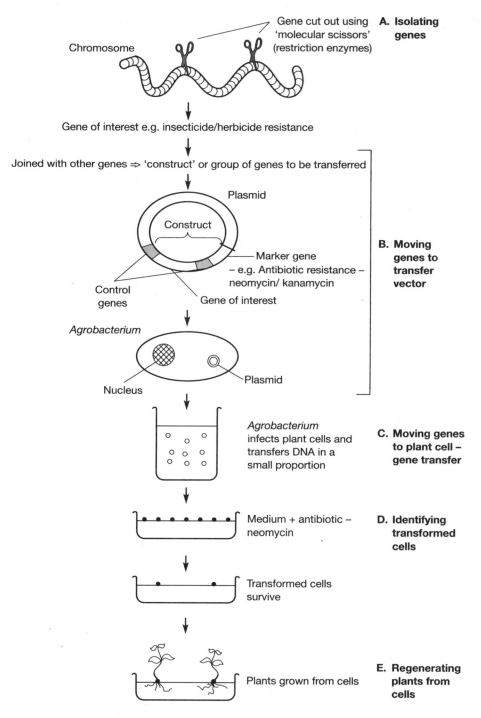

Figure 4.1 The process of genetic engineering.

- In cereals, such as maize and rice, 'biolistics' are used because Agrobacterium does not normally infect these types of plant (although techniques are being developed which mean it can be used). In biolistics, the DNA to be transferred is coated onto microscopic gold particles which are literally fired into the cells. Some DNA remains in the nucleus and is incorporated.
- In animals, the DNA construct is simply injected into the nucleus of a cell using a micropipette. In some cases it will be incorporated into the genome.

All of these methods are very inefficient and only a small proportion of cells are successfully modified. After the attempted transformation, the marker gene is used to identify the cells that have incorporated the new genetic material. For example, an antibiotic may be included in the culture medium so, if the cell has been genetically modified and acquired the appropriate antibiotic resistance gene, it will survive. Otherwise it will be killed by the antibiotic.

As well as transfer rates being inefficient, the genetic engineer is unable to determine where in the genome the genetic material will end up. If it disrupts important genes, it may have deleterious effects – by disrupting a vital biochemical pathway for example. So even those cells that have been genetically modified may not develop into 'normal' plants or animals and a lot of screening has to be undertaken.

4.3 What is being developed by whom?

All the world's major food crops have now been genetically modified. Over 60 species of plant have been field tested in Europe. Examples of the types of genetic modification being undertaken are shown in Box 4.2. The first crops grown commercially (largely in North America) include herbicide tolerant soybean and oilseed rape; insect resistant cotton and maize; tomatoes that ripen or soften more slowly; and potatoes that are resistant to a viral disease.

The main developers of GM crops are multinational companies formed from the old agrochemical companies. Through a series of acquisitions and mergers, they have gained the technical skills of genetic modification together with marketing outlets in the form of seed companies, which enables them to commercialise and market GM crops. The leading companies are DuPont (US), Novartis (Switzerland), Monsanto (US), Aventis (Germany/France), and AstraZeneca (Sweden/UK).

Box 4.2 Examples of the applications of genetic modification to crops and animals

Food Crops
- herbicide tolerance – allows crops to resist the effects of chemical weed killers
- insect resistance – allows crops to resist insect attack through the production of an insecticidal toxin by the crop
- male sterility systems – for hybrid crop production
- disease resistance – prevents crops developing viral or fungal diseases
- delayed softening in fruits – prolonging storage life
- altered oil characteristics – to fit processing needs
- nitrogen fixation – to transfer this ability to non-nitrogen fixing crops

Non-food crops
- flowers with modified colour and extended vase life
- trees with altered characteristics to make paper production easier
- plants to produce plastics and pharmaceuticals
- plants to assist in bioremediation of polluted sites

Animals
- increased growth rates – to reduce time to reach mature weight
- therapeutic substances in milk – to provide sources of medicines

Microorganisms
- production of enzymes or drugs – for use in food processing or as medicines
- degradation of pollutants – to clean up contaminated sites

Table 4.1. The estimated area of land sown commercially with GM crops worldwide (excluding China) in millions of hectares

Country	1996	1997	1998
USA		8.1	20.5
Canada		1.3	2.8
Argentina		1.4	4.3
Australia		0.1	0.1
Mexico		<0.1	0.1
Spain		0	0.015
France		0	0.001
South Africa		0	<0.1
Total	2	12	28

1998 saw a massive increase in the commercial growing of GM crops in North and South America (see Table 4.1). Of the 28 million hectares of GM crops planted worldwide in 1998, 71% (19.8 million) were herbicide resistant and 27% (7.7 million) were insect resistant (James 1998). This area is predicted to grow exponentially to 180 million ha in 2000, 400 million ha in

2001 and 900 million ha in 2002. While this growth has begun in the industrialised North, by 2001 almost half the world's GM crops will be in developing countries. Sales of GM crop seeds were $1.35 billion in 1998, and are expected to rise to $6 billion by 2005 and $20 billion by 2010. By then, GM crops are expected to form over 80% of the current $23 billion commercial seed market (Rural Advancement Fund International 1999).

4.4 The costs and benefits

The public debate around the use of genetic engineering in agriculture centres around the claimed benefits and risks of the technology. Both are hotly contested, both are partly theoretical. Box 4.3 gives examples of both.

4.4.1 The benefits

The industry and governments claim benefits will arise from GM crops for farmers, consumers, society more widely and the company producing the product.

The first wave of commercialised GM crops are seen as bringing benefits to farmers. Herbicide tolerant crops, where the crop has a gene that makes it resistant to the effects of a herbicide which would previously have killed it, are said to increase yields through better weed management and to reduce labour costs through easier (less use of mixtures) and reduced frequency of herbicide applications. Insect resistant crops, which have a gene coding for a toxin which kills insects feeding on the crop, reduce the time and expenditure involved in insecticidal sprays.

Box 4.3 Examples of the claimed benefits and costs of using GM in agriculture

Claimed benefits
- Promoting efficiency in farming – by reducing labour costs of herbicide or insecticide spraying for example.
- Increased yields – by reducing losses from pests and disease.
- Providing altered product characteristics to aid in food processing – such as tomatoes which soften more slowly and therefore have lower water content, facilitating processing into paste.
- Improving the nutritional value of food.
- Controlling fertility – to improve the purity of hybrid seed.
- Reducing fertiliser inputs through nitrogen fixation.
- Expanding the range of lands that can be used for agriculture – for example by growing crops tolerant to salt or drought.

▶

Box 4.3 (continued)

Possible costs

Direct environmental effects

- Gene transfer from the GMO to native flora or fauna – leading to new pests as a result of hybridisation.
- Unexpected behaviour of the GMO in the environment if it escapes its intended use and becomes a pest.
- Food web effects through harm to non-target species – for example, if the host range of a virus was increased it might affect beneficial species as well as the targeted species, or there might be secondary effects on the food web from the insect toxin contained in a crop.
- Harmful effects on ecosystem processes – if products of GMOs interfere with natural biochemical cycles (see p. 150).
- Wastage of natural biological resources if, for example, the use of a genetic modification to bring pest resistance in many difference species induces the emergence of resistance and loss of efficacy.

Indirect environmental effects

- Continuation of intensive agricultural systems – as a result of the requirement for high levels of external inputs.
- Impacts on biodiversity as a consequence of changes in agricultural practice – for example by altering patterns of herbicide use, effects on flora may be seen.
- Cumulative environmental impacts from multiple releases and interactions.
- Alterations in agricultural practices, for example, to manage any direct environment impacts such as the evolution of insect, herbicide or disease resistance in weeds.

Health

- New allergens being formed through the inclusion of novel proteins which trigger allergic reactions at some stage.
- Antibiotic resistance genes used as 'markers' in the GM food being transferred to gut microorganisms and intensifying problems with antibiotic resistant pathogens.
- The creation of new toxins through unexpected interactions between the product of the genetic modification and other constituents, for example.

Socio-economic

- Industrial competitiveness, jobs and investment could be affected by lack of adoption of the technology.
- Consumer choice may be restricted if labelling is not comprehensive.
- Patenting may affect farmers' ability to save seed freely for resowing in subsequent years and compromise the ability of poor farmers to compete.
- Ability to feed the world's population could be improved, or could be compromised if yield benefits are not realised.

However, claims of increased yields have been contested. According to Monsanto, the yield of Roundup Ready soybeans (RRS) in the US was 5% higher on average in 1996 and 1997 than that of conventionally bred varieties (Monsanto 1998). Independent analysis in Arkansas showed that only in 4/38 instances did RRS outperform the highest yielding varieties in the region (Lappe and Bailey 1999). The Mississippi Seed Arbitration Council has ruled that Monsanto's GM Roundup Ready cotton failed to perform as advertised in 1997 and recommended that nearly $2 million be paid to three farmers who had large losses (Union of Concerned Scientists 1998).

Although the ease and efficiency with which weeds can be controlled with herbicide is clear, there are concerns that such benefits will be short-lived because herbicide resistant weeds will emerge. In 1998 a farmer in Canada had problems with multiple herbicide resistant volunteer weeds (where seed shed at harvest germinates in the following season's crop) following the use of GM herbicide tolerant oilseed rape (Downey 1999).

The next phase of the use of GM is expected to be in ways which are considered to be beneficial to the consumer and retailer. Foods that bring benefits over and above their food value are known as functional foods or 'nutraceuticals'. Those currently under development include Monsanto's Laurical (a GM oilseed rape with increased laurate content which is claimed to lower blood cholesterol), and DuPont's GM soybean and oilseed rape (which are claimed to reduce the risk of heart disease by excluding *trans* fatty acids) (Brower 1998). AstraZeneca is focusing its research efforts on developing fruits such as tomatoes and bananas which have longer shelf lives.

The third wave of GM crops will consist of plants that are intended to replace factories as production facilities for drugs or other compounds.

The claimed benefits of the second and third wave GM crops have received less critical scrutiny and challenge, partly because they are in the development stage. However, public attitude research indicates that there will be hostility because benefits such as increased shelf life or improvements in processing are often considered trivial and not a justifiable use of GM techniques (Grove-White et al. 1997).

Will GM crops feed the world?

There have been much broader benefits claimed for GM crops such as their importance in promoting the competitiveness of industry and in creating jobs and wealth (which has been important in driving European policy for example). One of the most contentious claims has been that the use of GM in agriculture will have an important role in feeding a growing world population, and in preventing extinctions of wild species (see p. 44). For example it has been said that:

Without higher yields, the world would undoubtedly lose the wild forests and grasslands that still cover more than a third of the Earth's surface, because lower yield agriculture would require vastly more land [to feed increased population]. The demand will therefore be for more intensive agriculture ... embracing genetically modified crops.

Crowley et al. 1998

In 1998, Monsanto ran advertisements in the UK arguing that food biotechnology would feed 'starving generations' (*The Observer*, 2nd August 1998, 'Worrying about starving future generations won't feed them. Food biotechnology will'.) Their basic argument is that the population, which is currently 5.8 billion, is expected to reach 8 billion by 2020 and 11 billion by 2050 (Kendall et al. 1997). The increasing demand for food must be met without expanding the amount of land used for agricultural purposes (to protect biodiversity) and by addressing issues of soil erosion, salinisation, overgrazing and pollution of water supplies, and that GM crops are the best way to achieve this (Vasil 1998).

However, starvation is a result of poverty and unequal distribution, not lack of food. In 1994, food production could have supplied 6.4 billion people (more than the actual population) with an adequate 2350 calories per day, yet more than 1 billion people do not get enough to eat (Kendal et al. 1997).

Some argue that the way in which biotechnology is being applied, and the accompanying concentration of the seed market into the hands of a tiny number of large corporations, could threaten food security (the degree of certainty about future harvests) and the livelihoods of the world's poorest farmers in particular (McCrea and Mayer 1999).

Terminator technology, which results in the seed produced by a plant being sterile, has been particularly contentious. A chemical switch is genetically engineered into the crop. In the Terminator application, applying a chemical to the seed stops the production of a toxin that prevents germination. Seed sold by the company will germinate but seed produced by the plants grown would not germinate unless soaked in chemical again. The advantage to the company is that farmers have to buy seed each season. This puts up costs for farmers and for poor farmers who rely on farm saved seed, could undermine an important farming practice. Recently, companies have promised not to develop Terminator seeds.

There are also concerns that the way in which the technology is being applied is unlikely to be of benefit to developing countries in their efforts to feed their people (McCrea and Mayer 1999). Many of the applications, such as fruits which ripen more slowly, are geared to the rich markets of developed countries. Herbicide, insect and disease resistant crops may only have short-term advantages if resistant weeds and pests evolve. In any case the seed may be expensive and unavailable to poorer farmers. Thus the suspicion remains that the rhetoric of feeding the world may be little more than a marketing ploy to encourage GM adoption here.

Of course another approach is to question whether the potential benefits which are claimed for GM crops could be obtained *in another way altogether*. Organic agriculture or systems with greater emphasis on biological control methods may be able to provide the same, greater or different benefits. This is a view of benefits which is rarely taken – the traditional comparison is with the *status quo* alone.

4.4.2 Environmental risks

Many expert groups have considered the potential for environmental harm as a result of releasing GMOs into the environment, including the UK's Royal Commission on Environmental Pollution (1989) and the US's Ecological Society (Tiede et al. 1989). These analyses have focused on direct effects resulting from the genetic modification itself, such as gene flow to wild species (also called **genetic pollution**) or the ability of the crop to become invasive.

The potential for direct effects depends on the behaviour of the GMO in the environment and the particular genes which have been transferred. In the case of GM crops, if related wild plants are growing near by, there could be cross pollination and transfer of the foreign genes into native flora. The likelihood of this depends on a host of factors including the fertility of any hybrids formed, the relative position of the weeds and crop and how agricultural practices affect the outcome. Since one species of weed will not be genetically uniform, the likelihood of hybrid formation may even vary within a species. Thus predicting the likelihood of foreign gene flow is extremely complex and present knowledge remains uncertain. For crops such as sugar beet and oilseed rape, which evolved in Europe, related weeds do co-exist, have similar flowering periods and are compatible with the crop to varying degrees, so gene flow seems inevitable.

However, there is no direct evidence for harmful effects of GM crops following their growing in the field. The significance of observations in laboratories and from small-scale trials are disputed. On the one hand some say they are important signals of potential problems ahead; on the other, there are those who say the experiments create an artificial worst-case scenario, which would not be seen in the wider environment.

Gene flow

Some argue that gene flow from traditionally bred crops to native flora must have been taking place for a long time with no obvious ill-effects in the UK at least. However, elsewhere gene flow has caused serious weed problems, especially in developing countries because they are centres of biodiversity and weedy relatives are often found close by (Rissler and Melon 1993). For example, there are 22 species of wild rice in Asia, Africa,

Australia, Oceania and Latin America, many of which are important weeds and some of which have become more troublesome because of gene flow from cultivated rice (Cohen et al. 1999). Because the majority of today's crop species grown worldwide originated in the South, gene transfers to weedy relatives may be more likely to occur in the developing world than in, say, Europe or North America.

The impact of any transferred gene may depend on whether it confers an advantage on the plant receiving it. If the genes such as those giving disease or insect resistance are transferred into wild, weedy species under the right conditions they could give a considerable competitive advantage in the presence of the disease or insect attack. GM disease resistance uses genes from the disease virus itself to promote resistance by a poorly understood mechanism. This is very different from conventional methods of breeding disease resistant strains. As well as wild plants acquiring a new form of resistance, there could be recombination between the transferred genes and infecting viruses leading to the emergence of new viral strains.

As well as the gene causing the desired effect (such as disease or herbicide resistance), promoter and suppresser genes may have adverse effects. One common source of such genes is the cauliflower mosaic virus (CaMV). Studies looking at plant viral disease pathogenesis have shown that when transgenic brassicas (plants in the cauliflower family) containing CaMV sequences as suppressor or promoters are infected with CaMV, the functional transgene (such as herbicide resistance) may be switched off because the infecting virus recognises DNA which contains the same sequences as it does, binds with it and interferes with the functioning of the gene. This is known as homologous recombination and co-suppression. This is not just of research interest – commercial varieties of herbicide resistant oilseed rape (a brassica) containing CaMV sequences are in the final stages of approval, with the potential for crop failure (as a result of gene suppression) to occur should a CaMV virus infection arise.

Volunteer weeds

The GMO may also behave unexpectedly in the environment. A GM disease or herbicide resistant crop could become a troublesome weed in the right conditions. Crops from a previous sowing which persist on an area of land are called **volunteer weeds**; if they are herbicide resistant, farmers' weed control options may be made more difficult. This may be especially true for farmers who have fields of non-GM crops bordering those where a GM crop is grown. Pollen from oilseed rape can travel well over 1 km and thus cross fertilisation could result in a non-GM crop being partially pollinated by a GM crop. Completely unexpected herbicide resistant volunteer weeds could be the result. Organic farmers wanting to produce a GM-free crop will face similar problems if GM crops are grown close by.

Effects on biodiversity

Other concerns have been raised about wider or secondary effects on bio-diversity. The use of crops resistant to broad spectrum herbicides could allow farmers to apply more herbicide to their crops. This is because applying large amounts of herbicide to conventional crops can kill the crop, as well as the weeds. Increasing herbicide applications can alter weed flora and remove important food sources for birds already under pressure from conventional agricultural systems. GM insect resistant crops, where the toxin is expressed throughout the life of the crop, could harm non-target beneficial insects ingesting pests which have fed on the crop (Figure 4.2). If many different crops are modified in this way the effects on the food web could be very serious (through cascading effects – see p. 154). Research has shown that beneficial insects such as lacewings have reduced survival and reproduction when they eat pest species which have been fed on maize containing the most commonly used toxin in GM crops – Bt toxin, from the bacterium, *Bacillus thuringiensis* (Hilbeck et al. 1998). Monarch butterfly larvae have lowered survival when fed on pollen from Bt maize (Losey et al. 1999). Ladybirds have been similarly harmed by eating aphids which have fed on GM potatoes which contain a snowdrop lectin designed to make them insect resistant (Birch et al. 1999).

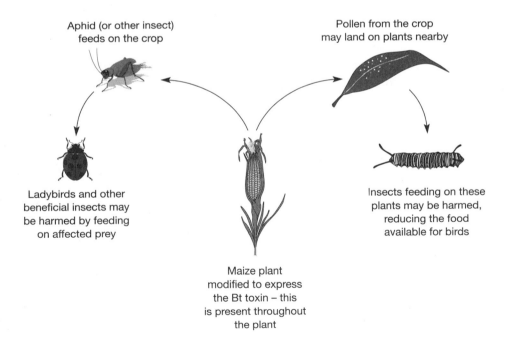

Aphid (or other insect) feeds on the crop

Pollen from the crop may land on plants nearby

Ladybirds and other beneficial insects may be harmed by feeding on affected prey

Insects feeding on these plants may be harmed, reducing the food available for birds

Maize plant modified to express the Bt toxin – this is present throughout the plant

Figure 4.2 Two possible impacts on biodiversity of growing insect resistant GM maize.

Pesticide resistance

Other unanswered questions include the likely rate of emergence of resistance in insect pests (Onstad and Gould 1998). The exposure to pesticides being experienced by insects feeding on a Bt crop is constant and very different from intermittent exposure to sprays. Since the toxin may also be expressed in the roots, soil invertebrates may be exposed in new ways. The fears that resistance may evolve quickly has led to the development of strategies to mitigate against this in the US, which involve the use of 'refuges' – areas of land planted with non-Bt crops – where Bt resistance will confer no advantage and so resistant strains would not have a selective advantage. Depending on whether conventional insecticides are sprayed in these areas, the recommended sizes of these refuges are from 20–40% of the crop area.

4.4.3 Human health risks

There are three main ways in which it is thought GM food could damage human health – the production of unexpected toxins and allergens and the transfer of antibiotic resistance genes to disease-causing organisms. The possibility of unexpected toxic effects was highlighted in the case of Dr Pusztai and the GM potatoes (Box 4.4).

Allergies

The incidence of food allergies is increasing; this is possibly linked with the growth in consumption of processed foods (Nestle 1996). There are certainly dangers if genes from well known allergenic species such as nuts are introduced to different foods (for example, when a brazil nut protein gene was transferred into soybean to improve its methionine content (Nordlee et al. 1996)). However, in such cases testing is reasonably straightforward as it is possible to conduct tests using human volunteers who are known to be allergic.

With other GM crops, however, the presence of novel proteins has raised safety concerns about the potential to cause *novel* allergies. Testing for new allergens is extremely difficult. Although the structures of many allergens are known and their characteristics (such as resistance to digestion) well recognised, there remain others which do not fit the classical picture.

Antibiotic resistance

Resistance to the antibiotics neomycin or kanamycin is one of the most commonly used marker genes in GM crops. Neomycin and kanamycin are not important drugs in clinical practice and therefore even if resistance

Box 4.4 Dr Pusztai and the potatoes

In August 1998, Dr Arpad Pusztai, of the Rowett Institute in Scotland, described to the press the results of his experiments comparing rats fed with GM potatoes containing a lectin gene (to make them resistant to insects) with rats in a control group which had been fed normal potatoes. Rats eating the GM potatoes showed growth and immune system impairment. In contrast to some other lectins (such as the one found in kidney beans), the lectin used in the experiments (which came from the snow drop) was not considered toxic to mammals.

Two days later Pusztai was sacked and prevented from speaking to the press. To reassure the public an independent audit report was published exonerating the potatoes. But the fire was ignited again when in February 1999, 20 international scientists criticised the audit report and supported Pusztai's original findings. The claim was also made that the genetic modification technique *itself* had caused some new toxin to be produced.

Finally, the gagging order was lifted on Pusztai and the Royal Society of London investigated the case. They reported in May 1999, saying that Pusztai's work was flawed, in part because of three problems with experimental design discussed in Chapter 1:

- Confounding variables – the normal and GM potatoes differed not only in the lectin gene, but also in their protein contents.
- Non-independence – separate measurements were made of different organs on the same rat specimens. But if a rat is underfed, many organs will be affected, so that these separate measurements will be interrelated and therefore not independent.
- Low power – there was high variability in the results, which meant that the power of the experiments was low.

However, the Royal Society also said this did not mean GM foods were inevitably safe.

Despite these problems, Dr Pusztai's work was finally published in *The Lancet* at the end of 1999.

was transferred this might not be a problem. However, the first commercially grown GM crop in Europe is a maize variety containing an ampicillin resistance gene as well as insect and herbicide resistance. This has raised considerable controversy because of the clinical importance of ampicillin and the risk of the antibiotic resistance gene being transferred to the bacterial flora in the intestine of animals eating the maize (which is intended for animal feed production) or in the soil. This resistance could eventually be transferred to human or animal pathogens, increasing clinical problems with antibiotic resistance. Because of these problems, companies are tending to phase out the use of antibiotic resistance genes.

4.4.4 Agriculture and food security

There are also risks associated with agricultural food production and security. By concentrating control of crop seeds into the hands of only five corporations, GM technology could give great political and financial power to companies which are outside democratic controls (see Chapter 3).

In the production of GM crops, the same alterations, such as the same insect resistance gene, are used across a whole array of species, raising the possibility of a new form of monoculture which crosses species. Because maintaining genetic diversity in crops may not be consistent with large-scale, global production, there are fears that diversity will be further eroded making huge areas of crops vulnerable to sudden failures as a result, for example, of disease or drought.

The introduction of GM crops in the US has already changed the farming culture because the crops are **patented**. This means that farmers cannot keep seed for resowing without the agreement of the company, which usually involves paying royalties. Monsanto have had contracts with farmers which state that they must use Monsanto's brand of glyphosate on Roundup Ready crops and that they must not keep seed for resowing. Monsanto has employed private detective agencies to police the agreement and asked farmers to inform on their neighbours if they think they are infringing the contracts. If these sorts of agreement are taken out in other countries, farmers who use saved seed could be seriously disadvantaged.

Other issues for farmers include the ability to produce organic produce (which does not allow the use of GM) and non-GM crops. Because pollen can travel many kilometres by wind or insects, the potential for contamination is great. Some farmers' businesses could therefore be threatened.

4.5 Regulations

In the UK and the rest of the European Union there is a regulatory framework laid down in Directives which are said to take a 'scientific' perspective and a 'precautionary approach' (see p. 84). This section considers these regulations.

The primary focus of both environmental and food safety regulations is on the genetic modification; the risk assessment is thus narrowly defined to include only the technical dimensions of the genetic modification. This leaves two areas of uncertainty. Firstly, inside the narrow framing there will be scientific uncertainty about the likelihood and scale of harm (for example, just how far pollen might travel). Secondly, there is uncertainty as to

Box 4.5 Environmental safety regulations in Europe

The environmental safety of GM organisms is addressed by a European Directive (see p. 165) called the 'Deliberate Release Directive' (90/220/EEC). In the UK, the Secretary of State for the Environment is advised by the Advisory Committee on Releases to the Environment (ACRE), a committee of experts. ACRE considers the safety of releases on a step-by-step, case-by-case basis. Each GM crop is tested in the laboratory, then in greenhouses and then in outdoor fields. The assumption is that the information from each stage will show whether it is safe to progress to the next. The focus is on the GMO itself and what effects it may have, such as becoming a problem weed or the foreign gene moving into related species.

There are various shortcomings to this approach:

- **A case-by-case approach precludes an assessment of cumulative impacts**. For example, one crop containing a toxin which kills insects may seem relatively innocuous. However, if many such crops are authorised, the toxin could affect the whole food web either by killing beneficial insect life or by removing an important food source for higher species. This is not specifically included in the risk assessment (see Chapter 8 for a similar example).
- **Secondary effects on biodiversity as a result of the effects of GMOs on agricultural practice and vice versa are not considered**. For example, the introduction of GM herbicide resistant crops will increase the use of some broad spectrum weed killers (GeneWatch 1998). By removing weeds more effectively, food sources for insects and birds will be reduced, possibly threatening bird populations.
- **Effects on other farming systems are not considered**. For example, the problems of cross pollination of organic and conventional crops. GM oilseed rape pollen can travel 1.5 to 2 km.
- **Small-scale trials cannot mimic the complexity of the natural environment**. Small-scale trials have limited statistical domain (see p. 23). Unexpected outcomes are probable and ACRE's chairperson, Professor John Beringer, has even acknowledged that 'We can't really learn anything from them [small-scale field trials].' (Anon 1998.)
- **Most experimental trials only provide information on economic characteristics such as yield, little of which is relevant to risk assessment** (Union of Concerned Scientists 1994). There is minimal research into ecological effects and, when undertaken, it is only conducted for one to two years. Ecologists have recommended that *at least* three years' data are needed (Kareiva et al. 1996). Therefore, there is little relevant information with which to make assessments of ecological safety.

whether the framing has included all the relevant criteria to avoid harm occurring (for example, there may be unexpected effects such as those claimed by Dr Pusztai). So environmental safety regulations leave much room for uncertainty, as explained in Box 4.5. Although things are beginning to change, in the past there has been no assessment of the impact of secondary effects on biodiversity or on farming practice and how this will affect the environment.

The food safety evaluation relies on a concept known as 'substantial equivalence' (see Box 4.6). Like the environmental risk assessments, this takes a very narrow view of safety, with no broader questions about public health being asked such as the impact on overall nutrition and health.

Box 4.6 Substantial equivalence

The concept of 'substantial equivalence' is used to determine if GM foods are safe. It involves a comparison of various characteristics of the GM food with existing conventionally produced foods.

Factors compared include the composition of macro- and micro-nutrients, and the presence of known toxins and of other anti-nutritional factors. For example, in potatoes:

- macro-nutrients = carbohydrate, protein, etc.
- micro-nutrients = vitamins, etc.
- known toxins = solanine

No further investigations are needed if the GM food is deemed 'substantially equivalent'. If it is deemed not equivalent, then toxicological and nutritional data are required.

The allergenic potential of introduced proteins and potential for transfer of antibiotic marker genes are assessed for all GM foods.

This approach has various shortcomings:

- **Unexpected changes are not screened for**, possibly leading to a false assumption of safety (Kuiper 1998).
- **Because the focus is on the transgene, crops may not be assessed in the context of use**. The substantial equivalence of Monsanto's Roundup Ready soybean, for instance, was established without considering the safety of the soybean when it had been sprayed with Roundup herbicide, even though this was the primary reason for its development (Padgette et al. 1995).
- **Questions about the likely allergenic effects of exposure to novel proteins will always be difficult** because: 'The allergenicity of specific proteins derived from known allergenic sources can be determined, whereas the potential allergenicity of proteins derived from sources of unknown allergenicity is much harder.' (Taylor and Lehrer 1996).
- **Short-term laboratory experiments with animals are not foolproof** (see Chapters 8 and 10).
- Because there is no segregation of GM from non-GM foods, **monitoring for adverse effects will prove difficult** if not impossible (i.e. there will be no control populations).

4.6 Conclusions

The debate about GM crops and foods is of huge political importance. Large corporations have invested billions in GM development and have much to lose. Politicians see it as the dominant technology of the next century, bringing jobs and wealth. Behind the fight about the risks of GM foods and crops is a much larger agenda about who controls food production, who takes the risks and who stands to gain. In many ways it is about how our democracies work and are organised. So whilst the arguments often appear to be about minute details of science, the backdrop is much larger and the stakes both in terms of risks and benefits are extremely high.

In this chapter we have looked at the risks of genetic modification – to the environment, human health and sustainable food production. However, all the issues are intertwined. Whether antibiotic resistance spreads from crops to organisms in an animal's intestines depends on environmental factors and farming practices. The extent to which biodiversity may be threatened by the use of broad spectrum herbicides depends on whether farmers observe the correct procedures. The scale of adoption of insect resistant crops will influence the extent to which there could be secondary effects on the food web. Whether farming practices are sustainable depends on what environmental harm occurs.

We have also seen that there is considerable uncertainty about the risks, whether they will be realised and how important they will be. There is uncertainty and dispute about what are the right questions to ask. The regulatory systems only take into account a certain proportion of the possible harm that may arise. As in many other areas of risk assessment, the process tends to be narrowed down as much as possible. Although this may seem sensible in an effort to make complex issues manageable, what might prove to be the important dangers may not be considered in the risk assessment, and irreversible harm might result.

The framing of risk assessment (what is taken into account and how harm is measured – against conventional or organic systems, for example) will drive the outcome of the assessment. For example, excluding effects on farming practices may lead to neglect of other farmers' ability to produce non-GM or organic crops. Research has shown that the framing is strongly influenced by the particular interests and position of the people involved in selecting the criteria (in other words, by contextual values – Chapter 2; Stirling and Mayer, 1999). For example, a belief that industrial competitiveness and jobs may be compromised if GM technologies are not adopted could act against the inclusion of wider issues for fear of stifling investment. However, as we have also seen in this chapter, the potential benefits of the technology are as contentious as the potential risks.

Alternatives, justification and need are not considered in conventional risk assessments, although there is evidence that many people believe they should be.

Getting the framing of the risk assessment right is important if there is to be wider agreement about the outcome of the evaluation. The US National Research Council (1996) has emphasised the importance of framing or 'risk characterisation' for the quality of the decision arrived at:

> In addition to the biological and physical outcomes that are typically covered, decision makers and interested and affected parties often need to know about the significant economic costs and benefits of alternatives, secondary effects of hazard events, or the efficacy of alternative regulatory mechanisms. (p. 29)

> A risk characterisation will fail to be useful if the underlying analysis addresses questions and issues that are different from those of concern to the decision makers and affected parties. (p. 29)

In the debate over GM crops, the whole risk characterisation has gone awry – it is simply not agreed upon and has resulted in heated argument. Many of the issues of concern to the public and others, such as secondary impacts on biodiversity or the future of agriculture, are not included in the regulatory system in Europe.

Therefore, in evaluating the risks of GM technology, it is not simply a case of science being able to determine whether something is safe or not. Science cannot resolve the issues even though some present risk assessment as if it were only to do with science. Uncertainties and ignorance will always be present, leaving question marks hanging over any risk assessment. To what extent the risks of GM crops and foods are predictable is impossible to say. So when politicians, scientists or regulators claim they are going to make a decision based on science alone, this can never be true. A whole host of social, political, cultural and economic factors will have shaped the evaluation process even before science is brought in to advise. These same factors will influence what importance is placed on the uncertainties in the risk assessment. It has proved difficult finding 'independent' experts to advise on the risks of GM crops and foods because links between industry and academia are growing in this area, leaving the risks to be judged by people who may have a general sympathy towards the technology (see Chapter 3).

Many of the arguments about GM crops and foods are fought out in terms of the science allowed under the narrow risk assessment system, as critics are accused of being 'unscientific' if they address wider issues. 'Safety' is the only arena open to debate, not the benefits, alternatives and justification which many wish to consider. Safety is supposed to be the domain of science alone. This is why there can be apparent hysteria over bits of scientific evidence which are provisional, as the Pusztai potato controversy showed. Preliminary data indicated the potential for harm to health from eating GM food and this threatened the whole industry. On both sides there was panic; the degree of reaction demonstrates just how high the stakes are, and the argument graphically demonstrated how science cannot pronounce unequivocally on safety.

If science is characterised as being able to determine safety, not only will the underlying social and political issues remain concealed, but the controversy will continue to rage. There is a danger that public anxieties over each successive 'revelation' of technology-induced threat will compound into a corrosive general attitude of fatalism, disillusion and distrust. Reassurances on the part of government or industry are increasingly coming to be seen as cynical exercises in financial or political damage limitation. Additional knowledge is needed and wider social input to risk characterisation is required if risk issues such as GM crops are to avoid becoming so polarised that social stability is threatened.

4.7 Summary

- Genetic modification involves the transfer of genetic material between species.
- Claimed benefits for this technology include the potential to help feed the world's growing population, increase the nutritional quality of foods and generate medicines and industrial materials.
- There are many possible risks involved, to the environment, health and society.
- Current regulatory frameworks and risk assessments are inadequate, because they do not consider the possible wider implications of the technology.
- The purely 'scientific' approach taken by the current frameworks cannot answer some of the most important questions regarding the application of GM technology. These questions need to be addressed openly and democratically, not only by scientists and others involved in the technology.

Further reading

Lappe, M. and Bailey, B. (1999) *Against the Grain. The Genetic Transformation of Global Agriculture*, Earthscan, London. Some of the global agricultural implications.

Nottingham, S. (1998) *Eat your Genes. How Genetically Modified Food is Entering our Diet*, Zed Books, London. A book aimed at the concerned consumer.

Old, R.W. and Primrose, S.B. (1994) *Principles of Gene Manipulation*, 5th Edition, Blackwell Science, Oxford. A good introduction to the science of genetic engineering.

Rissler, J. and Melon, M. (1993) *Perils Amidst the Promise*, Union of Concerned Scientists, Washington DC.

References

Anon (1998) *ENDS Report*, **283**, August, 22.

Birch, A.N.E., Geoghegan, I.E., Majerus, M.E.N., McNicol, J.W., Hackett, C.A., Gatehouse, A.M.R. and Gatehouse, J.A. (1999) Tri-tropic interactions involving pest aphids, predatory 2-spot ladybirds and transgenic potatoes expressing snowdrop lectin for aphid resistance. *Molecular Breeding*, **5**, 75–83.

Brower, V. (1998) Nutraceuticals: poised for a healthy slice of the healthcare market? *Nature Biotechnology*, **16**, 728–731.

Cohen, M.B., Jackson, M.T., Lu. B.R., Morin, S.R., Mortimer, A.M., Pham, J.L. and Wade, L.J. (1999) Predicting the environmental impact of transgene outcrossing to wild and weedy rice in Asia. 1999 BCPC Symposium Proceedings No 72: *Gene Flow and Agriculture: Relevance for Transgenic Crops*, pp. 151–157. British Crop Protection Council, Farnham, Surrey.

Crowley, P., Fischer, H. and Devonshire, A. (1998) Feed the World. *Chemistry in Britain*, July, 25.

Downey, R.K. (1999) Gene flow and rape: the Canadian experience. The 1999 BCPC Symposium Proceedings No 72: *Gene Flow and Agriculture: Relevance for Transgenic Crops*. British Crop Protection Council, Farnham, Surrey.

GeneWatch (1998) Briefing No 2 *Genetically Engineered Oilseed Rape: Agricultural Saviour or New Form of Pollution?* GeneWatch, Derbyshire.

Grove-White, R., Macnaghton, P., Mayer, S. and Wynne, B. (1997) *Uncertain World. Genetically Modified Organisms, Food and Public Attitudes in Britain*. Centre for the Study of Environmental Change, Lancaster University, Lancaster, 64pp.

Hilbeck, A., Baumgartner, M., Fried, P.M. and Bigler, F. (1998) Effects of transgenic *Bacillus thuringiensis* corn-fed prey on mortality and development of immature *Chrysoperla carnea* (Neuraptera: Chrysopidae). *Environmental Entomology*, **27**, 480–487.

James, C. (1998) *Global Review of Commercialised Transgenic Crops*: 1998. ISAAA Briefs No 8. ISAAA, Ithaca, NY.

Kareiva, P., Parker, I.M. and Pascual, M.P. (1996) Can we use experiments and models in predicting the invasiveness of genetically engineered organisms? *Ecology*, **77**, 1651–1675.

Kendall, H.W., Beachy, R., Eisner, T., Gould, F., Herdt, R., Raven, P.H., Schell, J.S. and Swaminathan, M.S. (1997) *Bioengineering of Crops: Report of the World Bank Panel on Transgenic Crops*. International Bank for Reconstruction and Development/World Bank, Washington DC.

Kuiper, H.A. (1998) Safety evaluation of genetically modified foods and animal feeds as a basis for market introduction. In: *Food Safety Evaluation of Genetically Modified Foods as a Basis for Market Introduction*, Ministry of Economic Affairs, The Netherlands.

Lappe, M. and Bailey, B. (1999) *Against the Grain. The Genetic Transformation of Agriculture*, Earthscan, London.

Losey, J.E., Raynor, L.S. and Carter, M.E. (1999) Transgenic pollen harms monarch larvae. *Nature*, **399**, 214.

McCrea, I. and Mayer, S. (1999) *AstraZeneca and its Genetic Research. Feeding the World or Fuelling World Hunger?* Action Aid, London.

Monsanto (1998) *Background. The Roundup Ready Soyabean System: Sustainability and Herbicide Use*, Monsanto, St Louis, 11 pp.

National Research Council (1996) *Understanding Risk. Informing Decisions in a Democratic Society*, National Academy Press, Washington DC.

Nestle, M. (1996) Allergies to transgenic foods – questions of policy. *The New England Journal of Medicine*, **334**, 726–728.

Nordlee, J.A., Taylor, S.L., Townsend, J.A., Thomas, L.A. and Bush, R.K. (1996) Identification of a brazil nut allergen in transgenic soybeans. *New England Journal of Medicine*, **334**, 688–692.

Onstad, D. and Gould, F. (1998) Do dynamics of crop maturation and herbivorous insect life cycle influence the risk of adaptation to toxins in transgenic host plants? *Environmental Entomology*, **27**, 517–522.

Padgette, S.R., Taylor, N.B., Nida, D.L., Bailey, M.R., MacDonald, J., Holden, L.R. and Fuchs, R.L. (1995) The composition of glyphosate-tolerant soybean seed is equivalent to that of conventional soybeans. *The Journal of Nutrition*, **126**, 702–716.

Rissler, J. and Melon, M. (1993) *Perils Amidst the Promise. Ecological Risks of Transgenic Crops in a Global Market*, Union of Concerned Scientists, Cambridge, MA.

Royal Commission for Environmental Pollution (1989) *The Release of Genetically Engineered Organisms into the Environment*, HMSO, London.

Rural Advancement Fund International (1999) RAFI Communique, January/February 1999 *Traitor Technology. The Terminator's wider implications*, RAFI, Canada.

Stirling, A.S. and Mayer, S.J. (1999) *Rethinking Risk. A Pilot Multi-criteria Mapping of a GM Crop in Agricultural Systems in the UK*, Science and Technology Policy Research Unit, University of Sussex.

Taylor, S.L. and Lehrer, S.B. (1996) Principles and characteristics of food allergens. *Critical Reviews in Food Science and Nutrition*, **36(S)**, S91–S118.

Tiede, J.M., Colwell, R.K., Grossman, Y.L., Hodson, R.E., Kenski, R.E., Mack, R.N. and Regal, P.J. (1989) The planned introduction of genetically engineered organisms: ecological considerations and recommendations. *Ecology*, **70**, 298–315.

Union of Concerned Scientists (1994) Experimental release of genetically engineered organisms. *The Gene Exchange*, **5**, 12.

Union of Concerned Scientists (1998) *The Gene Exchange*, Summer 1998.

Vasil, I.K. (1998) Biotechnology and food security for the 21st century: a real-world perspective. *Nature Biotechnology*, **16**, 399–400.

Wallace, H. (1999) Natural justice? *New Scientist*, **163** (2199), 46.

Chapter 5

Towards a sustainable response to climate change

P.M. Kelly

Editors' introduction

> The working groups gave nothing so much as the sense of a 'strong, almost desperate desire' to avoid noticing 'the elephant in the room'. That elephant is the need for a rapid, globally co-ordinated transition from fossil fuels to renewables. (Athanasiou 1996:68).

This chapter on the science and politics of global climate change could be taken to illustrate many of the main themes of this book. As Mick Kelly makes clear, although there is a broad scientific consensus over the main features of global warming, much uncertainty remains. Following the metaphor above (taken from one observer's description of an international climate negotiation), there are those who would doubt the existence of the elephant at all. Equally, the different rationalities and approaches to risk discussed in Chapter 3 are all represented; perhaps we should shoo the elephant politely away, and hope for the best? And what of the roles of the media and lobbyists, those crucial agents of persuasion? Who is getting to hear about the elephant, and who is trying to obscure it? All of these themes are dealt with below, but above all global climate change represents the ultimate test of the precautionary principle (see Chapter 3) and of how we use this to forge a sustainable future.

Science plays a central role in the global warming debate, because without it the problem of potentially catastrophic human-induced changes to the global climate would remain undiagnosed – science provides the only antennae with which to pick up the signal. But equally, the scientific uncertainties are particularly difficult to resolve in this case. Simple manipulative experiments (as described in Chapter 1, p. 21) are clearly impossible. But so are the 'natural experiments' discussed in section 1.6.3; although it may be possible to compare areas with different types of fisheries management (Chapter 7) or different nutrient loadings (Chapter 9), for example, there are no sub-sections of the global climate which could allow controlled comparison. Instead, climate models are tested on their ability to reproduce the past and current behaviour of the climate. There is always the possibility of *tautology* with such 'hindcasting' (p. 4), and there may be important climatic mechanisms which are simply unknown and so unaccounted for in the model; this chapter highlights the potential impacts of such 'climate sensitivity'. So the precautionary principle's insistence on action before full scientific certainty (see p. 84) is vital in this case.

Whilst the science of climate change is becoming more certain for broad global outcomes, it remains very uncertain for local conditions and their possible futures, as this chapter illustrates. This is partly because the global climate models are simply not fine-tuned enough to provide much consistent and accurate data at the regional and more local levels. For example, farmers, water companies, power utilities and others do not really see how their individual actions can alter climate futures bearing on their locality. So where decisions are being made at the local, rather than global, level about possible adaptation to climate change, or more removal of greenhouse gases, there is little scientific guidance. As the science develops, it is important that scientists increasingly act in partnership with local, as well as global, decision-makers, to come up with solutions appropriate to local conditions.

The role of the 'greenhouse sceptics', scientists who doubt the mainstream view and who are often funded by fossil fuel interests, is outlined below. Such scientists may disagree with the priority given to Type II, rather than Type I, errors by the precautionary principle (see p. 16). That is, they argue that it is best to wait and see how research develops, before attempting to counteract an effect which may not be real. But some people go further; in the words of a *New York Times* journalist: 'even in the unlikely event that the doomsayers are right about global warming, humanity will find a way to avert climate change or adapt, and everyone will emerge the better for it' (quoted in Athanasiou 1996: 79). This position is termed cornucopianism, the belief that 'all will be well'. Cornucopians are individualists in relation to risk (p. 81). Rather than simply question the re-evaluation of the importance of Type II, compared with Type I, errors implied by the precautionary principle, such people reject the whole *notion* of precaution. They use the uncertainties in science and the possibilities of technological innovation to oppose the precautionary principle and sustainable development on ideological and political grounds.

Given the high stakes involved, it is no surprise that the climate change debate should be so politicised. As this chapter makes clear, a central feature of the political debate is the role of equity, or fairness. Equity is enshrined in the version of the precautionary principle endorsed at Rio (see p. 85): 'In order to protect the environment, the precautionary approach will be widely applied by states *according to their capabilities*' (my emphasis). This aspect of the precautionary principle is particularly pertinent to global warming, since it is the rich countries of the North which have the greatest capabilities for change and which also bear the largest responsibility for past emissions.

A genuine commitment to equity would challenge many of the most important global economic and political structures. Yet it will be needed if the enormous task of building an international coalition capable of tackling global warming is to succeed. The scientists warning of global warming have been effective because they were able to reach consensus; for the precautionary principle to succeed, the decision makers and politicians must do likewise.

5.1 The challenge

Global warming, the change in climate induced by emissions of greenhouse gases such as carbon dioxide and methane, presents policy makers with a serious challenge. Greenhouse gas emissions are intrinsic to the dominant model of economic development, so reducing emissions substantially may require a fundamental change in patterns of growth. The impacts of climate change and sea-level rise could touch all aspects of life and coping with them could well prove costly. The climate threat is uncertain and poorly defined, hence identifying effective responses is not a straightforward matter. Finally, the timescale of the problem, decades and longer, is beyond the planning horizon of all but the most far-sighted decision makers. Global warming can, in fact, be viewed as the ultimate test of sustainability (Kelly and Granich 1995).

In this chapter, the basis for scientific concern regarding the climate threat is defined and key characteristics of the global warming problem are drawn out. There is a strong consensus that the science of global warming is sufficiently well-founded to warrant a precautionary reaction at this time, but the uncertainties that shroud understanding of the problem complicate identification of the most effective strategies. The development of the United Nations Framework Convention on Climate Change is described and current issues affecting implementation of this treaty are discussed. Finally, possible elements of a sustainable response to the threat of climate change are defined. Throughout this chapter, the term 'global warming' is used to describe the threat of environmental change posed by emissions of greenhouse gases resulting from anthropogenic (i.e. human) activity. The term 'climate change' is used to refer to both natural and anthropogenic variability.

5.2 Key characteristics of the global warming issue

5.2.1 Roots in the development process

The threat of global warming is the most striking indication of the transformation that has occurred in the relationship between humanity and the natural environment over recent centuries. The causes of the problem are clear – at least in general terms. They are the escalation in the demand for energy, the expansion of industry and the intensification of agriculture since the industrial revolution, all of which have led to increased atmospheric concentrations of **greenhouse gases** (see Box 5.1).

Take the major greenhouse gas, carbon dioxide, for example. The main source of carbon emissions is the burning of fossil fuels such as coal, gas and oil, responsible for adding around 5.5 GtC (gigatons or thousand million metric tons of carbon) to the atmosphere every year during the 1980s (Schimel et al. 1996). It is fossil fuel consumption that has underpinned the massive escalation in energy use in the industrialised nations over the past few centuries and it is the consumption of cheap local supplies of coal that is now supporting the rise in energy use in rapidly industrialising nations such as China and India (Rao et al. 1994).

Atmospheric concentrations of carbon are also increasing because of deforestation and changing land use, largely forced by agricultural expansion. The release of carbon as trees are burnt or decay added about 1.6 GtC to the atmosphere each year during the 1980s (Schimel et al. 1996). Agricultural expansion is also a major driving force behind the release of methane, another significant greenhouse gas, into the atmosphere (Prather et al. 1996). Methane is produced in the digestive systems of cattle, in rice paddy fields and as a by-product of land conversion.

Since the late 18th century, atmospheric carbon dioxide levels have risen by around 30% to a present-day value of over 360 parts per million by volume (Figure 5.1). Around half this rise has occurred since the 1950s. Methane concentrations have doubled over the past few centuries. The atmospheric concentration of nitrous oxide (another greenhouse gas) has risen from 280 ppbv in 1800 to over 310 ppbv in recent years.

Whether to drive industrial production and maintain economic growth or to feed the growing population of the world, the processes that are giving rise to the change in atmospheric composition are fundamental to the historical development of modern civilisation. It is not surprising, then, that the climate debate should be intensely political.

121

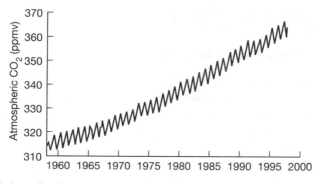

Figure 5.1 Carbon dioxide concentration, monthly values, at the Mauna Loa Observatory, Hawaii.

Data source: Carbon Dioxide Information Analysis Center at http://cdiac.esd.ornl.gov/

5.2.2 Vulnerability is widespread

There are many uncertainties concerning the detailed effects of global warming. See Watson et al. (1996, 1998) for state-of-the-art assessments. Nevertheless, it is possible to identify the major areas of impact (Kelly and Granich 1995)

- **Impact area 1.** Climatic zones will expand away from the equator towards the poles and ecological habitats will shift as climate patterns alter. While some species and ecosystems will be able to adapt, in many cases the speed of the change will be too fast and species, possibly whole ecosystems, could become extinct. The main threat will be to species and ecosystems in already vulnerable, marginal locations (towards mountain tops, near urban areas, and so on).

- **Impact area 2.** As temperatures rise, the oceans will warm, seawater will expand and glaciers on land will melt, resulting in a rise in sea level (perhaps by over 0.5 metre by the second half of the 21st century). Many of the world's major cities lie near sea level, as do valuable ecosystems and agricultural land. The main concern must be for those in the Third World who will not have the resources to protect themselves. Even today, thousands die in the storm surges which regularly flood the vulnerable Ganges delta in Bangladesh.

- **Impact area 3.** The northern continental interiors may dry out. This would have major implications for crop yields. The United States currently provides almost 90% of the world grain surplus. As that surplus is lost, prices will rise. Poorer nations suffering harvest failure will be unable to buy food on the world market. And, of course, food production in the developing nations is likely to be affected directly.

Some people and nations may benefit from the change in climate. Their climate may become more benign. They may have the resources to adapt. But those who are poor, and already vulnerable, will inevitably suffer. It is the widespread and serious nature of the potential consequences that explains why politicians are prepared to take action even though impacts are not yet evident and the science remains, to some degree, uncertain.

5.2.3 Understanding is limited

The climate system is complex and predicting the impact of global warming stretches scientific understanding to the limit. Box 5.1 outlines the main certainties in global warming science, the basis for concern. (See Warr and Smith (1993) for an accessible introduction and Houghton et al. (1996) for further technical information.) But for every global warming certainty, there is at least one major uncertainty – if not more. Here, we consider how critical uncertainties in scientific understanding limit society's ability to respond to the climate problem and have given rise to a polarised debate on the need for action.

For example, incontrovertible proof that global warming is occurring may not be available for some decades. While the warming observed over the past 100 years or so is not inconsistent with climate model predictions of anthropogenic impacts (Box 5.1), there are a number of other possible explanations for the warming trend: natural mechanisms of climatic change such as a change in the degree of volcanic or solar activity or in the distribution of ocean temperatures. Essentially, the temperature rise must surpass the natural variability in climate before natural hypotheses can be discounted and the greenhouse effect can be considered to have been firmly established as the prime cause. In any event, detecting trends in data which are variable can be extremely difficult (see Chapter 1), especially when the data have been collected in different ways at different times and places (Box 5.2). This is a critical uncertainty. If we cannot prove that greenhouse gas emissions are responsible for a past change in climate, then we have no 'smoking gun' to demonstrate to politicians just how real the problem of global warming is.

Moreover, while the trends in atmospheric concentrations are clear, as are the major sources of the excess greenhouse gas emissions (Box 5.1), there are important uncertainties in our understanding of the relationship between human activity, greenhouse gas emissions and the resulting change in atmospheric composition. For example, despite considerable progress in understanding the **carbon cycle** – how carbon is distributed and transferred between the rocks and soils, living matter, the atmosphere, oceans, and so on – there remains the **missing sink** problem

Box 5.1 The three areas of certainty in global warming science

Certainty 1: *There is no doubt that the greenhouse effect is a genuine mechanism and that a substantial change in atmospheric composition is underway*. Many of the gases being released as a result of human activity are greenhouse gases; not only carbon dioxide but also halocarbons such as the chlorofluorocarbons (CFCs), methane, nitrous oxide and surface ozone. Because of their molecular characteristics, these gases permit heat and light from the sun to pass down through the atmosphere to warm the earth's surface relatively unhindered, but they trap heat lost from the surface and the lower atmosphere and prevent it escaping back to space. This heat trap intensifies as concentrations of the greenhouse gases rise, warming the earth's surface and lower atmosphere. There is no doubt as to this basic mechanism. Without the natural greenhouse effect, the planet would be too cold to support life as we know it. And evidence of long-term trends derived from air trapped in ice cores demonstrates that the change in atmospheric composition that has occurred since the industrial revolution is without precedent during human history.

Certainty 2: *The global warming that has occurred since the mid-19th century is not inconsistent with model predictions of the likely effect of greenhouse enhancement over that period*. According to computer models, the change in atmospheric composition that has occurred over the past 100 years or so should already have resulted in warming of between a third and one degree Celsius. The world has, in fact, warmed by around 0.5°C over this period (Jones et al. 1999). The temperature of the planet is now higher than it has been at any time during the period of instrumental observations and, possibly, during the past 1000 years (Mann et al. 1998). The five warmest years in the global temperature record have all occurred during the 1990s. The causes of this trend could well be both natural and anthropogenic though, according to the latest assessment by the IPCC, 'the observed trend in global temperature over the past 100 years is unlikely to be entirely natural in origin.'

Certainty 3: *Assuming no concerted effort to curb greenhouse gas emissions, the surface temperature of the planet could rise anywhere between 1.5 and 3.0°C by the year 2100*. To place this change in climate in context, the temperature rise that brought the planet out of the most recent ice age was only of the order of 3 – 4°C. Even at the lower end of the range of uncertainty, global warming represents a substantial change in the planetary environment. According to current projections (Houghton et al. 1996), global temperature may stand over 1.5°C above the pre-industrial level by the year 2050 (Figure 5.2), a warming rate six times that experienced during the 20th century. It is necessary to go back 125 000 years to find a time when temperatures approached the level that could prevail by the mid-21st century.

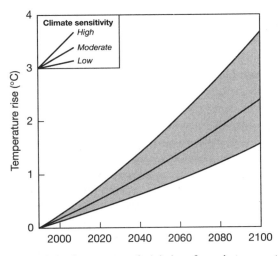

Figure 5.2 Projections of the future rate of global surface air temperature rise, based on an IPCC business-as-usual scenario (IS92a). The shaded range of uncertainty is defined by the climate sensitivity and ocean response.

Source: S.C.B. Raper (personal communication).

(Schimel et al. 1996). After being released into the atmosphere, some carbon remains there, creating the rise in atmospheric concentration and greenhouse warming, and a considerable proportion enters the oceans. But some of the carbon released as a result of human activities cannot be accounted for (*ignorance* about carbon pathways is an important source of uncertainty in the models – see p. 48). There are several possibilities that might account for the discrepancy. It may be that plant growth is being boosted by the greater availability of carbon dioxide in the air. Recent reforestation programmes in northern mid-latitudes may have resulted in more carbon storage. It is possible that the oceans may be taking up more carbon than observations and models suggest. Whatever the explanation, it will be difficult to have total confidence regarding modelled estimates of the benefits of any emission control strategy until this issue is resolved and understanding of the carbon cycle improves.

The third area of uncertainty considered here affects the projections of future global climate change. This uncertainty has two sources. First, it is not a simple matter to forecast the social, economic and technical developments which will determine the level of greenhouse gas emissions over coming decades. What rates of economic and population growth should be assumed? Will new technology become available? A range of plausible scenarios has to be developed rather than a single projection. Second, understanding of the manner in which the climate system will respond to the changing composition of the atmosphere is incomplete. For example, the effect on the climate system depends on a parameter known as the

---

Box 5.2 Taking the temperature of the planet

The global surface air temperature average provides a useful measure of the overall state of the climate system (Jones et al. 1999). It is based on observations from standard meteorological stations on land and from 'ships of opportunity' at sea. But constructing a reliable index from the millions of individual observations taken during the course of routine weather observation poses a series of problems.

First, there is the changing availability of data. Before the middle of the 19th century, instrumental coverage was limited to Europe, parts of Asia and North America and some coastal regions of Africa, South America and Australasia. By the 1920s, the only major land areas without meteorological instrumentation were some interior parts of Africa, South America and Asia, Arctic coasts and the whole of Antarctica. Today, surface observations are available for all areas but parts of the Southern Ocean. Over the past couple of decades, satellite data have afforded global coverage, although the shortness of this record limits the value of this database for climate change studies. Analysis of the effects of changing data coverage on the global surface air temperature average suggests that the longer-term trends in the data are reliable back to the late 19th century.

Second, there is the reliability of the individual series of observations. The most important causes of error, or 'non-homogeneity,' in climate series are: changes in instrument, exposure and measurement technique; changes in station location; changes in observation times and the methods used to calculate monthly averages; and changes in the station environment, particularly urbanisation. Before constructing a large-scale average, each individual record has to be tested for errors and accepted, corrected or rejected. There are also systematic errors or biases that can occur. For example, sea surface temperature data are used as a proxy for air temperature in marine areas as it is easier to measure the ocean temperature from a ship. But methods of measuring sea surface temperature have changed over the years. Originally, a bucket was slung over the side of the ship to sample the surface waters but nowadays the temperature of the water used to cool the ship's engine is sampled. There is a consistent bias between these two sets of measurements which must be removed from the data set if a reliable global average is to be calculated.

---

climate sensitivity. As temperatures rise in response to strengthening of the greenhouse effect, feedback processes will come into play, reinforcing or damping down the initial temperature change. For example, the snow and ice margin will retreat towards the poles. Snow and ice are more reflective than bare ground so as the snow and ice cover retreats, more solar energy will be absorbed by the ground, warming the overlying air and reinforcing the initial temperature change. This is **positive feedback**. But change in cloud cover may counter the warming trend, reflecting more solar energy back into space and creating a **negative feedback**.

It is uncertainty in the relative importance of these feedback processes that means we cannot predict with accuracy how global temperature will respond to a particular change in atmospheric composition. The rate of temperature change is an important factor for policy. Do we need to act immediately or can we afford to wait?

5.2.4 The greenhouse sceptics

The uncertainties in global warming science have fuelled argument regarding the urgency with which action should be taken. At the extreme ends of the spectrum are the more strident environmental organisations, claiming that society must move rapidly towards a 'fossil fuel-free future', and industrial lobbying groups countering that any limits placed on energy use will have dire economic consequences. Both groups cite scientific support for their positions. The environmentalists, for example, point to the continuing rise in global temperature, despite the uncertain origin of that trend. The industrial lobbyists have the so-called greenhouse sceptics in their camp.

The greenhouse sceptics are a group of scientists who believe that the scientific consensus regarding global warming is incorrect, even the result of conspiracy. For example, here is Nigel Calder, ex-editor of the journal *Nature* and a prominent critic of global warming science, commenting on the performance of climate models (Calder 1997):

> Drawn and coloured superbly by the computers, the maps looked as authoritative as a city street-plan. So if the computer covered the Great Lakes with a splodge of red to signify a 10 degree rise in winter temperatures, many people, even scientists, took the picture literally. When the silicon-brained artist saw fit to coat the American grainlands with orange to denote a 2-centimetre loss of soil moisture, experts started doing sums about the cost of irrigation. If you took the trouble to compare the maps from different computer modellers, any sense of awe was quickly dispelled. Although produced by similar programs, and with similar assumptions about the physical factors in climate, the painted maps looked very different. One promised drought in India, and another, floods. You could go around the world picking the regional forecast of your choice.

Calder's point about the disagreement often apparent between the results of different climate models, and indeed occasionally between different experiments (or *simulations*, see p. 29) with the same model, is correct. Uncertainty in the regional projections, largely the result of the low spatial resolution of the models (see Box 5.3), is a characteristic of the current development of this area of global warming science. And it is true that results are often presented with rather more care paid to artistic presentation than to the presentation of accompanying reservations and qualifications. Nevertheless, to draw the conclusion on the basis

---

Box 5.3 Modelling the climate system

Numerous mathematical models of the climate system have been developed, ranging from the very simple to the complex (Warr and Smith 1993). These computer-based models attempt to simulate the behaviour of the climate system from 'first principles' based on the fundamental laws which govern key physical, chemical and biological processes. The equations used in a climate model may be empirical (based on relationships observed in the real world), they may be the so-called primitive equations which represent theoretical relationships between variables, or they may be a combination of these two.

All models must simplify what is a very complex system. This is partly a result of incomplete understanding of the processes involved but largely a result of computational restraints. Simplification can take place in terms of spatial dimensionality, space and time resolution, or through neglect or simplification of the processes that are simulated. The simplest models are 'zero-order' in spatial dimension. The state of the climate system is defined by a single global average. At the more sophisticated end of the model spectrum lie the general circulation models (GCMs) which simulate processes in all three spatial dimensions: latitude, longitude and height. Whatever the spatial dimensions of a model, further simplification takes place in terms of **spatial resolution**. There will be a limited number of, for example, latitude bands in a one-dimensional model and a limited number of gridpoints in a model which simulates processes in both horizontal dimensions. Finally, the time resolution of climate models varies greatly, from minutes to years.

Verification of model performance is based on assessing how well they reproduce present-day climate. In general, the most sophisticated models capture the main characteristics of the climate system effectively but are limited in their ability to reproduce local detail. All models provide, at best, 'a cloudy crystal ball' in the words of one modeller, and their results must be treated with due caution.

---

of a critique of model performance that 'for computing the greenhouse warming, neither the understanding of meteorology nor the capacity of the computers was up to the job', as Calder does, goes way too far. Even though limited on the regional scale, climate models can still provide useful estimates of large-scale change. It is not the overall definition of the global warming problem that is uncertain – the big picture – but the fine detail.

Moving away from the extremes and towards the centre, we find commentators who favour a 'wait and see' approach, whereby action is delayed until stronger evidence is available, promoting research and prioritising expenditure that can be justified in terms of more immediate and certain benefits (see Table 5.1). Some go further and propose that global warming may, on balance, prove beneficial, with enhanced carbon dioxide levels, for

Table 5.1 Two contrasting philosophies regarding the urgency with which action to combat the climate threat should be taken

'Wait and See'	'No Regrets'
The scientific evidence for global warming is incomplete.	Global climate change is linked to other important problems of environment and development and the combined risks are serious enough to warrant urgent and bold initiatives, even if they impose a substantial cost.
Hastily contrived strategies could do more harm than good: the costs could lead to a loss of human welfare and their implementation could lead to the stifling of human activity.	Human welfare, by and large, will be enhanced through strong efforts to mitigate environmental effects.
With the passage of time we will know more about the global warming problem and how best to respond to it. New solutions may emerge over time.	Time is of the essence in view of the long timescales characteristic of the problem and the time needed to alter fundamental aspects of the development process to reduce emissions and adapt to the changing climate.
Investment in research reduces the risks associated with premature and costly measures based on incomplete information.	Potential costs should be factored into present-day investment calculations, offsetting the expense of early action.
We should 'learn then act,' so that optimal strategies can be determined on the basis of complete and accurate information.	We should 'act then learn,' adopting measures that favour experimentation, foresight and cost-effective preparation.

Based on Pachauri and Damodaran (1992).

example, promoting crop growth. In opposition, we find the 'no regrets' advocates (Table 5.1). Reacting to the same scientific uncertainties, we find another group advocating precautionary action at one level or another in view of the potential scale of the consequences of climate change. This latter position most closely reflects the consensus amongst the scientific community.

Underlying these contrasting positions are different attitudes towards risk or, more precisely, different attitudes regarding the acceptability of different types of risk (see p. 81). Those advocating a 'wait and see' approach consider that it would be unwise to risk present-day economic growth by imposing emissions control measures in order to combat the uncertain threat of future climate change, and, anyway, technological progress should bring a solution to the climate problem in time. Those proposing precautionary action to combat global warming believe that it would not be wise to risk jeopardising environmental and economic health as a result of climate change and, as the response to climate change need not be costly, emissions control would be a wise investment. For further information regarding the attitudes of the various climate protagonists, visit the Tiempo Climate Cyberlibrary at http://www.cru.uea.ac.uk/ tiempo/floor1/news/debate.htm.

5.3 Towards an international response

5.3.1 Cause for concern

There is nothing new about concern over global warming (Fleming 1998). In the closing years of the 19th century, the Swedish scientist Arrhenius calculated the effect of coal emissions on temperature and warned about the possibility of widespread warming. But the tools to take the research further were absent. Most climate records were no more than a few decades in length, too short to reveal long-term trends. Models of the climate system were rudimentary, limited by hand calculation as well as understanding of the atmosphere.

During the early 20th century, as climate records became longer, pioneering climatologists began to examine the time series for evidence of regular, predictable fluctuations and long-term trends. They produced the first evidence that large-scale climate was changing as collections of temperature records, largely for the northern middle latitudes, showed warming begin during the 1920s (Figure 5.3). At the same time, developments in atmospheric chemistry led to increased interest in the properties of carbon dioxide and a second wave of concern that the natural greenhouse effect might be enhanced by human activity arose.

This phase ended as cooling began to dominate the records of large-scale temperature then available during the late 1940s and 1950s (cf. the Northern Hemisphere data in Figure 5.3). Cooling was not consistent with the greenhouse theory and interest in the subject waned. Rapid advances in forecasting short-term weather meant that resources were concentrated here, at the expense of what was seen as the rather boring exercise of climatological book-keeping.

The roots of current scientific interest in the climate problem can be found in three separate developments during the 1960s and 1970s, two scientific and one societal (Kelly and Granich 1995). First, advances in computer technology allowed the development of sophisticated climate models, and the effects of the changing composition of the atmosphere provided an excellent experiment for these new tools. The model results demonstrated that changes in the greenhouse gas content of the atmosphere could generate a substantial change in climate. Second, the

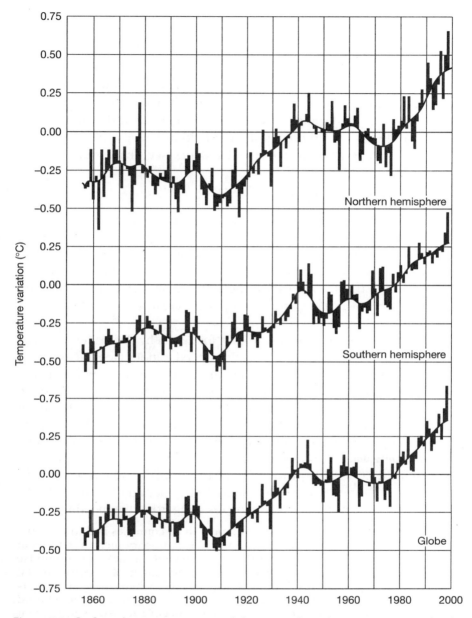

Temperature variation (°C)

Figure 5.3 Surface air temperature, annual departures from the 1961–90 mean, for the Northern hemisphere, Southern hemisphere and globe (Jones et al. 1999). The smooth curve reveals the longer-term variations.

Data source: Climatic Research Unit at http://www.cru.uea.ac.uk/tiempo/floor2/data/gltemp.htm

observational record of atmospheric composition and of large-scale climate improved substantially as a result of new atmospheric monitoring programmes begun in the late 1950s and concerted efforts to extend and correct climate databases during the second half of the 1970s. The observational evidence showed striking upward trends in greenhouse gas concentrations (Figure 5.1) and, from the late 1970s, renewed global warming (Figure 5.3). The final development, which led to the climate issue being considered an 'acceptable' subject of study as well as increased funding, was the broader concern about the environment which developed during the 1960s and early 1970s, culminating in the first United Nations Conference on the Environment held in Stockholm, Sweden, in 1972 (i.e. there was a change in contextual values, see Chapter 2).

5.3.2 From science to politics

During the 1980s, a succession of national and international scientific assessments of the issue documented the emerging consensus that, despite many uncertainties, the global warming problem should be taken seriously. The scientific community's concern was voiced at a series of conferences during the second half of the 1980s, culminating in a landmark meeting in Toronto in 1988, attended by both scientists and policy makers (Bodansky 1994).

In December 1988, responding to calls for action by the leaders of small island states at risk from sea level rise, the United Nations General Assembly recognized that 'climate change is a common concern of mankind' and called for a climate treaty. As a first step, the Intergovernmental Panel on Climate Change (IPCC) was established by the United Nations Environment Programme and the World Meteorological Organization. The aim of the IPCC was to provide the international community with technical guidance on dealing with the problem of climate change.

The initial IPCC reports provided the basis for discussion at the Second World Climate Conference in November 1991 (Jager and Ferguson 1991). According to the Ministerial Declaration resulting from that meeting:

> In order to achieve sustainable development in all countries and to meet the needs of present and future generations, precautionary measures to meet the climate challenge must anticipate, prevent, attack, or minimise the causes of, and mitigate the adverse consequences of, environmental degradation that might result from climate change. Where there are threats of serious or irreversible damage, lack of full scientific certainty should not be used as a reason for postponing cost-effective measures to prevent such degradation.

Precautionary measures, in this case, are those that would limit the scale or impact of global warming at little or no cost or else which have immediate benefits over and above reducing the climate problem. If, at a later date, it proves advisable to take further action then a start will have been made. If the present forecasts are not substantiated, little will have been lost.

The work of IPCC continued through the 1990s with a supplementary assessment in 1992 and major re-assessment in 1995. A third assessment is due in 2000/2001.

5.3.3 The climate treaty

The United Nations Framework Convention on Climate Change was ready for signature at the United Nations Conference on Environment and Development held in Rio de Janeiro in June 1992 and came into force in March 1994 (for a full discussion of the history and content of the Framework Convention, see Mintzer and Leonard 1994).

The objective of the Convention is '... to achieve ... stabilization of greenhouse gas concentrations in the atmosphere at a level that would prevent dangerous anthropogenic interference with the climate system. Such a level should be achieved within a time frame sufficient to allow ecosystems to adapt naturally to climate change, to ensure that food production is not threatened and to enable economic development to proceed in a sustainable manner.' Although superficially a very strong goal, this statement is rather subjective and vague. It proved difficult to reach agreement on a more precise wording; the vagueness was deliberate, to ensure a wide consensus as individual negotiators interpreted the statement to suit the interests of their particular constituency.

Reaching consensus has always been a key concern both during the deliberations of the IPCC and the more political debate that has characterised the negotiations surrounding the climate treaty. The reason for this concern is straightforward. Climate change is a global problem and, without the willing cooperation of the vast majority of the world's nations, significant progress in averting the threat cannot be made. At many key meetings, though, consensus has only been achieved after an all-night session before the final day and only then after substantial compromise. Political realities now shape the international response.

5.4 The politics of climate

The major political players during the climate negotiations can be defined as:

- The industrialised nations – some advocating strong action on the climate issue (such as the nations of the European Union) and some unwilling to forego dependence on fossil fuels (for example, the United States and Australia).
- The developing nations – some already heavily dependent on fossil fuels (India and China), many vulnerable to the impact of climate change

(small island states and the weaker economies), some fossil fuel producers (Venezuela and other oil states) and others compounding the climate problem through forest destruction (many nations in Southeast Asia and South America).

- Nations with economies in transition – heavy polluters with weak economies with considerable potential for growth.

Two major conflicts have characterised the history of the climate negotiations (Mintzer and Leonard 1994). First, there has been the reluctance of some nations or interest groups to accept that there is any need to curb fossil fuel emissions. The concern here is that emissions controls could damage economic growth. Similarly, some nations dependent on exploitation of forest resources have opposed any suggestion that controls might be placed on their use of their natural resources. Opposing this position are a number of industrialised nations committed to prompt action and many developing nations concerned that they are vulnerable to climate impacts, supported by environmental lobbying groups.

The second area of conflict centres on the North–South divide. The industrialised nations have been responsible for the bulk of greenhouse gas emissions to date (for this reason, industrialised nations alone committed to emissions controls when ratifying the Framework Convention). But it is the southern nations that are likely to experience the most substantial impacts because the resources available to them to offset adverse consequences are limited. The South has, therefore, exerted pressure on the North not only to take the lead with regard to emissions control but also to provide support to help the developing nations respond to the climate threat. Both these conditions of southern involvement in the process of dealing with global warming are met under the terms of the Framework Convention. One reason why the industrialised nations have accepted these conditions is that the involvement of the *industrialising* nations in the treaty process is critical for long-term success. It could be said that the developing world holds a loaded gun at the head of the industrialised North – in the form of its capacity to increase its own emissions in the future.

5.5 Current commitments

The diverse views of the negotiators, and the need to reach a consensus to ensure wide participation, meant that much of the text of the Framework Convention amounted to a compromise. Nevertheless, the Convention is considered a landmark in international environmental law. It is a global agreement with far-reaching consequences. It enshrines a commitment to sustainable development, including equity considerations, the concept of common but differentiated responsibilities, and, though in a rather circumspect fashion, the precautionary principle (see p. 84). Parties to the Convention take on a substantial list of commitments, ranging from emissions controls in the case of industrialised nations to regular reports on progress in implementing the treaty, an expanded research effort, planning for sustainable development and education programmes for all.

The Third Session of the Conference of the Parties to the United Nations Framework Convention on Climate Change took place in Kyoto in December 1997. The resulting Kyoto Protocol committed the industrialised nations to reduce their collective emissions of six greenhouse gases by 5.2% averaged over the period 2008–2012 (Bolin 1998; Yamin 1998). Carbon dioxide, methane and nitrous oxide reductions are to be from 1990 levels, the existing baseline. For three long-lived industrial gases – the hydrofluorocarbons, perfluorocarbons and sulphur hexafluoride – the baseline can be 1990 or 1995.

The Kyoto Protocol is considered a step in the right direction but, with carbon cuts of some 60% needed to halt global warming (Houghton et al. 1996), many had hoped for a stronger commitment to mark entry into the greenhouse century. But, again, consensus could only be achieved through compromise, which is reflected in the flexibility that was a characteristic of many aspects of the agreement. Some parties, such as the European Union, took on cuts of 8%. The United States reluctantly accepted a reduction target of 7%. Other nations may increase their emissions – Australia, for example, by 8% and Iceland by 10%.

Flexibility also extended to the manner in which commitments could be met (Jackson et al. 1998). Through **joint implementation**, parties may finance emissions reductions in other industrialised nations where reductions can be achieved at a lower cost and take credit for the outcome (Wirl et al. 1998). An **emissions trading mechanism** will permit industrialised nations to buy and sell emissions credits (Skea 1998). If any nation overshoots its emissions reductions target, it can sell the 'excess' emissions credit to another country, thereby offsetting the savings that nation will have to make. The **clean development mechanism**, funded by the industrialised nations, will finance emissions control measures in the developing world, encouraging these nations on a sustainable, low-emissions development path.

Three issues are likely to dominate the next stage of implementation of the climate treaty as we move into the new century.

- Given that many industrialised nations have failed to meet their initial target of stabilisation by the year 2000, how will compliance be encouraged, if not legally enforced (Yamin 1998)?
- There is likely to be much debate over joint implementation, the clean development mechanism and emissions trading. Is emissions trading, for

example, the most efficient means of achieving significant reductions, or is it just a device for industrialised nations to avoid responsibility for controlling their own emissions? There are serious questions to be resolved regarding monitoring, allocation of credit, fair play and justice. Might not the developing world lose out as the 'price' of emissions credits plummets as have other, more conventional southern commodity prices in recent decades?

- As emissions from southern countries increase, pressure will be on the South to accept limits on emissions trends. Under what conditions will southern nations accept formal targets? Will effective support be available from the historic polluters of the North to switch the South onto a greenhouse-friendly development path? (McCully 1991.)

5.6 Defining a sustainable approach to global warming

The international community has accepted the need for precautionary action to limit the threat of climate change. But what form should precautionary action take? In general terms, the response to global warming has two main parts (Bruce et al. 1996; Watson et al. 1996): the control of emissions sources and the promotion of emissions sinks (through, for example, forest expansion) to limit the change in atmospheric composition; and planned adaptation to minimise the impact of climate change and sea level rise.

Many opportunities are available to take action on both counts, through the adoption of new technology, land reform, altered lifestyles, and so on. What is of concern here, though, is not detailed measures and policies, but how we might define elements of an over-arching strategy consistent with the principles of sustainable development.

The Framework Convention on Climate Change contains within its text a clear commitment to equity between nations and to the process of sustainable development. Yet implementation of the Convention is becoming increasingly dependent on mechanisms such as emissions trading that flow from a neo-liberal economic philosophy and a belief in the effectiveness of unregulated globalisation and the free market. Whether or not there is a tension here depends on the perspective of the observer. Doyle (1998) has argued that the dominant paradigm of sustainable development is itself based on advancing globalisation and libertarian market systems. Nevertheless, it is undeniable that humanity is attempting to counter the effects of its inadvertent experiment on the climate system with a second, deliberate experiment in global economics. Then there is the tendency towards technocentric or 'top-down' strategies, to the neglect of important societal processes and cultural differences.

The first element of a sustainable approach to the climate problem is that it must take full account of the range of technical, social, economic, cultural and political processes that will determine effectiveness in a particular situation and guarantee equity, fairness, both within and between generations.

The second element of a sustainable strategy concerns priorities. We must take care that we do not neglect the needs of the present generation in order to protect those of the future. In fact, the resolution of the dichotomy between short-term needs and long-term concerns can be found in a strand of the precautionary position. If we can identify and adopt measures which have benefits in the here and now, as well as limiting the future problem of climate change, then the conflict disappears.

It is not difficult to find examples of such 'win–win' strategies. Reducing fossil fuel use by improving the efficiency with which energy is used and deploying energy conservation measures represents an extremely cost-effective approach that will reduce the rate of depletion of finite reserves and save money, as well as limiting emissions (Goldemberg et al. 1988). On the impact side, Kelly and Adger (1999) argue that adaptation can be promoted in coastal Vietnam through measures such as poverty reduction, risk-spreading through income diversification and protection of common property management rights – all goals consistent with present-day development priorities.

The second element of a sustainable approach must be the careful assessment of priorities, placing long-term concerns in the context of the full range of present-day demands and aspirations.

While a win–win strategy may suffice for the early precautionary stage of the response to global warming, the problem of uncertainty is not solely a characteristic of this phase. It is unlikely, for example, that definite forecasts of the long-term climatic future will ever be available. Predicting the underlying socio-economic trends that shape the evolution of greenhouse effect can never be precise and there are other, inherently unpredictable, factors which also affect climate. Yet many sectors of human activity require planning on timescales not dissimilar to that of climate change: forestry, agriculture, water resource management. Where long-term planning is necessary, the optimal strategy must be based on caution (one might almost say humility), diversity and an acceptance that a selected approach might have to be abandoned in the light of experience and changing circumstances. We might term this a co-evolutionary response (Norgaard 1994). Such a strategy must be based on:

- monitoring (with sufficient power, see p. 25) – so that change and its consequences can be detected promptly
- awareness and empowerment – so that prompt action can be taken at every level of society as circumstances change

- staged implementation – so that any step taken in the wrong direction is a small one
- diversity – so that a range of approaches is available enabling matching with different socio-economic and cultural circumstances
- flexibility – so that options are kept open, knowledge is gained through the experience and different measures can be deployed as circumstances alter
- continual evaluation and re-evaluation – so that ineffective approaches can be quickly modified or replaced

The third element of this sustainable approach to the climate problem is therefore that it must be characterised by caution and staged implementation based on flexibility, diversity, continual evaluation of performance and an informed community.

The three elements defined here are by no means the whole story. There are many other aspects that require examination if we are to develop a truly sustainable strategy. How can we take full account of non-market values (such as aesthetic or intrinsic values, see p. 145) in assessing the costs and benefits of different measures? How do we resolve the trade-offs that must inevitably occur between benefits in different areas? Do we have the consultative procedures necessary to ensure adequate community involvement (see p. 88)? The questions are endless. While the impact of climate change is still relatively slight, we have the opportunity to examine carefully the full range of response options available to us, questioning their relative efficiency, their costs and benefits, so that we can develop an effective, equitable and sustainable approach.

5.7 Summary

- Greenhouse gases, such as carbon dioxide, methane and nitrous oxides, trap heat in the lower atmosphere.
- The atmospheric concentration of these gases has increased markedly in the last century or so, largely as a result of industrial and agricultural practices.
- The scientific consensus is that this changing atmospheric concentration is at least partly responsible for the current warming trend, and that it will cause further planetary warming and sea level rise in the future.
- There are many uncertainties in the science, arising, for example, from uncertainties about the strength of feedback mechanisms and ignorance about the carbon cycle. These uncertainties are used by the greenhouse sceptics to argue that the scientific consensus is wrong.
- The United Nations Framework Convention on Climate Change is an international agreement which attempts to tackle the threat of global

warming. In order to maintain consensus, it contains many compromises, and uses new and controversial economic instruments such as emissions trading.

- Given the high stakes and uncertainties involved, a sustainable response to climate change must guarantee equity, it must look for win–win solutions and it must be implemented flexibly and with monitoring.

Further reading

Grubb, M., Vrolijk, C. and Brack, D. (1999) *The Kyoto Protocol: A Guide and Assessment*, Royal Institute of International Affairs/Earthscan, London. Comprehensive assessment of the latest stage of the climate negotiations.

Jepma, C.J. and Munasinghe, M. (1998) *Climate Change Policy: Facts, Issues and Analyses*, Cambridge University Press, Cambridge. Up-to-date and accessible account of climate policy issues, including a concise summary of global warming science based on the Second Assessment by the Intergovernmental Panel on Climate Change (IPCC). For a more technical account, see the various IPCC reports cited in the text of this chapter (Houghton et al. 1996; Watson et al. 1996, 1998).

Mintzer, I.M. and Leonard, J.A. (eds) (1994) Negotiating Climate Change: The Inside Story of the Rio Convention, Cambridge University Press, Cambridge. Detailed account of the development of the UN Framework Convention on Climate Change.

O'Riordan, T. and Jäger, J. (eds) (1996) *The Politics of Climate Change: A European Perspective*, Routledge, London. Contrasting responses to the climate problem from different European nations.

References

Athanasiou, T. (1996) *Slow Reckoning. The Ecology of a Divided Planet*, Vintage, London.

Bodansky, D. (1994) Prologue to the Climate Change Convention. In: Mintzer, I.M. and Leonard, J.A. (eds) *Negotiating Climate Change: The Inside Story of the Rio Convention*, Cambridge University Press, Cambridge.

Bolin, B. (1998) The Kyoto negotiations on climate change: A science perspective. *Science*, 279, 330–331.

Bruce, J. Hoesung Lee and Haites, E. (eds) (1996) *Climate Change 1995: Economic and Social Dimensions of Climate Change*. Cambridge University Press, Cambridge.

Calder, N. (1997) *The Manic Sun: Weather Theories Confounded*, Pilkington Press, London.

Doyle, T. (1998) Sustainable development and Agenda 21: the secular bible of global free markets and pluralist democracy. *Third World Quarterly*, 19, 771–786.

Fleming, J.R. (1998) *Historical Perspectives on Climate Change*, Oxford University Press, New York.

Goldemberg, J., Johansson, T.B., Reddy, A.K.N. and Williams, R.H. (1988) *Energy for a Sustainable World*, Wiley, New York.

Houghton, J.T., Meira Filho, L.G., Callander, B.A., Harris, N., Kattenberg, A. and Maskell, K. (eds) (1996) *Climate Change 1995: The Science of Climate Change*, Cambridge University Press, Cambridge.

Jackson, T., Begg, K. and Parkinson, S. (1998) The language of flexibility and the flexibility of language. *International Journal of Environment and Pollution*, **10**, 462–475.

Jager, J. and Ferguson, H.L. (eds) (1991) *Climate Change: Science, Impacts and Policy. Proceedings of the Second World Climate Conference*, Cambridge University Press, Cambridge.

Jones, P.D., New, M., Parker, D.E., Martin, S. and Rigor, I.G. (1999) Surface air temperature and its changes over the past 150 years. *Reviews of Geophysics*, in press.

Kelly, P.M. and Adger, W.N. (1999) Assessing vulnerability to climate change and facilitating adaptation, *CSERGE Working Paper, GEC 99-07*. Centre for Social and Economic Research on the Global Environment, Norwich/London.

Kelly, P.M. and Granich, S.L.V. (1995) Global warming and development. In: Morse, S. and Stocking, M. (eds) *People and Environment*, UCL Press, London.

Mann, M.E., Bradley, R.S. and Hughes, M.K. (1998) Global-scale temperature patterns and climate forcing over the past six centuries. *Nature*, **392**, 779–787.

McCully, P. (1991) The case against climate aid. *The Ecologist*, **21**, 244–251.

Mintzer, I.M. and Leonard, J.A. (eds) (1994) *Negotiating Climate Change: The Inside Story of the Rio Convention*, Cambridge University Press, Cambridge, 392 pp.

Norgaard, R.B. (1994) *Development Betrayed*, Routledge, London.

Pachauri, R.K. and Damodaran, M. (1992) 'Wait and See' versus 'No Regrets': comparing the costs of economic strategies. In: Mintzer, I. M. (ed) *Confronting Climate Change: Risks, Implications and Responses*, Cambridge University Press, Cambridge.

Prather, M., Derwent, R., Ehhalt, D., Fraser, P., Sanhueza, E., and Zhou, X. (1996) Radiative forcing of climate change: other trace gases and atmospheric chemistry. In Houghton, J.T., Meira Filho, L.G., Callander, B.A., Harris, N., Kattenberg, A. and Maskell, K. (eds) *Climate Change 1995: The Science of Climate Change*, Cambridge University Press, Cambridge.

Rao, P.G., Kelly, P.M., Hulme, M. and Srinivasan, G. (1994) Climatic change, greenhouse gas emissions, future climate and response strategies: the implications for India. *CSERGE Working Paper, GEC 94-22*, Centre for Social and Economic Research on the Global Environment, Norwich/London.

Schimel, D., Alves, D., Enting, I., Heimann, M., Joos, F., Raynaud, D. and Wigley, T. (1996) Radiative forcing of climate change: CO_2 and the carbon cycle. In: Houghton, J.T., Meira Filho, L.G., Callander, B.A., Harris, N., Kattenberg, A. and Maskell, K. (eds) *Climate Change 1995: The Science of Climate Change*, Cambridge University Press, Cambridge.

Skea, J. (1998) The role of emissions trading in implementing the UN Climate Convention. *International Journal of Environment and Pollution*, **10**, 454–461.

Warr, K. and Smith, S. (1993) *Science Matters: Changing Climate*, Open University, Milton Keynes, 282 pp.

Watson, R.T., Zinyowera, M.C. and Moss, R.H. (eds) (1996) *Climate Change 1995: Impacts, Adaptations and Mitigation of Climate Change: Scientific-Technical Analyses*, Cambridge University Press, Cambridge.

Watson, R.T., Zinyowera, M.C., and Moss, R.H. (eds) (1998) *The Regional Impacts of Climate Change: An Assessment of Vulnerability*, Cambridge University Press, Cambridge.

Wirl, F., Huber, C., and Walker, I.O. (1998) Joint implementation: Strategic reactions and possible remedies. *Environmental & Resource Economics*, **12**, 203–224.

Yamin, F. (1998) Climate change negotiations: an analysis of the Kyoto Protocol. *International Journal of Environment and Pollution*, **10**, 428–453.

Chapter 6

Why conserve wild species?

Mark Huxham

Editors' introduction

In Britain, the most important conservation areas are known as 'Sites of Special Scientific Interest' (SSSIs), which must be selected according to a 'scientific framework'. The European Union designates conservation areas (SPAs, see p. 165) on scientific (as opposed to social or economic) criteria, and US conservation legislation also relies heavily on scientific concepts such as 'ecological balance'. These examples demonstrate a widespread and persistent belief that the conservation of wild species and habitats is essentially a scientific business. A new science, conservation biology, has developed recently to deal with the task.

Chapters 2 and 3 showed how scientific approaches usually reflect a 'technical rationality', the hallmark of which is the attempt to predict, manipulate and control the natural world. Much of conservation biology fits this pattern. Its journals are full of technical papers addressing questions such as 'what is the best shape for a nature reserve?' and 'how small can the population of this species become before being in severe danger of extinction?'. These are questions about how to achieve particular outcomes. They can be very difficult to answer because of the problems in meeting some of the requirements for good experimental science discussed in Chapter 1 (see p. 152 for an example of confounding factors). What these questions do not address is the motivation for asking them in the first place: *why* should we try to preserve wild species?

Chapter 2 introduced *cost–benefit analysis* as one approach that attempts to answer such 'why' questions in a scientific (or perhaps pseudo-scientific) manner. Perhaps we should conserve species because the costs of doing so are outweighed by the benefits? As this chapter shows, the balance of costs and benefits for conserving most species is not clear, and it is likely that many species are not particularly 'useful' to human beings. Most conservation biologists are motivated by values that go far deeper than such 'rational' assessments of what wild species are worth.

That *contextual values* underlie and inform all areas of science was made clear in Chapters 2 and 3. However, these values are usually implicit; they are not frequently discussed and scrutinised by the scientists working under their influence. In fact, many scientists would argue that values have no place in the operation of science, and that an open identification with any particular value system could lead to bias (see p. 49). Conservation biology, in contrast, is an example of a scientific field where values are often openly acknowledged and identified as being of primary importance. One of the founders of the discipline, Michael Soulé, makes clear his own motivation: 'planetary tragedy is also a personal tragedy for those who feel compelled to devote themselves to the rescue effort.' Being a conservation biologist is a way of 'pledging our support for life'. There is no fact/value divide here. So conservation biology gives an excellent example of how facts and values are intertwined in complex fields of applied science, and in particular of how the values underlying the science are of more importance than the science itself. In contrast to the impression given by much of the legislation, a rational and sensible approach to conservation may not focus on science at all; perhaps, instead of Sites of Special Scientific Interest, it would make sense to designate 'Sites of Special Ethical Interest', or just 'Beautiful Places'? This chapter looks at some of the reasons why.

Because the science of conservation biology acknowledges its ethical roots, it is particularly open to interaction with, and enrichment by, lay citizens. The benefits of biodiversity include a combination of ecological understanding and sensory/aesthetic enjoyment. The more individuals can visit and appreciate a changing conservation area, the more the function of wildlife and amenity carry meaning. For example, in Germany families visit organic farms (which usually support more biodiversity than conventional farms); people can see how animals are treated and how organic beer is made. They receive guided tours of the farm and can see the wildlife that lives there. So the organic food industry comes to life, and the appreciation of organic produce is an experience, not just a culinary memory. Such active engagement with biodiversity enhances its meaning and value to people. We learn from this that people's perception of concepts such as biodiversity does not stand still: it evolves as the culture changes and the science comes alive in the minds of the participants.

6.1 Introduction

The ones that are lost don't interest me very much. R. North

I saw a monkey and it was fun. Ghanaian schoolgirl

All species go extinct. So at one level, all efforts to conserve species are futile. As an argument against conservation this is as sensible as proposing that life-saving medicine is a waste of time, since we will all die eventually. What matters is how long we might reasonably expect the species, or the individual, to survive. There is now abundant evidence that species are dying much too 'young'; that we are entering a period of mass extinctions, caused by human activity (Ehrlich and Ehrlich 1992).

Two questions need to be addressed in the face of this mass extinction: should we try to stop it? And if so, how? Our answers to these questions will ultimately depend on why we value species in the first place. In this chapter, I consider the three main categories of argument used by conservationists, and illustrate their strengths and weaknesses by looking at one or two specific examples of arguments within each category. The role that science plays in these arguments varies from one of central importance to one of irrelevance. Given the aims of this book, I concentrate on those arguments that rely most heavily on science. I look at the implications of these arguments for the strategies chosen by conservationists, and consider how they have been used in conservation legislation. My focus is on the conservation of species, rather than habitats. However, there is much overlap between arguments in favour of, and policies directed at, species and habitat conservation.

6.1.1 Chimney sweep or cherished child?

Why have, or cherish, children? Three possible reasons are: 1. Children are gifts from God; it is our sacred duty to cherish them. 2. Children contribute to the family income; in poor families the work of children is vital for survival. 3. Every child is a person of infinite value in their own right, and deserves to be respected and cherished for who they are. These three positions can be further summarised as being: 1. for God's sake; 2. for the parents' sake; 3. for the children's sake.

Approaches to valuing (or cherishing) other species can be classified in very similar ways. By analogy, humans might value species because they are part of God's divine creation (the **theocentric** – centred upon God – approach); for what they can do for us (the **anthropocentric** – centred upon man – approach); or because they are intrinsically valuable in their own right (the **biocentric** – centred upon life – approach). The main arguments used in each approach are summarised in Figure 6.1.

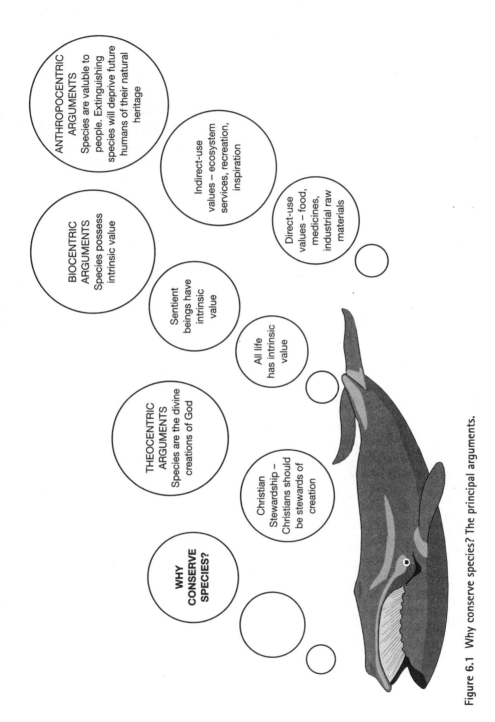

Figure 6.1 Why conserve species? The principal arguments.

6.2 Theocentric arguments

Who has let the wild ass go free? Job 39:5

What does God think of conservation? People of all religions are increasingly asking this question, and usually they attempt to answer it through reference to holy scripture. A brief outline of the Christian position is given here; this is also relevant to Judaism and Islam (because these faiths also regard the 'Old Testament' as holy writ). Other faiths, particularly eastern religions and paganism, take a very different and on the whole more benevolent view of nature. For further discussion, see Northcott (1996).

6.2.1 Christian stewardship and God's covenant

- *The idea* all species form a part of God's divine creation, and it is a Christian's duty to protect them.
- *Policy implications* all of creation deserves respect and protection.

During the flood, humans and animals were thrown together in a cramped, dangerous and smelly existence. When they could at last disembark, God declared:

Behold, I establish my covenant with you and your descendants after you, and with every living creature that is with you, the birds, the cattle and every beast of the earth with you, as many as came out of the ark. Genesis 9:9

This makes clear God's concern for all the animals, not just for Noah; He promises never to abandon them to catastrophe again. On the basis of this and other similar passages, some Christians argue that it is a religious duty to respect nature. In particular, they interpret the famous Genesis verse, in which God grants man dominion over 'the fish of the sea, and over the birds of the air, ... and over every creeping thing that creeps upon the earth' (Genesis 1:26), as meaning that man must have **stewardship** (responsible care), rather than ruthless mastery, over nature.

Religious arguments such as this suffer from two main problems. First, they are unlikely to influence atheists or people of other faiths. Second, they are often open to re-interpretation even by people of the same faith. Historically, most Christians have interpreted Genesis as giving man the right to do what he wants with the world; passages where man is told to 'fill the earth and subdue it' (Genesis 1:28) support this traditional view.

6.3 Anthropocentric arguments

6.3.1 The direct-use values of non-human species

Humans use biodiversity and its products for food, fuel, industrial raw materials and medicines. Although the bulk of humanity is sustained by only some 20 different cultivated crops, many people in the Third World (or Majority World) continue to rely on wild species, and a wide range of species could be utilised as food (Myers 1997). Global ocean fisheries, which provide 100 million tonnes of protein-rich food every year, rely entirely on wild animals (see Chapter 7). However, the range of species eaten by people remains relatively small. More important for the future is the potential for wild species to provide useful genetic traits which could be transferred to food crops, either through conventional breeding or genetic engineering. The notion of nature as a vast treasure trove of genetic resources is a powerful argument for conservation (although there are reasons for concern about how this resource might be exploited – see Chapter 4). Because we don't know which traits may be useful, or where they may be found, conservationists argue that it is sensible to conserve all species, rather than just edible ones. The strengths and weaknesses of this approach are illustrated in the case of medicines below. For a discussion of the actual and potential value of wild species to agriculture and industry, see Myers (1997).

The natural pharmacy

- *The idea* most species have never been assessed for their medicinal properties, and they could contain cures to many or most diseases.
- *Policy implications* all species should be conserved, but particularly those, such as plants and fungi, that have traditionally proved to be most useful.

Up to 57% of all prescription medicines in the USA contain compounds originally derived from wild organisms (Grifo et al. 1997). Classic examples include the contraceptive pill and penicillin. Poorer communities have an even greater reliance on natural products; most of the world's population still relies predominantly on traditional remedies, consisting largely of plant extracts, for their health care. Many of our best-known medicines come from tropical organisms. For example, the antibiotics streptomycin and neomycin come from tropical soil fungi, and drugs derived from the Madagascan rosy periwinkle (*Catharantus roseus*) have revolutionised the treatment of childhood leukaemia. But cures can be found in all parts of the world. One famous example is taxol, derived from the Pacific Yew tree

(*Taxus brevifolia*) native to the USA, which has great promise in the treatment of breast cancer (Chivian 1997 and references therein). The oceans remain virtually unexplored for their medicinal potential, which again could be enormous; current work involving extracts from *Bugula neritina*, a marine bryozoan, could lead to treatments for leukaemia.

It is not accidental that most medically important compounds are found in organisms such as plants and invertebrates. Vertebrates possess immune systems, but invertebrates and plants must rely on synthesising chemicals to deal with infections; it is these compounds that become the precursors of medicines. For conservationists, the natural pharmacy argument has special appeal because it applies particularly to organisms, like the small and obscure bryozoans, that cannot compete for the public's affection with big vertebrates like deer and bears; no matter how ugly or unknown, all should be preserved. In addition, plants and animals with the highest concentrations of defensive compounds are likely to be found in crowded conditions. For example, a plant growing slowly in the deep shade of a tropical forest needs to survive innumerable attacks by insects and microorganisms before it can reproduce. In contrast, a 'weedy' species growing in an open area will grow fast and reproduce quickly, before it suffers too much insect damage; such species will therefore usually have lower levels of defensive chemicals. So the natural pharmacy argument also gives particular emphasis to the conservation of mature ecosystems with high biodiversity, such as rain forests and coral reefs.

So it is likely that many therapeutically valuable compounds remain undiscovered. But finding these compounds is exceedingly difficult. Since the 1940s, pharmaceutical companies have been searching for new drugs by taking thousands of wild species and screening them for biological activity. Such random screening requires huge effort, often for no returns. The US National Cancer Institute found only one marketable anticancer compound during the screening of 35 000 species of plant (Aylward 1995). No new classes of antibiotic have been discovered for over 25 years, and some bacteria are now resistant to all known classes. So there is an urgent need to speed up the discovery of new drugs and treatments. A number of new techniques are being used or developed (Box 6.1). Whilst some of these, such as automated high-throughput screening, promise to enhance the potential for discovering new medicines from nature, most offer alternative routes. Recent years have seen a shift away from the use of natural products in searching for drugs (Nisbet and Moore 1997), and this trend could continue or accelerate if new techniques prove effective. Some commentators have already declared that 'the reign of trial and error' in pharmaceutical development is drawing to a close (Aylward 1995 and references therein).

Box 6.1 New approaches in the search for novel medical treatments

- **Rational drug design** – the use of computer-aided techniques to make drugs 'designed' to fit target sites on molecules.

- **Combinatorial chemistry** – starting with a few simple 'building blocks', chemists can now synthesise huge 'libraries' of compounds for medicinal screening.

- **Gene therapy** – this new field for medicine aims to insert genes into defective cells. This might involve replacing genes defective from birth, or treating diseases such as cancer by inserting genes that code for toxins to kill cancerous cells.

- **Genome sequencing** – the structure of all the genes (the genomes) of some bacterial strains are now known. This will allow new drugs to be targeted at particular sites on these genomes.

- **Automated screening** – new screening techniques will allow many tens of thousands of compounds to be screened for biological activity in a single day.

In conclusion, the natural pharmacy argument remains a strong justification for species conservation, but is vulnerable in two ways. First, if a species has already been screened and shown to be useless, this means it can be lost. Second, the whole approach could be undermined by advances in medical technology (if, for example, we could one day simply design and synthesise new drugs from scratch). Similar points can be made for other direct-use arguments.

6.3.2 The indirect–use values of non–human species

Chains of being and webs of life

> From Nature's chain whatever link you strike,
> Tenth, or ten-thousandth, breaks the chain alike. A. Pope

> Plants and animals, remote in the scale of nature, are bound together by a web of complex relations. C. Darwin

The metaphor of a chain of being, extending from God down to the simplest invertebrate, is an ancient one. As Pope makes clear, the chain is only as strong as its weakest link. If this is broken, the whole chain fails. A similar but extended concept is that of the web of life. All organisms are linked, not in a chain, but by a dizzyingly complex net of relationships involving feeding on, competing with, infecting and helping each other. As Darwin emphasised, this view of life implies **interdependence** – what happens to one species will affect all the others.

This interdependence underlies the notion of a 'balance of nature'. Ecologists and others speak of natural communities being 'in balance', having 'stability' or being 'at equilibrium'. If this is the case, how much disturbance can a community withstand before this balance is upset, and what happens if it does become unbalanced, are important questions. Suppose an obscure and apparently worthless species is driven to extinction. If this loss results in knock-on effects, then species that are considered valuable may also be lost, and the ecosystem as a whole may become degraded.

Ecologists distinguish between the **structure** and **function** of ecosystems. The number and types of species, and the ways in which those species interact, are the main structural characteristics of ecosystems – the 'biological scaffolding' on which they are built. An idea of the structure of an ecological community can be given by constructing a **food web** of that community (Figure 6.5). Functional characteristics of ecosystems describe what those ecosystems do – they might include, for example, the cycling of nutrients, the stabilisation of soil, the production of biomass and the regulation of atmospheric gases. The benefits that humans derive from ecosystem functions are called **ecosystem services**. These will vary between ecosystems. For example, mangroves provide nursery grounds for commercially important fish species. Forests provide timber and act as a sink for CO_2, helping to stabilise global climate (see Chapter 5). Streams provide irrigation for crops and remove and detoxify wastes. Human beings have a very immediate interest in the maintenance of these services; they have been estimated to have a global value of $33 trillion per year (Costanza et al. 1997). But such estimates are illustrative only; even if we had the money, most ecosystem services could not be substituted artificially. Human life on the planet would cease to be possible without them.

A vital question for conservation, therefore, is how many species can be lost before the functional characteristics of the affected ecosystem are seriously degraded?

Functional integrity – the biodiversity/ecosystem function debate

- *The idea* reducing the number of species in ecosystems will reduce the ability of those systems to function, and therefore to provide essential ecosystem services.
- *Policy implications* if ecosystem services are affected by the loss of even a few species, then all species should be conserved. If ecosystem services are robust in the face of species loss, a smaller number need be conserved.

In order to ensure a supply of clean drinking water, New York City has recently invested $1–1.5 billion in the restoration of the natural watershed for the city. The ecosystem service in this case – water purification – is pro-

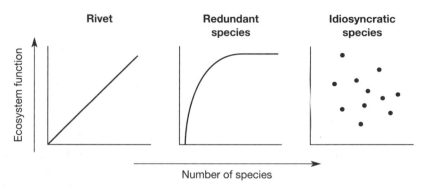

Figure 6.2 Three possible relationships between ecosystem functions and the number of species.

vided by a biological community dominated by trees. Without any trees, the ecosystem service disappears. But would it make any difference to New York's water if the forests in its watershed had only two species of tree, rather than 15–20? There are a number of possible ways in which ecosystem functions may change as species are lost; the three most often discussed are shown in Figure 6.2.

- **The rivet-popping hypothesis**. If all species contribute to ecosystem function, the removal of any will damage the ability of the ecosystem to function. The rivet-popping hypothesis likens species to the rivets that hold an aeroplane together. If a lunatic starts to remove these rivets during flight, the plane will become gradually weaker and bits will start to fall off; this might initially be inconvenient (the toilet door falls off) but will soon be disastrous (the wing falls off). If species are like rivets, they should all be conserved.

- **The idiosyncratic response hypothesis**. Perhaps the identity of the species that are lost will determine how the ecosystem responds? Losing just any species might not matter, but losing particularly significant ones will (see p. 153). If this is the case, the relationship between ecosystem services and the number of species will depend on the order in which species are lost; if the important ones are lost early on, ecosystem function will plummet. If they are conserved, all may be well. Unless we know which species are important, it is impossible to predict how ecosystem functions will respond as species are lost.

- **Redundant species hypothesis**. Losing a kidney does not mean losing your life; since human beings have two kidneys, but can function quite happily with one, there is *redundancy* in the provision of kidneys. Perhaps ecosystems are like this too? As long as there is the minimum number of species needed to maintain ecosystem functions, then losing species may have little effect. In ecology, **functional groups** are defined as groups of species that share common biogeochemical attributes (or that do similar 'jobs' in ecosystems). For example, all the decomposers that act to recycle nutrients could be classified as belonging to one functional group. Provided all the important functional groups are represented within an ecosystem, it may make no difference to ecosystem function how many species each group contains. If there is much redundancy within ecosystems, then many species can be lost without affecting ecosystem functions. However, losing species will mean that the ecosystem is more vulnerable if it is stressed in the future; once you've lost one kidney, it is disastrous to lose another. So redundancy in ecosystems may play an important part in ensuring that they are resistant in the face of environmental stresses (Tilman 1997).

Which of the hypotheses is true?
Deciding between these hypotheses will be difficult, not least because of the presence of **confounding variables** (see p. 22 and Figure 6.3). Ideally, a test of these ideas needs to change the variable of interest, species number, whilst holding other variables constant, and measure the resulting changes in ecosystem function. Recent studies designed to do this, using plant-based terrestrial systems, have found productivity was systematically reduced as species number declined (Tilman 1997; Hodgson et al. 1998 and references therein). Productivity may thus conform to the rivet-popping hypothesis, although the work to date suggests that once species richness becomes high, adding further species has little impact on productivity. This finding concurs with knowledge about agricultural systems; farmers have known for many years that growing two crops together – intercropping – can be more productive than growing either one on its own. Ecological theory can explain this increase in productivity through the idea of complementary resource use. If different species can live successfully under different resource conditions, then combining species will allow the 'resource space' to be used more fully. For example, plants differ in the amount of light they need to grow, with some species better adapted to shady conditions and others flourishing better in full sunlight. Growing 'shade' and 'sun' species together will allow a fuller use of the available resource (sunlight) than growing either of them on their own.

Of the three relationships, the rivet-popping hypothesis would demand the most urgent action if shown to be generally true. Some empirical studies, and ecological theory, suggest that it *may* be true, at least for some functions in some ecosystems. However, interpreting the results of these experiments is difficult (see Figure 6.3 and Hodgson et al. 1998), and few types of community have yet been studied, limiting the **domain** of the experiments (see p. 23); in particular, marine and animal-dominated communities remain largely unexplored. So we are far from a consensus on which, if any, of the three hypotheses may be nearest to the truth.

Low diversity treatment
Eight individuals of two randomly selected species. By chance, no large or medium species are included. Overall biomass is therefore low.

High diversity treatment
Eight individuals of four randomly selected species. By chance, these include one large species and one medium one. Overall biomass is therefore high.

Species pool
A pool of nine different species of plants is selected for the experiment. These species all vary in size and other characteristics.

Figure 6.3 Experiments to measure the effects of changing diversity on ecosystem function aim to alter the number of species between treatments, without altering other variables (such as the number of individuals). But random sampling effects make that difficult. In this case, the number of individuals remains constant, but biomass is altered between treatments because the two species in the low diversity treatment are both small.

Are some species special? Keystones and foundationstones

- *The idea* not all species are equal. Some play particularly important roles in maintaining the structure and function of ecosystems.
- *Policy implications* if some species are particularly important, conservation efforts should be directed specifically at those species.

As the idiosyncratic-response hypothesis suggests, some species do have larger impacts on their communities than others. Often it is obvious which are important; the removal of the species that contributes most to the overall biomass (such as the dominant species of tree in a forest) will have dramatic effects. Such species could be described as **foundationstone species**. In contrast, and more interestingly, there are also **keystone species** which are much more important than their, often relatively small, biomass would suggest. Removing keystone species affects not only their immediate predators, prey or competitors, but has **cascading effects** which impact on species that do not directly interact with the keystone species, and which lead to a change in the whole community (Figure 6.4).

Since keystone species are so important, their conservation is necessary if we want to conserve their ecosystems. A policy of identifying and protecting keystone species may therefore be sensible. However, there are three major problems with this approach.

First, finding keystone species is difficult. The only convincing way to do it is to see what happens to communities when the species is removed. Experiments to do this are very difficult for many organisms (consider removing just one species of phytoplankton from a patch of ocean) and to remove all the species in turn from even moderately diverse communities is a daunting task. Some of the classic examples of keystone species come from unintended 'experiments'. For example, after sea otters (*Enhydra lutris*) were hunted to near-extinction in the northwestern USA, the population of sea urchins, their principal prey, exploded and removed the kelp and other large seaweeds that formed the basis of the local biological com-

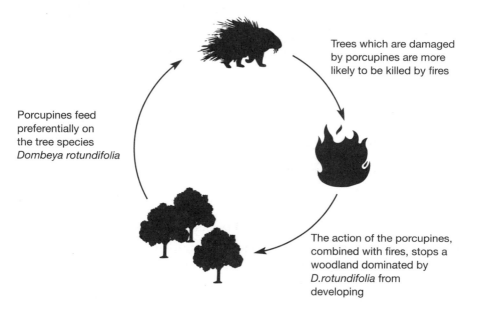

Trees which are damaged by porcupines are more likely to be killed by fires

Porcupines feed preferentially on the tree species *Dombeya rotundifolia*

The action of the porcupines, combined with fires, stops a woodland dominated by *D.rotundifolia* from developing

Figure 6.4 Are porcupines a keystone species? Yeaton (1989) predicted that removing them would cause cascading effects, leading to a change in the type of woodland at their field site.

munity (Estes and Palmisano 1974). Although such events are instructive, conservationists cannot rely on them; waiting to see when disaster will strike is not a sensible option.

Second, although a species may play a keystone role in one community, it may be unimportant in another. For example, the starfish *Pisaster ochraceus* is a keystone species in exposed rocky shores, but may be unimportant in sheltered sites only tens of metres away (Menge et al. 1994). So the keystone status is context-dependent – it relies on the particular biological interactions and physical influences in a community – and the hunt for keystones would be necessary in every different community.

Third, there may be many communities with no keystones at all. Intensive investigation of the food web in the Ythan estuary, in Scotland, has so far revealed an incredibly complex community (Figure 6.5) but one with few species with large interaction effects, and no keystones (Figure 6.6). A conservation policy directed solely at keystones would ignore such communities.

In conclusion, whilst conserving keystones is necessary to conserve the communities of which they are a part, a policy directed at their conservation would be difficult to implement and would ignore some, and possibly many, natural communities.

Aesthetics, spirituality and recreation

And since to look at things in bloom, fifty years is little room,
about the woodlands I will go, to see the cherry hung with snow.
A.E. Housman

Wild species have always inspired poetry and song, awe and admiration, love and wonderment. One of the most compelling arguments for conservation is that we derive such great aesthetic, spiritual and cultural sustenance from nature. Living things are the most complex products of cosmic evolution; who would argue that losing them does not diminish the amount of beauty and wonder in the world? Species are also part of a country's heritage, often as important to national identity as flags and anthems – think of how Americans regard the bald eagle (*Haliaeatus leucocephalus*), or how New Zealanders call themselves 'kiwis'. People express their love of wild species in many ways, from bird watching to simply enjoying the thought that magnificent species like whales exist, even if they personally will never see one. The appeal to aesthetic, spiritual and cultural values could be termed the art gallery argument.

The art gallery argument

- *The idea* species should be conserved for their beauty and ability to inspire us.
- *Policy implications* beautiful and inspirational species should be conserved.

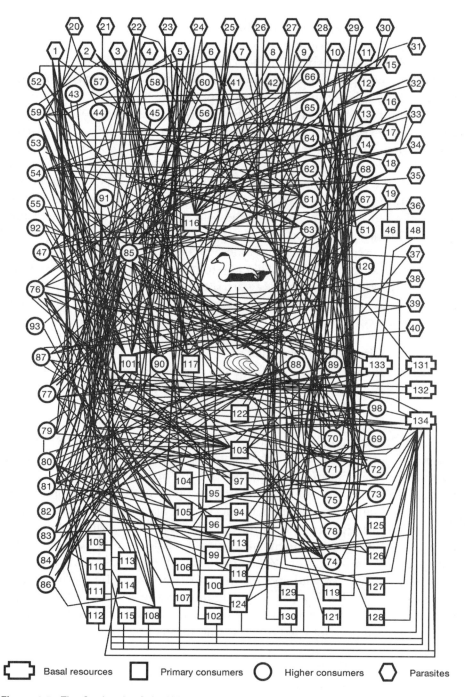

Figure 6.5 The food web of the Ythan estury, which is one of the best-documented webs in the world.

Numbers refer to Huxham et al. 1996.

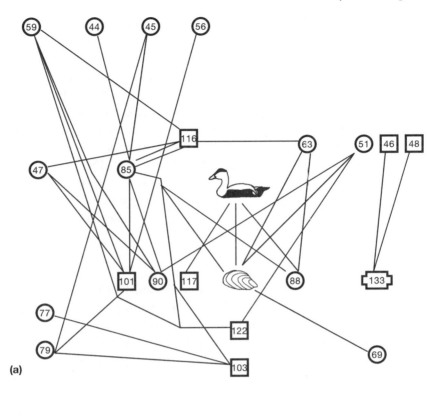

(a)

(b)

Figure 6.6 (a) Energetically important links in the Ythan web. (b) Functionally important links in the Ythan web; there are no keystone species recorded in this system.

Even ugly species possess what Paul Ehrlich has aptly termed a 'beauty of wonder'. If you look closely enough at a fly or a tapeworm, you will marvel at how exquisitely adapted it is to its way of life. So perhaps it is enough to say that we should conserve species because they are wonderful? But relying on political support for conservation based on aesthetics or spiritual inspiration could let many species go unlamented to extinction. Surveys have shown that people's views of animals vary widely, from very positive feelings towards pets such as dogs and birds such as robins and swans, to mostly negative feelings towards invertebrates and dangerous species such as snakes. Similar rankings are found in a number of cultures (Kellert 1996), although people in non-industrial societies may take a less positive view towards wildlife in general, viewing it with fear and hostility (Kellert 1996: 149). Of the species that are liked, those that have a direct use or that have a high profile are preferred. Since most species are not charismatic vertebrates with high profiles, like whales, and since most species live in non-industrialised countries, aesthetics could provide a poor foundation for conservation arguments. As one scientist put it during the Brent Spar debate (see Chapter 8), 'no one is going to damage the economy for the sake of a few worms.'

Do future generations matter?

Imagine an engineer who knowingly builds a faulty bridge, using cheap materials and pocketing the money saved. His actions are no better if the bridge is built in a far-away country rather than in his home town – if a catastrophe happens the distance between him and any victims makes no difference to his guilt. If difference in space is irrelevant, then so is distance in time; people in the future, who are not yet born, should figure in our moral judgements. This insight is central to the notion of sustainable development, and is often described as the need for **intergenerational equity**. As I have indicated, some of the anthropocentric positions above, such as the natural pharmacy argument, are likely to lose force with the passage of time. Others, however, will probably increase in importance. More people are seeking out the aesthetic, spiritual and recreational experiences wilderness and wild animals can offer. This trend is likely to continue and intensify as human beings become more urbanised and wilderness increasingly rare. So to remove these things deprives not only people now, but also a potentially huge number of nature lovers who are yet to exist.

6.4 Biocentric arguments

Where does value, or worth, come from? The discussion so far has assumed that it derives solely from humans. On this account, valuable things are like a currency; if people think the dollar in your pocket is valuable then it is, but the value can change dramatically (through inflation or a stock market crash) and could even disappear entirely (through the use of 'electronic money' or a revolution?). Any value that is found in the non-human world is issued like a driving licence. If a species passes the tests, then it is given some value, but this could be withdrawn by the human authorities at any time if we discover that the species isn't worthy after all.

The biocentric approach rejects this idea of value, and states that non-human species can have value quite regardless of what humans think of them; the value is issued more like a birth certificate, with no tests required to gain it and no possibility of it being recalled (it is *intrinsic*). Here, I outline two of the ways in which philosophers have attempted to demonstrate this value – for a more comprehensive account, see Fox (1996).

6.4.1 Is pain the answer? The sentience approach

- *The idea* animals which can suffer, or which can 'have a point of view', are intrinsically valuable.
- *Policy implications* policy should respect the value of sentient organisms.

Traditional western thought has excluded non-human animals from moral concern, because other animals cannot talk, are not self-conscious, are not highly intelligent or are not rational. A strong strand of opposition to this tradition has grown from **utilitarian** philosophy (see p. 59). In 1789, Jeremy Bentham wrote that the morally important question is not 'can they reason? nor can they talk? but, can they suffer?'. After all, babies and some disabled people cannot talk, are not self-conscious and might not be able to reason; this does not mean that it is acceptable to mistreat them. This insight has been developed, most notably by the philosopher Peter Singer, to form the ethical basis of the modern animal liberation movement. The logic underlying utilitarian ethics is compelling, and follows the form of a simple syllogism (see p. 3). If we accept the axiom that suffering is bad, and that happiness is good, and we believe that an animal is capable of experiencing these things, then it is morally wrong to inflict suffering on that animal unless there are strong moral arguments in favour of doing so. The task for the utilitarian, then, becomes one of deciding where to draw the line; just what kinds of animal can suffer? Peter Singer would extend the moral community as far as oysters, others might restrict it to higher vertebrates. It is clear that many types of life form, especially plants, cannot be included.

Identifying pain as the key to value would allow the destruction of any number of species as long as it was done painlessly. An alternative criterion is that of sentience. Broadly speaking, the sentience approach argues that moral value comes from the ability to have a point of view. If what happens to an organism matters *to it* then it has intrinsic value; its value to itself is independent of what we think, and its welfare should be of moral concern to us. What matters to organisms is not just the avoidance of pain, but also the fulfilment of their natural behaviours. One reason it is wrong to kill a human being painlessly (even if the person has no friends or relatives who would suffer bereavement) is that by doing so you are robbing them of all those experiences that they might expect to have had. Similar arguments apply to other sentient organisms.

The implications of this conclusion are profound for human– animal interactions. But what grounds does it give for conserving species? As a conservation ethic the sentience approach leaves much to be desired. It cannot apply to plants and other non-sentient beings. It values individual animals, rather than species *per se*, and it places no higher value on an individual of a rare species than on a common one. Nevertheless, in many real situations it might form the basis of a powerful argument in favour of conservation. Consider, for example, a proposal to 'reclaim' an area of estuary used by fish and migratory birds for agricultural land. Such reclamation will displace the sentient organisms who rely on the habitat, probably leading to their deaths from starvation, something which is clearly wrong under the sentience approach. However, the approach can also lead to conflicts with conservation objectives; cases where large (sentient) herbivores such as deer need to be culled in order to protect rare (non-sentient) plants are common.

6.4.2 The life approach and deep ecology

- *The idea* all living things, and possibly non-living parts of ecosystems as well, have intrinsic value.
- *Policy implications* all life and living systems need to be treated with moral respect.

Can we extend the moral community beyond sentient beings? The life approach and deep ecology are two related ways in which people have argued that we can. Some versions of these philosophies rely primarily on intuition (see Box 6.2) to demonstrate their points. Although intuition can be a powerful guide, a problem arises when others do not share your intuition – how can others be convinced that your intuition is correct? So a rational foundation is also important.

Albert Schweitzer, and others since, have argued for a 'reverence for life'. Deep ecologists take this a step further and include ecosystems. One of the first explanations of what came to be known as a deep ecology posi-

---

Box 6.2 It's the end of the world as anything knows it

Philosophers often play mind games, by describing fanciful situations which help illuminate their arguments. Here's a variant of one used by deep ecologists to illustrate intrinsic value.

Suppose that a deadly virus escapes from a biological warfare laboratory and eliminates all animal life on the planet. You are the last living animal, and you also happen to be the president of the USA. You too are infected and will die in minutes. Would it be morally wrong for you to push the red button, releasing a final show of nuclear fireworks to mark your death? By doing this, you might destroy all remaining plant life on the planet, and you would certainly be acting gratuitously and peevishly. But since no sentient organisms will be affected, does this matter?

Deep ecologists argue that if you think it would be *wrong* (rather than just pointless and stupid) to destroy all remaining life in this scenario, this is because you intuitively appreciate the intrinsic value of life.

---

tion was that of the pioneer American ecologist Aldo Leopold, who believed 'A thing is right when it tends to preserve the integrity, beauty and stability of the biotic community. It is wrong when it tends otherwise.' The main rational argument for extending intrinsic value beyond only sentient beings is that all life forms are self-organising, self-maintaining entities, and that some non-living things, such as ecosystems, may be seen in this way too. Because such systems act in such a way as to maintain themselves, they can be said to embody an interest in themselves, and thus to possess intrinsic value.

By emphasising the value of biotic integrity, and of all forms of life, deep ecology overcomes some of the problems associated with the sentience approach. However, it remains difficult to see just how non-sentient life can have interests. As Singer (1993) says, although we might speak of a plant having an interest in finding water and light, we are speaking metaphorically. Without consciousness, the plant can't be aware of whether its interests are fulfilled; its welfare cannot be affected one way or another, and it remains on the same level as a river having an 'interest' in finding the sea. In addition, Leopold's ethics might struggle if stability and integrity are not necessarily related in biological communities (see p. 150). So although deep ecology may seem intuitively appealing, it has yet to develop firm foundations.

A summary of the arguments discussed so far is given in Table 6.1

Table 6.1 A summary of conservation arguments, along with an indication of the role science plays in each one

Argument	Strengths	Weaknesses	Role of science	Further reading
Theocentric				
Christian stewardship	Could appeal to millions of believers	Relies on faith and disputed interpretation	Irrelevant	Northcott 1996
Anthropocentric				
Natural pharmacy	May apply to millions of species, including obscure and ugly ones	Could be undermined by advances in medical science	Central	Kunin and Lawton 1996
Functional integrity	May apply to millions of species, including obscure and ugly ones	Could be undermined by advances in ecological science	Central	Daily 1997
Art gallery	Easily understood and appreciated by anyone interested in nature	Likely to exclude most species	Marginal ('scientific wonder')	Kellert 1996
Biocentric				
Sentience	Firm ethical foundations	Limited to sentient organisms	Important (in determining where sentience lies)	Singer 1993
Life approach	Encompasses all living things	Lacks firm ethical foundations	Marginal	Singer 1993

6.5 Legislation

This section considers how the main arguments for conserving species outlined above have influenced policy, by looking at a selection of important conservation legislation, at international, regional and national levels (Table 6.2), which illustrate a range of justifications.

Table 6.2 A selection of international and national conservation legislation

Law or treaty	Main aims	Justifications
International law		
International Convention for the Regulation of Whaling, 1946	The sustainable exploitation of whale species	Direct-use value of whale meat
RAMSAR convention, 1971	Protection of wetlands and wildfowl	Environmental services and indirect-use values
Convention on International Trade in Endangered Species of Wild Fauna and Flora (CITES), 1973	Regulation of trade in endangered species to protect them from extinction	Direct- and indirect-use values
Convention on Biological Diversity, 1992	Regulation of benefits from exploiting biodiversity	Intrinsic value, direct- and indirect-use values
European law		
Directive on the Conservation of Wild Birds, 1979	The protection of all species of naturally occurring birds in the European Union	Ecological balance and natural heritage
Directive on the Protection of Natural and Semi-natural Habitats and of Wild Flora and Fauna ('Habitats Directive'), 1992	Contribute to sustainable development through conserving habitats and species endangered within the EU	Preservation of natural heritage for future generations
United States law		
Marine Mammal Protection Act, 1972	Conservation of populations of marine mammals	Ecosystem integrity
Endangered Species Act, 1973	The conservation of all endangered species in the USA	Direct and indirect use
United Kingdom law		
Wildlife and Countryside Act, 1981	Conservation of listed species and sites	Indirect use
New Zealand law		
Resource Management Act, 1991	Sustainable management of natural resources	Intrinsic value, direct- and indirect-use values

6.5.1 International agreements

International agreements are an essential part of the conservation effort. However, individual states participate voluntarily in such agreements, and can withdraw at any time, so public pressure is vital to their success. Two examples are discussed here:

International Convention for the Regulation of Whaling (1946)

This convention established the International Whaling Commission (IWC) to regulate whaling, in response to chronic overfishing of whale stocks. The justification was entirely on the basis of the direct-use value of whales – primarily meat. The work of the IWC scientific committee, in determining the size of whale stocks and safe levels of harvest, means science should play a central role in this convention. In reality, most member states no longer hunt whales, and the IWC has become a vehicle for limiting whaling on other grounds. For example, the British government now opposes whaling for humanitarian (intrinsic value) reasons, even though it accepts the scientific models which show that small numbers of some species can now be hunted without threatening the long-term viability of the stocks. Whaling nations such as Norway and Japan argue that they are justified under the convention in hunting some whales, and that non-whaling countries are attempting to change the rules in using non-scientific arguments.

Convention on Biological Diversity (1992)

This convention was one of five major documents signed at the United Nations Conference on Environment and Development (the 'Earth Summit') in Rio de Janeiro. Although it begins with a recognition of the intrinsic value of biodiversity, its principal aim is to promote the sharing of benefits from exploitation of wild species (for medicines, new crops, industrial applications, etc.) between the companies that develop new products and the nations from which the species are taken. Funding for the convention is proving difficult. The USA has yet to ratify it because it might restrict the US biotechnology industry, and there is resentment in the Majority World at the notion that the poor should act as caretakers for the world's genetic resources, waiting passively until the rich exploit their potential.

6.5.2 The European Union

All EU environmental policy is guided by a series of **Environmental Action Programmes**. The first (in 1973) framed eleven underlying principles for all subsequent environmental legislation. The only principle that says *why* conservation is important is number 3: 'Exploitation of nature and natural resources which causes significant damage to the ecological balance must be avoided. The natural environment ... is an asset which may be used, but not abused.'

The EU can enact several types of legislation. The most important for environmental matters is the **directive**; this sets out goals which all member states must achieve. The two most important directives concerned with species conservation are the **Directive on the Conservation of Wild Birds (1979)** (the 'Birds Directive') and the **Directive on the Protection of Natural and Semi-natural Habitats and Wild Flora and Fauna(1992)** (the 'Habitats Directive'). The Birds Directive aims to conserve populations of all naturally occurring species of bird by prohibiting the deliberate killing of birds and taking of their eggs, and through designating 'special protection areas' (SPAs) to protect the habitat of rare species. The main justification for the Directive is that birds represent a common heritage, and that their decline 'represents a serious threat to the conservation of the natural environment, particularly because of the biological balances threatened thereby'. The Habitats Directive aims to conserve all species that are endangered, or likely to become so, within the EU, principally by designation of 'special areas of conservation' (SACs). The main stated justification is simply that 'threatened habitats and species form part of the community's natural heritage'.

6.5.3 The USA

The **Endangered Species Act (1973)** is the most important species conservation law in America. Its purpose was stated as preserving species that are of 'aesthetic, ecological, educational, historical, recreational and scientific value to the Nation and its people'. According to the Act, these criteria can apply to all species, excepting bacteria, viruses and insect pests. The debate in Congress preceding the act was influenced by arguments for the intrinsic value of all species and for the necessity of species conservation to preserve ecosystem function (Nash 1989). These sentiments did not make it into the final version, and conservation was justified on direct and indirect use to humans, but in practice there has been little attempt to show that species listed for conservation under the Act are of 'value' to the nation in one of the ways listed above; even where species have no obvious aesthetic, educational, historical or recreational values, it has been assumed that they must have ecological or scientific value.

6.5.4 United Kingdom

The **Wildlife and Countryside Act (1981)** protects listed species and provides for the designation of protected areas as Sites of Special Scientific Interest (SSSIs). It builds on previous laws, in particular the

National Parks and Access to the Countryside Act (1949), which first introduced SSSIs. As the name suggests, the stated motivation for protecting these areas was scientific. Discussion preceding the act had emphasised that the conservation of these sites should be justified on 'scientific' (rather than, for example, aesthetic) grounds, since it was felt that 'science' was more likely to gain public respect (Sheail 1995). Cyril Diver, one of the people most influential in establishing the SSSI system, was explicit in his belief that conservation was justified on the grounds of providing open-air laboratories, since reserves would be 'a first class experiment in population dynamics which they (scientists) could not possibly afford to set up for themselves'.

6.5.5 New Zealand

Conservation in New Zealand is unusual for three reasons. First, many of the indigenous species occur nowhere else (they are **endemic**). Second, it must attempt to reconcile European and Maori aspirations. Third, it is formally linked with tourism and recreation. The **Resource Management Act (1991)** combines some of these elements. Its purpose is to 'promote the sustainable management of natural and physical resources', with 'sustainable management' meaning managing the use, development and protection of resources, and being justified on the basis of intergenerational equity. While the emphases of the Act include protection of indigenous biota, preservation of the natural character of aquatic ecosystems and safeguarding the relationship of Maori culture with their ancestral lands and other resources, other matters to be recognised include intrinsic values of ecosystems, amenity values, the ethic of stewardship and its equivalent in Maori culture and religion, 'kaitiakitanga'.

6.5.6 Overview of legislation

The list above represents a small sample of law relevant to species conservation, but includes a wide range of justifications. These are important, because the words used will often determine how the law is interpreted in controversial cases. Those acts or treaties which enforce conservation on the basis of a narrow range of arguments – in particular, those which rely most on scientific and direct use justifications – seem most vulnerable to shifts in knowledge or values. For example, many difficulties have been encountered by those nations wishing to use the International Whaling Commission to ban or severely restrict whaling. Since the Whaling Convention was designed to allow sustainable whaling (i.e. it was based only on the recognition of direct-use values of whales), if a species can be scientifically shown to have a sufficiently large population, then it can be hunted, regardless of other arguments (such as those based on intrinsic value). Similar difficulties could arise for other legislation based on ecological criteria, such as the US Marine Mammal Protection Act (1972). This prohibits the reduction of marine mammal populations 'beyond the point at which they cease to be a significant functioning element in the ecosystem of which they are a part'. As we saw in the case of the Ythan (p. 155), many species are likely to have little or no functional impact and therefore could lose protection. Similarly, the notion of ecological balance is difficult to define, and its relationship to diversity is unknown – the use of this as a justification (for example in European legislation) is therefore unwise. British ecologists thought that 'science' would give conservation prestige. The record of destruction of SSSIs in the UK suggests that arguing for conservation for purely 'scientific' reasons is not effective.

Legislation based on broader arguments is less vulnerable. For example, the Endangered Species Act in the US appeals to all direct- and indirect-use values and can thus be applied to virtually all species. But even this has left room for dispute. An early controversy over the Act involved the construction of a dam at Tellico, Tennessee, which threatened the snail darter, a protected species of fish. Proponents of the dam argued against protecting the fish because 'You cannot eat it. It is not much to look at. It is a slimy colour' (quoted in Nash 1989: 178); that is, it has no obvious direct- or indirect-use values. The dam was eventually constructed. If the Act had included other justifying arguments (such as intrinsic value) then such failures would be less likely. There is a tendency among some conservationists to dismiss arguments not based on 'hard' science or economics as uninfluential or flawed. This is a mistake. The most important anthropocentric arguments, based on direct-use values and ecological integrity/function, are the most vulnerable to changes in knowledge. Legislation invoking the broadest range of justification (such as the EU Habitats Directive) and combining different values which will matter to different groups of people (such as the New Zealand Resource Management Act, which includes reference to Maori religious/cultural values) is more likely to achieve the goal of conservationists: the protection of as many species as possible.

6.6 Summary

- Arguments for conserving wild species can be based on the value of those species to God, to human beings, or to themselves.
- All the arguments have weaknesses, but taken together they make an overwhelming case for conservation.
- Science is particularly important in informing anthropocentric arguments. However, it can be difficult to demonstrate the truth of these

arguments scientifically (for example, because of confounding variables and limitations in experimental design).

- Science may also undermine some of the anthropocentric arguments, through technological progress or changes in knowledge.
- Conservation legislation based on narrow justifications is vulnerable to changes in knowledge and attitudes.
- Conservation legislation therefore needs to be based on a range of arguments and justifications if it is aimed at preserving maximum biodiversity.

Further reading

References giving useful further reading on the various arguments for conservation are given in Table 6.1. For a very accessible introduction to all of the main positions, see Fox, W. (1996) A critical overview of environmental ethics. *World Futures*, 46, 1–21.

References

Aylward, B. (1995) The role of plant screening and plant supply in biodiversity conservation, drug development and health care. In: Swanson, T. (ed) *Intellectual Property Rights and Biodiversity Conservation: An Interdisciplinary Analysis of the Values of Medicinal Plants*, Cambridge University Press, Cambridge.

Chivian, E. (1997) Global environmental degradation and biodiversity loss: implications for human health. In: Grifo, F. and Rosenthal, J. (eds) *Biodiversity and Human Health*, Island Press, Washington.

Costanza, R., d'Arge, R., de Groots, R., Farber, S., Grasso, M., Hannon, B., Limburg, K., Naeem, S., O'Neill, R.V., Paruelo, J., Raskin, R.G., Sutton, P. and van den Belt, M. (1997) The value of the world's ecosystem services and natural capital. *Nature*, **387**, 253–260.

Daily, G.C. (ed) (1997) *Nature's Services. Societal Dependence on Natural Ecosystems*, Island Press, Washington.

Ehrlich, P.R. and Ehrlich, A.H. (1992) The value of biodiversity. *Ambio*, **21**, 219–226.

Estes, J.A. and Palmisano, J.F. (1974) Sea otters: their role in structuring nearshore communities. *Science*, **185**, 1058–1060.

Fox, W. (1996) A critical overview of environmental ethics. *World Futures*, 46, 1–21.

Grifo, F., Newman, D., Fairfield, A., Bhattacharya, B. and Grupenhoff, J. (1997) The origin of prescription drugs. In: Grifo, F. and Rosenthal, J. (eds) *Biodiversity and Human Health*, Island Press, Washington.

Hodgson, J.G., Thompson, K., Wilson, P.J. and Bogaard, A. (1998) Does biodiversity determine ecosystem function? The Ecotron experiment reconsidered. *Functional Ecology*, **12**, 843–856.

Huxham, M., Beaney, S. and Raffaelli, D. (1996) Do parasites reduce the chances of triangulation in a real food web? *Oikos*, **76**, 284–300.

Kellert, S. (1996) *The Value of Life; Biological Diversity and Human Society*, Island Press, Washington.

Kunin, W. and Lawton, J. (1996). Does biodiversity matter? Evaluating the case for conserving species. In: Gaston, K. (ed) *Biodiversity: A Biology of Numbers and Difference*, Blackwell, Oxford.

Menge, B.A., Berlow, E.L., Blanchette, C.A., Navarrete, S.A. and Yamada, S.B. (1994) The keystone species concept: variation in interaction strength in a rocky intertidal habitat. *Ecological Monographs*, 64, 249–287.

Myers, N. (1997) Biodiversity's genetic library. In: Daily, G.C. (ed) *Nature's Services. Societal Dependence on Natural Ecosystems*, Island Press,Washington.

Nash, R.F. (1989) *The Rights of Nature, A History of Environmental Ethics*, 1st Edition, The University of Wisconsin Press, Wisconsin.

Nisbet, L.J. and Moore, M. (1997) Will natural products remain an important source of drug research for the future? *Current Opinion in Biotechnology*, 8, 708–712.

Northcott, M. (1996) *Environment and Christian Ethics*, Cambridge University Press, Cambridge.

Sheail, J. (1995) War and the development of nature conservation in Britain. *Journal of Environmental Management*, 44, 267–283.

Singer, P. (1993) *Practical Ethics*, 2nd Edition, Cambridge University Press, Cambridge.

Tilman, D. (1997) Biodiversity and ecosystem functioning. In: Daily, G.C. (ed) *Nature's Services. Societal Dependence on Natural Ecosystems*, Island Press, Washington.

Yeaton, R.I. (1989) Porcupines, fires and the dynamics of the tree layer of the *Burkea africana* savanna. *Journal of Ecology*, 76, 1017–1029.

Chapter 7

Why does fishery management so often fail?

Callum M. Roberts

Editors' introduction

In common with all the case studies in this book, fisheries management involves dealing with huge uncertainties. But it differs from the other topics covered in important ways. Humanity has been fishing for thousands of years; the Maglemosians, who lived on the shores of the Baltic 10 000 years ago, left huge shellfish middens as evidence of their reliance on marine resources. And early civilisations were quickly faced with the problem of how to manage these resources; it is likely that groups of people have been actively managing fisheries for at least 3000 years.

So in contrast to the other case studies discussed, the fundamental problems faced by fisheries managers are not new. And the science of fisheries management, which exists to inform these managers, is a well established discipline employing thousands of practitioners worldwide. The failures of fisheries management, as documented in this chapter, cannot therefore be blamed on the 'shock of the new', on ignorance and inertia in the face of a novel and unexpected threat.

Chapter 2 (p. 42) introduced the problems associated with uncertainty in complex scientific models, and the models used by fisheries scientists certainly provide good examples of these problems. Many fisheries models rely on large amounts of data, particularly on catch sizes, provided by the fishers themselves. But as discussed in this chapter, there are incentives for fishers to misreport their catches, so there is often great *measurement uncertainty* in the models. In addition, some of the most important ecological knowledge required by the models, such as the relationship between how many adult fish there are in a population and how many young fish they will produce, is often not available, so modellers must make assumptions leading to doubts about the *representation* of the models (p. 46). For these reasons, fisheries management supports the rule of thumb suggested in Chapter 1 that simple models, which are not as vulnerable to these problems, are often preferable to more complex ones, and this chapter gives some examples of such models. However, the main difficulties in fisheries management arise not from the science, but from the political, economic and social factors which influence how the scientific advice is acted upon.

Chapter 3 discussed how environmental decisions are the result of a process of lobbying, bargaining and claim making by 'agents of persuasion'. Many fisheries are managed by setting limits on the tonnage of each species of fish which can be taken each year, and these fisheries provide annual examples of the difficulties and drawbacks that can be inherent in such decision making. The advice of fisheries scientists informs a process involving fishers, civil servants and politicians. As discussed in this chapter, the final recommended catches are often wildly, and dangerously, different from those recommended by the scientists. The process can leave scientists feeling ignored, fishers feeling disdainful of scientists (whose advice in the past has not always been correct) and politicians feeling trapped in the middle. Some of the difficulties in this process may come from the very different approaches to risk adopted by the participants. Chapter 3 described four different categories of risk taker: individualists, hierarchists, egalitarians and fatalists. Nearly all fishers stress independence, self-reliance and freedom from regulation and regimentation as important aspects of their work; they are classic individualists. They live lives that are radically different from those of most land-dwellers. They work for hours on end, in often freezing temperatures, standing on moving decks which could at any moment pitch them into an early grave. It is not surprising, therefore, that their approach to risk contrasts markedly with the hierarchical outlook of the scientists.

Given the uncertainty in the science, the different perceptions of risk and the classic problems of managing a largely open access resource, fisheries management is notoriously difficult. The future may lie in more participatory and inclusive decision making (as described in Chapter 3); since policing any agreements is difficult, management decisions must have the broad support of most of the stakeholders, in particular the fishers, before they will work. An important start in this process is to find scientific prescriptions for fisheries management which can be accepted, understood and policed.

Once again fisheries management shows how science is only a small component in the pattern of decisions that ultimately influence the nature of common resource management. Where stakeholders are not involved in the early stages of decision making, they may be resistant to the observations of scientists. Their alienation from the process of taking hard management decisions makes it difficult for them to accept the premises of scientific uncertainty. To include stakeholders in such decisions requires a different kind of interaction between science and policy, which is open to principles of trustworthiness, fairness and negotiation. The outcomes of such approaches are rarely more accurate in strict scientific terms, but they permit the science to be better incorporated into the cultural outlooks of those most affected by the predictions and decisions made.

7.1 The expansion of global fisheries

The technology used to pursue and capture fish has advanced rapidly in the past 200 years. Today's fishing fleets are more deadly to fish than ever before. The sheer enormity of their nets beggars belief. Before they were banned in the Pacific, drift nets 14 miles long would be set to sieve the oceans. The largest trawl net could swallow a fleet of 12 jumbo jets whole (Greenpeace 1993). Boats are guided to their prey by satellites. They scan the ocean floor with fish finders developed from the technology of anti-submarine warfare. They hunt their quarry by day and night and can operate in conditions which in former times would have sent boats scurrying for port. But paradoxically, for all this dazzling technical wizardry, it is as hard today for fishers to make a living as it was for their great-grandparents, perhaps even harder.

Our growing ability to catch fish is reflected by the growth of global fish landings (Figure 7.1), which peaked in the late 1980s at around 90 million tonnes per year. Taken at face value this trend looks healthy, with increasing catches mirroring a rapidly growing human population. But the reality is that global fisheries are living on borrowed time. Fishing is often referred to as 'harvesting' which gives the impression of harmlessly removing excess production. In fact this is the generally expressed objective of fishery management: to catch the maximum yield that a population can sustain. However, experience has been different. Most stocks (an economic analogy for populations) are being removed faster than they can reproduce and so are actually being mined rather than harvested.

Global fisheries are worth some $70 billion per year (Kemf et al. 1996). The fisheries of places like the USA and Europe are overseen by sophisticated national and international networks of fishery scientists and managers. Despite their efforts, fisheries have continued to collapse. For example, the conservation-minded Canadian government was taken by surprise when its formerly prolific cod stocks went spectacularly bust in 1992 (Hutchings et al. 1997). The International Commission for the Conservation of Atlantic Tuna (ICCAT) has for the last 30 years presided over a 90% decline in the fishery it was set up to manage, leading one observer to rename it the International Conspiracy to Catch All Tunas (Safina 1998b)!

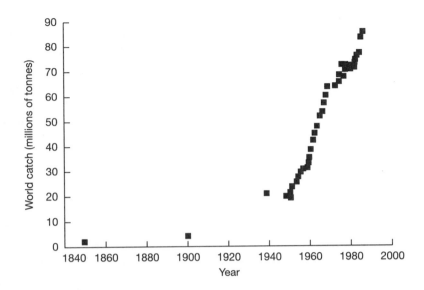

Figure 7.1 Growth of global fish landings.
Redrawn from Hilborn (1990).

Why is it that we are so incapable of managing fisheries? Is it scientific understanding we lack or are there other reasons why fisheries collapse?

In this chapter I first describe the objectives of fishing and current approaches to management, before explaining some of the many reasons why those methods usually fail. I also explore how fishing has been transforming marine ecosystems leading to an urgent need for conservation initiatives to be focused on the sea. I show how marine reserves, areas closed to fishing, could lead to more precautionary management of fisheries at the same time as protecting ecosystems. Finally, I describe how politics often conflicts with sustainable resource management.

7.2 The objectives of fishing

In theory, catching fish can increase the productivity of a stock. Figure 7.2a shows population growth of a single species following the form of the **logistic function**. According to this, at low population densities there is unconstrained exponential growth in population size. However, as population levels continue to increase, resources become limiting and growth slows, eventually to zero at the **carrying capacity** of the environment. This relationship can be re-plotted as population growth rate versus population size (Figure 7.2b). Maximal growth rates occur at intermediate population sizes. Theory suggests that fishing increases population growth rate by reducing animal densities to levels below which resources are limiting.

173

There is a second way in which fishing can boost growth. Most fishing gears are size selective, preferentially removing larger fish. Over time fishing reduces the average size of fish in a population. Individual growth in body size of a fish follows a similar pattern to that of logistic population growth (Figure 7.2a). Young fish grow fastest and growth slows as fish age. Reducing average body size also reduces average age and so exploited populations have a higher proportion of fish growing at maximal rates. In combination with reduced population densities, fishing increases the rate of production of catchable biomass. These effects are captured in the classic relationship between fish catch and level of fishing effort (Figure 7.2c).

The catch versus fishing effort relationship forms the essence of the **surplus yield model** that underlies most fishery management efforts. The surplus yield is the extra productivity that is released by the process of fishing. As fishing effort increases so fishers are rewarded with increasing total catches. However, above an intermediate level of fishing intensity, known as the **maximum sustainable yield** (MSY), catches begin to fall. The point of MSY corresponds to the point of maximal growth for a fish stock (Figure 7.2b). Fishery managers try to set fishing effort at a level which will lead to

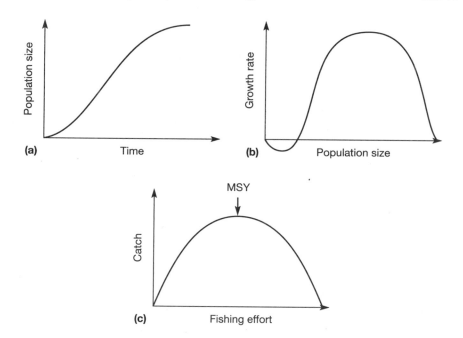

Figure 7.2 (a) Logistic population growth of a single species. (b) Population growth rate versus population size. In this figure, the population densities can fall to such low levels that the species cannot reproduce effectively. (c) The classic catch versus fishing effort curve that encapsulates the surplus yield model of fishery production. The apex of the curve corresponds to the point of maximum population growth rate in (b), and represents the maximum sustainable yield (MSY).

these maximum catches. In other words, they aim to maintain population densities of the target fish species at intermediate levels that will support the highest level of productivity. On paper, this objective seems sensible, so why does management go wrong? There are four classes of reason for management failure:

- practical problems (inadequate tools)
- problems with the underlying theory
- inadequate data
- political constraints.

I will explain the basis for all of the problems but begin by looking at the practical problems with management.

7.3 The limitations of conventional management tools

To try to hit the MSY point, managers must restrain fishing effort, otherwise more and more fishers would enter the fishery until fishing effort was well above the level needed to deliver maximum catches. Managers occupy a position somewhat like that of United Nations peacekeepers keeping an uneasy truce between a hugely armed aggressor and a peaceful foe. Technology acts to make fishing easier, fishery managers were invented to make it harder. However, managers have limited options for controlling fishing and the tools they use to attain management targets are blunt instruments (Table 7.1).

Conventional management tools include restrictions on gear, fishing effort, or landings. Gear restrictions include measures such as limits on mesh size or on the kinds of gear that can be used (Table 7.1). For example, fish traps have been banned from coral reefs off Florida and Bermuda because they are so unselective and a wasteful way of catching fish (Butler et al. 1993). Mesh sizes on trawl nets can be increased to allow fish to grow larger before being caught. However, managers face a dilemma when setting mesh sizes in multispecies fisheries that include differently sized fish: do they set the mesh size large enough to maintain breeding stocks of the largest species, and lose out on catching smaller fish, or do they keep a smaller mesh and risk losing the larger species altogether?

Mesh size limitations have other drawbacks. Trawls that are full of larger fish pressed against the net, a solid wall of fish flesh, will retain undersized fish behind them. These fish will be hauled on to the deck and will likely be dead by the time they are dumped over the side.

There is a tendency for most fisheries to become overcapitalised (see Box 7.1). Restrictions on effort are used to try and reduce the fishing power of a

Table 7.1 Some common fishery management tools currently in use and their limitations

Management measure and purpose	Problems
Restrictions on fishing effort	
Limiting days spent at sea	Can be undermined by increasing fishing power of vessel. Could force fishers to go to sea in dangerous conditions.
Limiting numbers of vessels in fishery	Number of vessels reduced, but the fishing power of the remaining ones may be increased.
Closed areas	Partial closures often lead to capture of the fish that are the subject of the measure as by-catch in permitted fisheries. Complete no-take areas overcome this. However, both complete no-take and partial closures may lead to increased fishing intensity elsewhere.
Closed seasons	Leads to 'derby fisheries'. Could force fishers to go to sea in dangerous conditions.
Restrictions on landings	
Total allowable catches (TACs) and quotas	Require large amounts of information on stocks to set accurately. Undermined by lack of gear selectivity.
Size limits	Lower size limits lead to the capture of the largest, most reproductively valuable fish. Usually ineffective for fish that change sex at a certain size, leading to reduced spawning success. Upper size limits sometimes used for these but undersized or oversized fish discarded often die. Especially ineffective for deeper water species as almost all by-catch dies.
No landing of 'berried' females	Designed to protect breeding female crustaceans, but there may be by-catch mortality of females caught and discarded.
Prohibited species	Ineffective if the species continues to be caught as by-catch and suffers high mortality on release.
Gear restrictions	
Prohibition of gears	Generally effective, if well enforced.
Net mesh size restrictions	Ineffective in multispecies fisheries, since mesh sizes are generally too small to protect the largest fish caught. Ineffective in full trawls as the meshes close up as the catch increases.
Limitations on gear size (e.g. length of drift nets or long-lines) or design (e.g. use of turtle excluder devices on shrimp trawls)	Can be overcome by setting multiple gears or using illegal gear modifications.

fleet and can be imposed in a number of ways. For example, there may be limitations on the amount of gear a fisher is allowed to set. Another tool is to limit the number of days that fishers are allowed to spend at sea, an unpopular measure leading to vessels being tied up at the dock for long periods. Alternatively, there may be a fishing season imposed, limiting the period during which a species may be landed. For extremely vulnerable species the season lengths can be very short. Before they moved to a different system of management, annual catches of Halibut in Alaska were landed in just 48 hours (Parfit 1995). Such short seasons encourage fishers to invest in more powerful fishing gears in order to compete effectively in what become 'derby fisheries'. This is economically inefficient. Short seasons may also be dangerous, perhaps forcing fishers to go to sea under difficult conditions. Limits on seasons also fail to prevent a species being caught at other times. They only prevent it being landed.

Another way in which stocks can be protected is if some areas are declared off limits to certain kinds of fisher or for certain periods when stocks are most vulnerable. For example, the 'plaice box' is a large area in the southern North Sea that is closed to beam trawlers of above 20 m long in order to protect juvenile plaice (Clarke 1998). The 'mackerel box' off the south-west coast of England is designed to protect over-wintering juvenile mackerel (Rogers 1997).

Total allowable catches (TACs) represent another tool to restrain effort. Once a quota has been filled the species can no longer be landed. However, TACs may be ineffective. Preventing a species being landed does

---

Box 7.1 Boom and bust in fisheries

Most fisheries begin with little or no regulation. A new stock is discovered or opened to fishing, perhaps as a result of the development of a new kind of fishing gear, perhaps because of the depletion of more desirable stocks. At this stage governments often encourage the development of the fishery by offering subsidies or cheap loans for fishers to gear up and exploit the species. In many cases government support is motivated by an economic crisis in the fishing industry as a result of prior over-exploitation of other stocks. Fishers rapidly enter, leading to a boom phase. The problem is that too much capital enters the fishery too fast (**overcapitalisation**), overshooting the level of capacity that would be sustainable. The fishery enters a phase of increasing regulation and diminishing returns, a bust phase. Regulations are usually implemented too slowly to halt the stock's decline and fishers are forced to find other, underexploited stocks to move on to and the whole cycle begins again in a process known as **sequential overexploitation**.

Adapted from Camhi (1996).

not guarantee that it will not be caught as fishers may continue fishing to fill quotas of other species and simply discard catches of over-quota species. To overcome this difficulty, it is possible to implement a quota on by-catch ('by-catch' describes all non-target species caught accidentally). By-catch quotas will lead to a fishery being shut down when a quota for by-catch of a non-target species has been reached. This approach has been experimented with in Alaskan fisheries but it requires all boats to carry observers to record by-catch and this is expensive.

Another form of quota system involves the imposition of a 'bag limit' or vessel quota, allowing a person or boat to land only a certain number or weight of fish at a time. However, this can lead to a problem known as high-grading. Where fishers spend long periods at sea there is pressure on them to land the most valuable species they can catch. Lower value species are therefore discarded until the hold is filled with the most valuable species, wasting a great deal that could have been landed and sold, albeit at a lower price.

Most fisheries are managed with a mix of the above tools. As a fishery encounters problems there is a tendency for management measures to proliferate as managers try one approach after another to try to control effort. The problem is that the tools cannot deliver precise management targets. Fishery management proceeds like a series of experiments that nobody is sure will work. The repeated failure of tools to deliver decisive results erodes the confidence of fishers that managers know what they are doing. Once this confidence has been lost, it is hard to get fishers to abide by the measures and so the likelihood of success falls still further.

7.4 The failure of fishery theory

Even if the tools used to deliver management targets were more precise, fishery management could still fail because the models upon which it is founded are inadequate. Consider the surplus yield model. The first limitation of this model is that it considers only one species at a time. This simplifying assumption is necessary to make the mathematics tractable, but no species exists in isolation. Some species are predators, others prey, many are both, and there may be complex food web effects of fishing (see p. 150). Yet this model assumes that changes in population size are due to fishing alone. In fact, simultaneous fishing of a predator of a target species could increase population size of that target species. Fishing of a prey species could decrease it, so affecting fisheries for the target species.

The surplus yield model, as originally formulated, also assumes that a species' environment has no effect on population size. However, we have long known that environmental variability in the sea has profound effects on population size of marine species. Compared to terrestrial animals, exploited marine species tend to produce vast quantities of offspring that disperse widely on ocean currents. In the 19th century, scientists estimated that if all their offspring survived to adulthood then 'it would take only three years to fill the sea so that you could walk across the Atlantic dry-shod on the backs of cod' (Alexandre Dumas, *Le Grande Dictionaire de Cuisine*, 1873).

Only a tiny fraction of the offspring produced by fishery species survives to **recruit** to fisheries (recruitment is the term used by fishery scientists to denote the time at which a fish first becomes vulnerable to capture). Most species produce vast numbers of offspring, and far greater than 99% of all of them die young. Tiny variations in mortality rates can lead to huge differences in the numbers of animals that survive the dispersal phase. For example, if a fish population produces 100 billion eggs and mortality is 99.99% over the dispersal phase, then a total of 10 million will survive to become juvenile fish. However, if instead mortality is 99.28% then 720 million will survive dispersal, a 72-fold difference. Environmental variability can have such effects on mortality. For example, in some years climatic conditions are better for the plankton prey of fish larvae and so larval survival is higher. In other years conditions will be less favourable for production of their prey or may have boosted populations of their predators. Fishing acts on populations that vary widely in response to environmental signals, but the surplus yield model ignores this.

A further problem for a manager is estimating the level of stock that maximises yield. Figure 7.2c implies that the MSY point lies at roughly half of the unexploited population size. However, if fish are exploited everywhere, then how are we to know what the unexploited stock size is (that is, there are no controls – see p. 22)? In practice, we 'guesstimate' it by modelling from an estimate of natural mortality rate (which is itself extremely difficult to measure). There is a second problem though. Unlike the symmetrical catch versus effort curve in Figure 7.2c, real data suggest that curves are actually skewed sharply to the right for most fish stocks and skewed to the left for whales (Sidney Holt, pers. comm.). Since effort and catch data are generally unavailable over a wide enough range to see the shape of the relationship from real data, relationships are usually modelled. This again leads to oversimplification and uncertainty.

The relationship between spawning stock size and recruitment has been a subject of great interest and debate. If you know the underlying shape of this relationship you should be able to predict future recruitment, and therefore catches, from present stock abundance data. Figure 7.3 shows

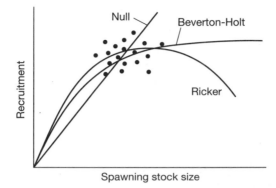

Figure 7.3 Three possible relationships between spawning stock size and subsequent recruitment. The Ricker curve and the Beverton–Holt curves are the forms most commonly assumed for marine fishery species.

Redrawn from Parma (1998).

several theoretical relationships between stock and recruitment. However, real data show a great deal of variability and it is usually impossible to discriminate between possible underlying relationships (see Figure 1.6). For this reason most managers have made the assumption that recruitment is independent of the size of the spawning stock, at least over the range of stock sizes they typically encounter (managers make a methodological value judgement, see p. 56.). However, there is one point on the graph that we can be totally certain of: there will be no recruitment if spawning stock is zero. Among the possible relationships, the two most commonly used, the Ricker curve and the Beverton-Holt relationship (Figure 7.3), both suggest a rapid fall in recruitment at low stock sizes. Assuming recruitment is independent of stock size encourages risky management decisions not to cut fishing effort when stock sizes are low.

7.5 The problem of inadequate data

Poor data quality is a general problem for fishery managers no matter what models they base their advice upon. Managers usually have to rely heavily on data gathered from the fishery itself. Such data suffer from several drawbacks. Firstly, measurements of stock size are based on proxy measures, rather than absolute measures. The proxy measure used most often is catch-per-unit-effort (CPUE). As population density falls, fish get harder to catch and so CPUE falls. Trends in CPUE are often used to infer changes in the underlying stock size. There are two problems with this. Fishers do not fish at random, they seek out the areas where fish are most common and therefore easiest to catch. If a fishing fleet pursues a dwindling stock into a smaller and smaller area of its range then a relatively high CPUE might be sustained right up to the point at which the population is extinguished. This is what happened in the case of the northern cod stock of Canada. Fishery managers interpreted sustained CPUE levels as an indication that the stock was healthy until it was too late and the stock collapsed (Hutchings et al. 1997).

The second problem with CPUE data is that fishing power increases over time and so a unit of effort, for example one hour of trawling, is not equivalent between a boat of the 1950s and one of the 21st century. Larger engines, sophisticated fish finding devices and gears that can fish over rough ground, all lead to a gradual increase in the efficiency of each unit of effort. A time series of constant CPUE may actually mask a steep decline in stocks that would only be revealed if CPUE were adjusted for changes in fishing power.

7.5.1 By-catch, discards and 'black landings'

Relying on data from fisheries themselves carries other risks. Fishers do not land all that they catch. Sometimes they do not declare all that they land (i.e. the data will be biased, see p. 49). The first problem is referred to as discarded by-catch, the second as 'black landings'. The net result is that you cannot rely on landings data to determine the total fishing mortality to which a stock has been exposed.

By-catch occurs because fishing gears are unable to target species independently of one another. A trawl engulfs almost all species within its path, a purse seine will catch herring and the fish that prey on them, a trap will catch most species curious enough and small enough to enter it. Levels of by-catch vary widely between gears and fisheries. Shrimp and prawn fisheries are among the worst, with 5–10 kg of animals caught for every 1 kg of catch landed (Dayton et al. 1995). Much of the by-catch consists of juvenile fish that could have been caught elsewhere later in their lives. For example, juvenile cod are caught by the million in beam trawl fisheries for plaice in the southern North Sea (McGlade et al. 1997). Juvenile or undersized fish are simply dumped over the side of the boat, unrecorded and usually dead. Fishing is a remarkably wasteful process. Imagine that every time you wanted to slaughter a sheep you had to kill ten lambs as well. This is what fishing does.

A central plank of fishery management in Europe is the **Total Allowable Catch** (TAC). TACs are set annually for each fish stock and quotas divided up among the fishers of European Union nations. However, unselective fishing gears cannot simply stop catching a species once the quota has been filled. Unless it has a very large mesh, a trawl is incapable of distinguishing cod from haddock from whiting. If there are still whiting to be caught, you keep trawling. But you also catch cod, only now you have to discard it over the side – dead. A recent estimate suggests that as much as 20% of total global fish catches are simply discarded over the side of boats (Camhi 1996). What use is a quota system that doesn't take into account by-kill?

Fishers hate to throw away good fish that have been caught through hard work under dangerous conditions. There is a great temptation to keep over-quota by-catch. Some of it finds its way to ports and is sold clandestinely. Such black landings could make up a significant proportion of catches. In Scotland, for example, one estimate put the amount of cod illegally landed in the early 1990s as between 100% and 200% of declared catches (ICES 1995)!

Ignoring by-catch mortality and black landings leads to serious underestimation of total fishing mortality for a species. However, fishery managers have little to go on and their estimates of by-catch mortality have large confidence limits. Because traditional management models, such as MSY, rely on data which are either uncertain or unavailable, the outputs from these models are **unreliable** (see p. 45).

7.6 The road to safer management 1: avoidance of recruitment overfishing

From the 1950s through to the 1980s the emphasis of fishery management was on maximising sustainable catches, based largely on the theoretical framework of the surplus yield model (Cushing 1988). Now the emphasis is gradually shifting towards the goal of sustaining catches over the long-term rather than seeking maximal yields over shorter timescales. There are two forms of overfishing that managers seek to avoid: **growth overfishing** and **recruitment overfishing**. Growth overfishing occurs when fish are caught too small, before they have realised their potential value. Recruitment overfishing is more serious and occurs when fish are removed faster than they can replace themselves, so putting future catches at risk.

How do you avoid recruitment overfishing? Fishery managers in the USA have begun to use a measure referred to as **spawning potential ratio** to gauge the vulnerability of a stock to recruitment overfishing (Mace and Sissenwine 1993). The spawning potential ratio is the amount of spawning stock present expressed as a percentage of the spawning stock that would be present if the species was not exploited. The Ricker and Beverton-Holt relationships between stock size and recruitment (Figure 7.3) show recruitment rapidly rising with spawning stock up to a certain point before levelling out or falling. The ratio of spawning stock size at the point of this levelling out, to the size of the unexploited spawning stock, is referred to as the **replacement spawning potential ratio**. Most managed stocks in the USA are now subject to management trigger points based on values of the spawning potential ratio below which the stock must not fall in order to avoid recruitment overfishing. This value is usually set at the level of the replacement spawning potential ratio.

What level of spawning potential ratio is sufficient to avoid recruitment overfishing depends on the shape of the stock versus recruitment relationship. Some species suffer recruitment overfishing at much higher levels of spawning potential ratio than others. They are more vulnerable to overexploitation. Mace and Sissenwine (1993) measured values of replacement spawning potential ratio for 91 stocks in the USA and Europe, representing 27 species. The average value was around 20%, meaning that for the average species recruitment overfishing can be avoided by maintaining the spawning stock size above one fifth of its unexploited size. However, average values hide a broad spread of vulnerability. Some species faced recruitment overfishing if their spawning stocks fell to below three-quarters of their unexploited size, indicating severe vulnerability to overexploitation. For most species values were lower and 80% of stocks would be considered safe from recruitment overfishing if a spawning potential ratio no lower than 35% were maintained. However, there is a cloud on the horizon. Managers seeking to maintain replacement levels of spawning potential ratio face exactly the same problems as their predecessors who sought to deliver targets of fishing mortality that matched maximum sustainable yields. The tools at their disposal are highly imprecise, and the data they require (such as the correct shape of the stock size versus recruitment curve) are often not available.

7.7 Multispecies fisheries, fish value and extinction risk

I have already described how lack of fishing gear selectivity makes it hard to target separate management measures at different fish species even though it is necessary to do this for them to work. But use of unselective gears also leads to more serious problems. No two species respond to fishing in the same way. They differ in size, behaviour and life history characteristics in such ways as to make them more or less vulnerable to fishing mortality. Some species are highly resilient and can maintain viable populations even at extreme fishing intensities. Other species can only withstand very low levels of fishing.

Figure 7.4 shows how species' responses to fishing vary in relation to life history. Ecologists sometimes use the terms 'r-selected' and 'K-selected' as a shorthand to denote different ends of a life history spectrum. R-selected species tend to be short-lived, reproduce early and recruit prolifically; sardines, anchovies, herring and sand-eels are examples. Their terrestrial mammalian analogues can be found in the rodents, species that live fast and die young. By contrast, K-selected species tend to grow more slowly,

Why does fishery management so often fail?

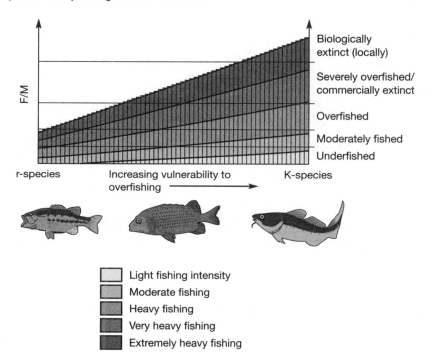

Figure 7.4 A species' response to fishing is dependent on its life history characteristics. This diagram shows the response of 60 hypothetical species (one column for each) from a multi-species coral reef trap fishery. Species are arrayed in a spectrum from r-selected to K-selected species. The y axis shows a measure of the effects of fishing on populations, represented as the ratio of fishing mortality to natural mortality (F/M) that a species experiences. Vulnerability to fishing mortality is indicated by the height of the columns, and each column shows the effects of five different levels of fishing effort from light to intense exploitation. r-species tend to be much more resilient to fishing mortality than K-species. At the highest levels of effort, the most vulnerable species would be completely eliminated from an area.

Reproduced from Roberts (1997) with permission.

mature late, and may invest much more in fewer offspring produced over long life spans. Sharks, groupers, halibut and rockfish can be numbered among species with such life histories, in the same way that rhinoceros and elephants are on land. R-selected species generally experience high levels of natural mortality while for K-selected species adult mortality is low. Consequently, r-species tend to be far more resilient to fishing mortality than K-species. In other words, you can fish harder for r-species than for K-species without over-exploiting them.

This spectrum of vulnerability greatly complicates the management of multispecies fisheries. Ideally, managers must hold fishing effort at different levels adjusted to each species' capacity to tolerate fishing mortality. However, a lack of fishing gear selectivity compromises this objective. For example, 72 species of fish and shellfish are caught by a Jamaican trap fishery (Sary et al. 1997). If a manager sets the mesh size of the traps large enough to allow big fish like groupers to grow large enough to reproduce, then the fishery would miss out on all the smaller species. If you set the mesh size small enough to catch little fish, all the groupers get caught and these species are lost. Many species have disappeared from large areas of the Caribbean as a result of this dilemma (Roberts 1997a). Sharks are especially vulnerable to overfishing because they are large, easy to catch and produce only a small number of young. Sharks were once common in the world's oceans but many are now threatened by fishing.

There was a time when people believed that economics could prevent the extinction of any exploited marine species. The argument goes that it will become too expensive to keep catching fish before they become rare enough to be biologically endangered. Unfortunately this is false. In multispecies fisheries, catches of more resilient species can maintain the commercial viability of the enterprise and species that cannot cope with such fishing mortality continue to be caught whenever they are encountered. The California white abalone provides a classic example. Abalones are herbivorous molluscs that live in shallow rocky habitats. They are prized in the Far East and can fetch hundreds of dollars per kilogram. In the 1960s densities of up to 10 000 white abalones per hectare were commonly encountered throughout the species' range in California and Mexico (Malakoff 1997). By the middle 1990s heavy exploitation had reduced the population to a last few dozen individuals and the species now seems doomed to global extinction (Tegner et al. 1996). But the abalone fishery continues, despite the loss of white abalone, since profitability has been maintained by rising prices and catches of the co-occurring black, red, pink and green abalones.

Some species of fish increase in value as they become rare, so that it pays to catch them regardless of how abundant they are. Take for example the Atlantic Bluefin Tuna. Average fish cost around £10 000 and the most expensive ever sold reached a phenomenal £50 000 (Safina 1998b). These fish are so valuable that boats fishing for them off the eastern US coast employ aircraft to spot them before swooping in for the kill. They are then flash frozen and airfreighted to Japan (Safina 1995). What chance does a tuna have against this massive firepower?

However, a species need not be valuable to become threatened. In the waters off the eastern coasts of North America the barn-door skate has been forced to the brink of extinction by capture in trawls. This species ceased long ago to be common enough to support a fishery but, even though now almost extinct, individuals are occasionally scooped up as by-catch in trawls (Casey and Myers 1998). Again, their plight highlights the problem of lack of selectivity of fishing gear.

7.8 Ecosystem effects of fishing

Increased fishery production has been sustained by a process known as **sequential overexploitation** (Box 7.1). The process of sequential overexploitation is evident throughout the world and can be seen in the trend towards capture of animals from lower and lower in food webs as the larger, more desirable predatory species are removed (Figure 7.5; Pauly et al. 1998). Average trophic levels are lowest in the Mediterranean, the region that has been intensively fished for longest.

People rarely think of fishing as having more than a relatively trivial effect on ocean ecosystems, but fisheries now remove an incredible 24–35% of the total primary production from continental shelf and upwelling systems of the oceans. These areas account for 95% of the world's catches (Pauly and Christensen 1995). A recent calculation suggests that an area equivalent to half of the entire global expanse of continental

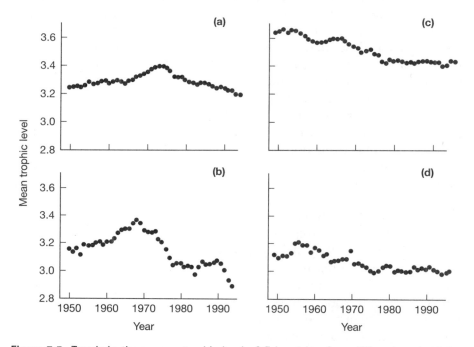

Figure 7.5 Trends in the average trophic level of fish catches from different parts of the world: (a) North Pacific, (b) Northwest and Central Atlantic, (c) Northeast Altantic, and (d) Mediterranean. Trophic level represents the level in a food web at which a species typically feeds, increasing from 1 (primary producers) to around 5 (top predators). Pauly et al. (1998) describe each species' trophic level as a fraction, representing the average level at which they feed (since many species feed on others from several different trophic levels). In most places the trophic levels of landings have declined in a process known as fishing down marine food webs. People are now eating species they used as bait 20 or 30 years ago.

Redrawn from Pauly et al. 1998.

shelf is hit by trawls each year (Safina 1998a). Each square metre within intensively fished areas such as the North Sea and Gulf of Maine is swept by trawls three or four times a year. Fishing is having just as profound an effect on marine ecosystems as agriculture does on land.

A serious drawback of conventional management approaches is that they focus on target species without considering possible repercussions of fishing at ecosystem scales that might undermine the long-term viability of fisheries. Figure 7.6 shows the dramatic change in the composition of groundfish communities on George's Bank off the eastern US coast. Over a period of 23 years communities shifted from dominance by valuable groundfish species such as cod, haddock and flounder, to dogfish and rays. The latter species appear to have benefited from the removal of competing fish and through scavenging

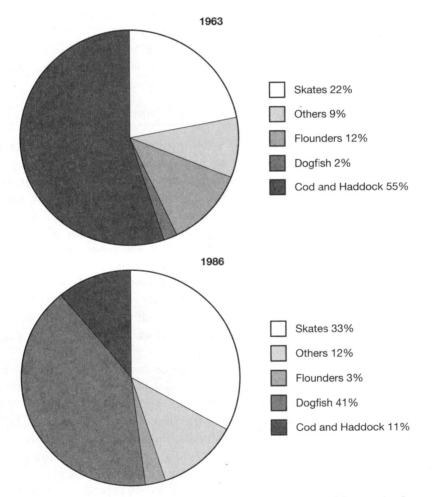

Figure 7.6 Changes in the composition of demersal fish communities on the George's Bank off the east coast of the USA.

Redrawn from Stork and Samways (1995), adapted form Anthony (1993).

discarded fish and animals injured by trawls. The fishing industry eventually switched to catching these dogfish, repackaged for the consumer as 'cape shark'. Now, dogfish too have been overexploited and the once highly productive ecosystem of this shallow bank is impoverished.

Non-target species can also be indirectly threatened by fisheries. For example, we now compete directly with many marine predators for prey fish. In the Bering Sea, stocks of walleye pollock have been reduced by 80% through trawling. The pollock form the main prey of Steller's Sea Lions and reproductive success of sea lions has fallen sharply (Camhi 1996). There is an unexpected twist to this tale. Killer whales that once fed on sea lions have switched to eating sea otters, possibly precipitating a recent collapse in otter numbers from over 50 000 to around 10 000 (Estes et al. 1998). Loss of sea otters has caused an increase in abundance of herbivorous sea urchins and led to the destruction of kelp forests. Cascading effects of fishing like this may cause ecosystem structure to change radically (see p. 154; also Steneck 1998). Managers need to take a broader view of the fisheries they oversee.

7.9 The road to safer management 2: no–take marine reserves

A means of putting the ecosystem back into fisheries management has been suggested in the form of no-take marine reserves, areas that are permanently closed to all forms of fishing. The theory behind no-take reserves is simple. If you protect fish from getting caught they live longer, grow larger and produce an exponentially increasing number of eggs (Bohnsack 1996). Animals inside reserves contribute to the replenishment of stocks in fishing grounds through the export of their eggs and larvae on ocean currents during the larval dispersal phase (Roberts 1997b).

As populations inside reserves increase, a growing number of fish will move out of them into the less crowded fishing grounds. Where well enforced reserves have been in place for several years or more, fishers have taken to 'fishing the line' along reserve boundaries to take advantage of the higher catch rates this spillover delivers.

A rapidly growing body of theory and practice suggests that reserves can help fishery management in important ways. Just like other tools they are a way of rebuilding spawning stocks, but this time without the risk that fish will be caught as by-catch and thrown over the side. Unlike the complex MSY models, no-take reserves do not rely on data that are difficult or impossible to obtain. They have the additional advantage of being simple and easily understood. Modelling work suggests that they can decrease the year-to-year variability of fish populations, acting like a reservoir of reproduction pouring out offspring to keep fishing grounds topped up (Sladek Nowlis and Roberts, in press). This will make catches more predictable, the manager's job easier and fishers' income more reliable. The existence of permanent no-take reserves can act as an insurance policy against management failure. Because biological uncertainty means that sometimes managers give the wrong advice, and politicians often ignore good advice, fishery management badly needs such a precautionary approach.

Migratory species, as well as sedentary ones, can benefit from no-take reserves. If reserves are established in nursery areas, they will protect juveniles from being caught before they have grown large enough to be valuable. Many migratory species also pass through migration bottlenecks, areas where the population aggregates together and becomes even more vulnerable to capture. For example, mackerel gather off south-west England to spawn. Fisheries often target such aggregations. Protecting them with no-take reserves could significantly reduce fishing mortality.

No-take reserves can also address many of the conservation concerns caused by fisheries. They can protect sensitive habitats from destruction by heavy fishing gears. No-take areas can help sustain prey populations upon which seabirds and mammals depend. However, they will only achieve their full conservation benefits if they are closed to all forms of fishing. Partial closures will provide only partial benefits and will suffer from the same problem as conventional tools: that of targeting management at species rather than ecosystems. There has been a tendency for fishery managers to regard closures as single species measures, but reserves will fail to improve management much if used in this way.

It may seem that no-take reserves are a new development but in fact they are as old as fishing itself. There have always been places that were too deep, too dangerous or the bottom too rough to fish. Improvements in fishing technology have opened up more and more of them to exploitation and the area of the seas that is not fished has grown smaller and smaller. Unfished areas probably played a vital role in supporting past fisheries and no-take reserves are a means of recreating them.

7.10 Politics and fisheries

Ecological systems are inherently complex and there is a large degree of uncertainty in our predictions for the future. Politicians dislike uncertainty and would prefer clear-cut predictions of future fish yields upon which to base policy. Given predictions with a wide range of error it is all too easy to avoid tough decisions to protect stocks. Politicians would rather hope for the best than take action that will have immediate economic impacts on the fishing industry. The cynical treatment given to scientific advice by politicians can be seen annually at the meeting of European Union fishery ministers at which annual quotas are set. For example, in 1998 scientists advised cuts in fishing mortality averaging 18.4% for nine stocks of fish in waters south-west of England and Eire. In response, ministers *increased* Total Allowable Catches by an average of 1.1% (M. Pawson, pers. comm.). For the west Channel plaice a cut of 34% was recommended and the TAC was increased by 30%! Ironically, avoiding hard decisions in the short-term risks much greater economic hardship over the long term. Unfortunately, politicians rarely take a long-term view. All too often their actions are driven by electoral cycles rather than a desire to protect the long-term viability of the fishing industry.

The demand for hard predictions by decision makers may also lead to managers failing to explain fully to politicians the uncertainties underlying their recommendations. Hutchings et al. (1997) have suggested that the Canadian Department of Fisheries and Oceans played down valid differences of opinion in interpretation of figures on the status of cod in advice to ministers (because of contextual values – see p. 56 – the department felt that it had to make its science appear more certain). This set the scene for the spectacular collapse of the fishery. Hutchings was sued for libel for stating something that has become painfully evident to everybody outside the management agency – that short-term politics has no place in fishery management.

The same criticism of ministers acting for short-term political advantage rather than long-term prudence has been levelled at governments that set bank interest rates. The solution has been to establish independent central banks to adjust interest rates. Fisheries would benefit much from independent management by agencies that have no direct political interest.

7.11 Summary

- Fishery management fails for many reasons. Firstly, the models that underlie conventional management usually consider only one species at a time and ignore the ecosystem in which the species is embedded. Fish populations are highly variable and fluctuations are driven by a multitude of interacting factors as well as the intensity of exploitation.
- Secondly, the data that traditional models require are complex. Much of the data are collected by the fishing industry itself and may be biased (omitting by-catch, discards and illegal landings of over-quota fish). A trend of sustained catch per unit effort may suggest all is well with a stock but technical innovations may mask what has actually been a decline.
- Thirdly, management fails because the tools used to deliver targets cannot be used to regulate fishing with precision.
- Rather than attempt to deal with the uncertainties and complexities of fisheries management by applying more complex scientific models, a better route may be to apply *simpler* ones, such as no-take reserves.

- The use of no-take marine reserves could build insurance into management. Insurance is needed because there is so much uncertainty in fisheries, both of biological and human origin. Reserves can put fishery management on a more precautionary footing.
- Politicians look to the short-term while fisheries management is concerned with the long-term. Uncertainty in predictions too often leads to risky decisions by politicians. Ultimately, fishery management must be divorced from short-term political expediency.

Further reading

Botsford, L.W., Castilla, J.C. and Peterson, C.H. (1997) The management of fisheries and marine ecosystems. *Science*, 277, 509–515. This provides a good summary of the ecosystem impacts of fisheries.

McGoodwin J.R. (1990) *Crisis in the World's Fisheries. People, Problems and Politics*, Stanford University Press, California. An excellent introduction to some of the anthropological, sociological and political issues.

Roberts, C.M., and Hawkins, J.P. (1999) Extinction risk in the sea. *Trends in Ecology and Evolution*, 14, 241–6. This paper documents how fisheries are increasingly threatening the extinction of marine species.

References

Anthony, V.C. (1993) The state of groundfish resources off the northeastern United States. *Fisheries*, 18, 12–27.

Bohnsack, J.A. (1996) Maintenance and recovery of reef fishery productivity. In: N.V.C. Polunin and C.M. Roberts (eds) *Reef Fisheries*, Chapman & Hall, London.

Butler, J.N., Burnett-Herkes, J., Barnes, J.A. and Ward, J. (1993) The Bermuda fisheries: a tragedy of the commons averted? *Environment*, 35, 6–15, 25–33.

Camhi, M. (1996) Overfishing threatens sea's bounty. *Forum for Applied Research and Public Policy*, 11, 5–15.

Casey, J.M. and Myers, R.A. (1998) Near extinction of a large, widely distributed fish. *Science*, 281, 690–692.

Clarke, B. (1998) *No Take Zones (NTZs). A Realistic Tool for Fisheries Management?* Marine Conservation Society, Ross-on-Wye.

Cushing, D.H. (1988) *The Provident Sea*, Cambridge University Press, Cambridge.

Dayton, P.K., Thrush, S.F., Agardy, M.T. and Hofman, R.J. (1995) Environmental effects of marine fishing. *Aquatic Conservation of Marine and Freshwater Ecosystem*, 5, 1–28.

Estes, J.A., Tinker, M.T., Williams, T.M. and Doak, D.F. (1998) Killer whale predation on sea otters linking oceanic and nearshore ecosystems. *Science*, 282, 473–476.

Greenpeace (1993). *It Can't Go on Forever: The Implications of the Global Grab for Declining Fish Stocks*, Greenpeace International, Netherlands.

Hilborn, R. (1990). Marine biota. In: B.L. Turner, W.C. Clark, R.W. Kates, J.F. Richards, J.T. Mathews and W.B. Mayer (eds) *The Earth As Transformed by Human Action*, Cambridge University Press, Cambridge.

Hutchings, J.A., Walters, C. and Haedrich, R.L. (1997) Is scientific inquiry incompatible with government information control? *Canadian Journal of Fisheries and Aquatic Science*, **54**, 1198–1210.

ICES (International Council for the Exploration of the Sea) (1995) *Report of the Study Group on Unaccounted Mortality in Fisheries* ICES CM 1995/B:1, ICES, Copenhagen.

Kemf, E., Sutton, M. and Wilson, A. (1996) *Marine Fishes in the Wild: A WWF Status Report*, http://www.panda.org/research/fishfile2/fish1.htm

Mace, P.M. and Sissenwine, M.P. (1993) How much spawning per recruit is enough? *Canadian Specialist Publications in Fisheries and Aquatic Science*, **120**, 101–8.

Malakoff, D. (1997) Extinction on the high seas. *Science*, **277**, 486–488.

McGlade, J., Price, A., Klaus, R. and Metuzals, K. (1997) *Recovery Plans for the North Sea Ecosystem, with Special Reference to Cod, Haddock and Plaice*, World Wide Fund for Nature, Godalming.

Parfit, M. (1995) Diminishing returns. *National Geographic*, **188**, 2–38.

Parma, A.M. (1998) What can adaptive management do for our fish, forests, food and biodiversity? *Integrative Biology*, **1**, 16–26.

Pauly, D. and Christensen, V. (1995) Primary production required to sustain global fisheries. *Nature*, **374**, 255–7.

Pauly, D., Christensen, V., Dalsgaard, J., Froese, R. and Torres, F. (1998) Fishing down marine food webs. *Science*, **279**, 860–863.

Roberts, C.M. (1997a) Ecological advice for the global fisheries crisis. *Trends in Ecology and Evolution*, **12**, 35–8.

Roberts, C.M. (1997b) Connectivity and management of Caribbean coral reefs. *Science*, **278**, 1454–7.

Rogers, S.I. (1997) *A Review of Closed Areas in the United Kingdom Exclusive Economic Zone*. Centre for Environment, Fisheries and Aquaculture Science, Science Series Technical Report 106, Lowestoft.

Safina, C. (1995) The world's imperilled fish. *Scientific American*, **273**, 46–53.

Safina, C. (1998a) Scorched-earth fishing. *Issues in Science and Technology*, **14**, 33–6.

Safina, C. (1998b) *Song for the Blue Ocean*, Henry Holt and Company, New York.

Sary, Z., Oxenford, H.A. and Woodley, J.D. (1997) Effects of an increase in trap mesh size on an over-exploited coral reef fishery at Discovery Bay, Jamaica. *Marine Ecology Progress Series*, **154**, 107–20.

Sladek Nowlis, J. and Roberts, C.M. (2000) Protecting biodiversity and sustaining fisheries through marine fishery reserves. *Fishery Bulletin*.

Steneck, R.S. (1998) Fishing, trophic cascades, and the structure of coastal ecosystems: does overfishing create trophic cascades? *Trends in Ecology and Evolution*, **13**, 429–30.

Stork, N.E. and Samways, M.J. (1995) Inventorying and monitoring. In: V.H. Heywood and R.T. Watson (eds) *Global Biodiversity Assessment*, Cambridge University Press, Cambridge.

Tegner, M.J., Basch, L.V. and Dayton, P.K. (1996) Near extinction of an exploited marine invertebrate. *Trends in Ecology and Evolution*, **11**, 278–280.

Chapter 8

The sea dumping debate

Gillian Glegg

Editors' introduction

The human population recently passed the six billion mark, and is expected to rise to at least ten billion by the end of the 21st century. As waste management and disposal options are already limited, this swelling population could lead to massive pressure on the world's current waste sinks, and increasing efforts to find new sites for waste disposal. One obvious possibility is to increase the use of the world's oceans. In the words of two leading oceanographers:

> We forecast that the disproportionately high degree of protection being currently afforded to the oceans will be reduced, and demands to exploit them will increase. (Angel and Rice 1996).

But in contrast to the prediction above, recent policy changes in Europe have increased the restrictions on waste disposal at sea. This chapter considers the science behind these decisions, and looks at whether scientific knowledge is sufficient to decide whether to relax the 'disproportionately high degree of protection' that the oceans enjoy.

Two approaches to answering the question 'what is the impact of dumping this waste?' are outlined in this chapter. In the context of sea disposal, both these approaches are beset with fundamental problems of the sort described in Chapter 1. The first, prospective assessment, makes a prediction of likely impacts based on toxicological studies conducted on the waste in the laboratory. The main difficulty here is ignorance about the relevant *statistical domain* (see p. 23). Will the results obtained in the laboratory, using one or a few species for a short period of time in a controlled environment, really be relevant to the wide oceans? The second, retrospective assessment, measures impacts after the waste has been dumped. But ecological monitoring in the oceans, in common with epidemiology (see Chapter 10) usually suffers from a lack of *power* (see Box 1.4, p. 25). This means it is often impossible to say whether there has been an effect, and so Type II errors (p. 16) are likely.

How should policy makers deal with this uncertainty? Despite the difficulties in predicting and measuring impacts, there are strong arguments in favour of using the deep oceans for waste disposal, and political incentives to move waste away from where people can see (or smell) it. In addition, decisions to dump waste at sea have been supported by the expert judgement of marine scientists. For example, in the high profile case of the Brent Spar discussed in this chapter, most scientists who commented publicly agreed with Shell that the disposal of this one redundant oil storage platform would have a negligible environmental impact, and was a safer option than disposal on land. As an editorial in the specialist journal *Marine Pollution Bulletin* put it: 'There can be little doubt that a rational balancing of the expected environmental effects favours deep sea disposal' (McIntyre 1995).

However, opponents of sea dumping have rarely based their arguments solely on scientific risk assessments of individual dumping decisions. Instead, they argue against setting dangerous precedents (perhaps one oil installation is innocuous, but how about fifty?), question the long-term effects of multiple and/or continuous discharges, and discuss the wider issue of how to reduce the production of waste in the first place. These concerns are not irrational, but they do go beyond the scope of scientific risk assessments. Rather than interpreting conflicts over sea dumping as a clash between rational science and emotional scaremongering (as much of the press did after the Brent Spar affair), it is often more accurate to describe a clash between *different* rationalities, a *technocratic* rationality (see p. 67) and a *cultural* one.

Chapter 3 discussed the role of the media, and of the wider political process, in determining environmental decisions. The sea dumping debates provide excellent illustrations of these factors. In the case of both the Brent Spar and sewage sludge dumping, explored in this chapter, environmental organisations were able to use arresting images to gain coverage for their views in the media. This allowed them to mobilise public support to their arguments. The political context at the European level was also crucial in determining the outcomes. The European Union has an increasing emphasis within its environmental policy on the Precautionary Principle (see p. 84) and shared responsibility between nations. Sea dumping by the UK was seen as contravening these principles and running counter to the long-term goal of reducing pollution inputs to the North Sea. In the face of these wider objectives and forces, scientific risk assessments played a relatively minor role in the final decisions.

8.1 Introduction

The oceans cover 71% of the earth's surface, have an average depth of 3.8 km and contain 1370 million km^3 of water. So will dumping a few boatloads of waste really make any difference? This chapter investigates whether we are in a position to answer this question. Dumping at sea has been common for over a hundred years, but many countries have now stopped the intentional dumping of most kinds of wastes at sea from ships. This chapter considers the reasons, scientific and otherwise, behind this change in policy.

At first sight there are advantages to ocean dumping (Angel 1992). Many waste disposal policies rely on maximising the dispersion of wastes so that dilution will be high enough to minimise damage (the 'dilute and disperse' approach). The oceans are huge and so high dilution may be expected. Dumping at sea also puts geographical distance between people and the waste. The land is very crowded with life whilst the sea is vast and relatively empty. The deep-sea, bottom-dwelling organisms most likely to be affected by sea dumping are of little direct use to humans (but see p. 147).

There are also obvious disadvantages associated with dumping wastes at sea. If the dilute and disperse motto is fulfilled, the waste will be irretrievable; if problems associated with that waste arise at a later date, there is little that can be done. Mixing and transport of water and wastes in the oceans is not as predictable or well understood as we might imagine and so wastes may become concentrated in unexpected places. If wastes are disposed of on land, there will often be political pressure from nearby residents to reduce the volume and toxicity of waste. In the long term, this could lead to less waste being produced in the first place. The deep oceans have no such local constituency.

Ocean dumping of sewage sludge started in the UK around the end of the 19th century. Increasing urbanisation had led to increased quantities of sewage and industrial waste being discharged to rivers. This had caused major water quality problems and even resulted in the Houses of Parliament in London being closed one summer because of the filthy stench. Therefore there was a need to move sewage out of sight (and sniff). Dumping sewage sludge at sea from purpose-designed vessels seemed an obvious solution.

This practice was followed in many other countries, notably Ireland, Germany and the USA. Other wastes were also dumped including liquid and solid industrial wastes, nuclear wastes, unwanted weapons and dredge spoil. Dumping continued unchallenged until the 1970s when concerns started to be raised. Here were a few industrialised countries dumping wastes in the seas on which many nations depended, and possibly contaminating fish or other marine resources.

At around the same time a series of international conventions were set up to manage marine waters (Box 8.1; Birnie and Boyle 1992). In 1982 the United Nations Convention on the Law of the Sea (UNCLOS) was introduced in an attempt to provide a global framework for the protection of the marine environment and the management of its uses and resources. Dumping at sea was one of these uses and this law was key in clarifying that pollution of the seas and oceans could no longer be regarded as an implicit freedom – all countries had to regulate and control pollution to protect the seas for everyone.

Box 8.1 International regulation of sea dumping

The United Nations conference on the Human Environment, which was held in Stockholm, Sweden in 1972, recommended that governments introduce controls on waste dumping at sea and consider an international system of regulation. Shortly afterwards the London Convention on the Prevention of Marine Pollution by Dumping of Wastes and other Matter was adopted by 25 nations (Birnie and Boyle 1992). This global international agreement, which now has over 70 signatories, was originally created as a means of regulating waste dumping from ships, planes or platforms in order to prevent pollution, but it has now seen several categories of waste dumping banned altogether.

The London Convention (LDC) forbids the dumping of waste without a permit. Wastes are categorised according to their content, with the most dangerous materials, such as mercury, cadmium and organohalogen compounds being on a Black list (Annex I). Less harmful materials such as copper, zinc, lead and organosilicon compounds are on the Grey list (Annex II). Dumping of Black list substances is forbidden while dumping of Grey list materials is allowed only with a special permit. All other wastes require a general permit. The LDC also outlines the criteria that must be met before a permit to dump waste is issued by the relevant national authorities. These criteria cover the characteristics of the material to be dumped; the site and method of disposal; the possible impacts on the area, and the adequacy of the science available for making such an assessment; and, importantly, the availability of land-based alternatives to marine dumping.

The Oslo Commission was also established in 1972 to prevent pollution as a result of waste dumping at sea but it only covered the North East Atlantic and had 13 signatories. In recent years it has combined with the Paris Commission (which was established to prevent marine pollution as a result of discharges from land-based sources) to form the OSPAR Convention on the Protection of the Marine Environment of the North East Atlantic (OSPAR 1992). The Oslo Commission regulated dumping operations in this area and worked to bring about an end to dumping and incineration of industrial wastes in advance of the London Convention deadlines.

The North Sea Conference, which has representatives from all the North Sea states, meets at irregular intervals to work to improve quality of the environment and to estimate the impacts that humans are having on it. The North Sea Task Force, which worked under the auspices of the Paris Commission and the International Council for the Exploration of the Seas (ICES), was responsible for undertaking research to enable a much improved understanding of the North Sea and its circulation patterns, inputs and dispersion of contaminants and ecological conditions. The results were published in the 1993 Quality Status Report (NSTF 1993) which, although it did not answer all the questions asked, did demonstrate how difficult the original task was.

Table 8.1 The quantity of wastes dumped at sea by the UK in 1990 (MAFF 1994)

Waste type	No. of licences	Quantity (wet tonnes)
Liquid industrial	5	228 000
Solid industrial	7	4 919 654
Sewage sludge	19	11 633 579
Dredged material	121	36 151 174

Table 8.1 shows the quantity of wastes dumped at sea by the UK in 1990. Of these wastes only dredge spoil is still being dumped by 1999 and there is no timetable for it to end. Why is this? Were these decisions made because of direct evidence of ecological harm, or were political and ethical considerations more important? No one reason can be given for the decisions to end the disposal of these wastes at sea. Whilst environmental science played a role in making these decisions it was not always the most significant feature.

This chapter considers the debate surrounding dumping of materials at sea. It initially discusses the assimilative capacity, an approach which has guided waste disposal activities for many years and which can be seen as the forerunner to, and in some ways the opposite of, the precautionary principle (see p. 84). The discussions surrounding two examples of wastes – sewage sludge and dredge spoil – are then examined in detail, and for each the science, technology and policy which has led to the current situation is considered.

8.2 Assimilative capacity

The assimilative or environmental capacity has been proposed for many years as a policy tool to control waste discharges to the marine environment (Stebbing 1992). It states that a particular action is only allowed if the harm it causes falls below an acceptable threshold. It has been defined by the United Nations Environment Programme's Group of Experts on Scientific Aspects of Marine Pollution (GESAMP 1986) as:

> **A property of the environment defined as its ability to accommodate a particular activity or rate of activity without unacceptable impact.**

The assimilative capacity therefore assumes that a certain quantity of waste can be absorbed by an environment without any significant, unacceptable change in its condition and, importantly, that this quantity can be specified. In order to apply the concept, it must be possible to determine scientifically the likely impacts of a waste. However, a value judgement is also explicitly required in defining when any impact moves from acceptable to unacceptable.

An example of how the assimilative capacity approach is used can be seen in the derivation of Environmental Quality Standards (EQSs) which are used widely in Europe (see p. 224). These are maximum allowable concentrations of certain contaminants in the environment, and their value depends not only on the nature of the contaminant but also on the uses of the environment into which it will be discharged. For example, in defining EQSs for copper Mance et al. (1984) consider the uses of copper, its chemistry and behaviour in the environment, typical concentrations found in the environment and toxicity data. They conclude that for marine waters the EQS for dissolved copper should be 5 micrograms per litre, although note that higher concentrations are acceptable in areas 'where a history of copper contamination has allowed acclimatisation, or where the presence of organic matter may lead to complexation of copper'.

In theory, two routes could reasonably be followed to determine the assimilative capacity of an environment into which waste is dumped. One option is to conduct a **prospective assessment** before dumping to attempt to predict its effects. The second option is to monitor the environment after dumping is carried out for evidence of the capacity having been exceeded (Figure 8.1 summarises a few of the possible impacts); this is a **restrospective assessment**. In most cases both of these aspects will be considered, but whichever option is chosen, a number of difficult scientific questions must be addressed.

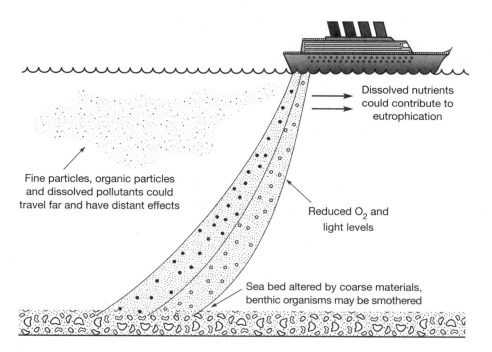

Dissolved nutrients could contribute to eutrophication

Fine particles, organic particles and dissolved pollutants could travel far and have distant effects

Reduced O_2 and light levels

Sea bed altered by coarse materials, benthic organisms may be smothered

Figure 8.1 A few of the possible impacts of dumping a waste at sea.

8.2.1 Prospective assessment of waste

Identifying the constituents of concern

Which of the many chemicals likely to be contained within the waste represent the most significant threat? Some chemicals, such as the highly toxic metals mercury and cadmium, or the pesticides DDT or lindane, will be recognised already as pollutants about which there is national or international concern and legislation. The procedures used to select these most dangerous chemicals are considered in Box 8.2. Restrictions on the use and disposal of these known pollutants should mean that they are present in low concentrations, if at all. However, there are around 100 000 manufactured chemicals on the market in Europe today. In addition, in industrial wastes many more chemicals can be found which are by-products of industrial

---

Box 8.2 Selection of dangerous chemicals

In many international agreements concerning the marine environment (e.g. OSPAR) three properties are highlighted as being of most significance when assessing the risks posed by individual chemicals. These properties are **toxicity, persistence** and **tendency to bioaccumulate**. Usually a pollutant must exhibit at least two of these characteristics before it is selected for special treatment. For example, if a chemical is highly toxic and does not break down in the environment then it could present a serious threat. Likewise, even if a chemical was only toxic at a relatively high dose, if it persisted in the environment and had a tendency to accumulate in fatty tissues, it could build up to high concentrations within animals, which might then exhibit signs of poisoning.

Byrne (1988) and Agg and Zabel (1990) discuss the use of these properties in a risk assessment scheme to define the UK's Red List of 'most dangerous pollutants'. In this scheme the properties for each pollutant are categorised as high, medium or low and a flow chart is used to determine which chemicals represent the greatest threat as shown in Figure 8.2. This looks straightforward, but obtaining the numbers to fill in these boxes can be anything but simple.

Byrne (1988) incorporates three types of toxicity data – acute, chronic and toxicity to higher animals. The test used to assess acute toxicity is a 96-hour LC_{50} (lethal concentration) assay in which the animals (usually fish or invertebrates) are exposed under laboratory conditions to the pollutant in solutions of various concentrations, to determine the concentration at which 50% of the population will die within 96 hours. These assays expose one species to one chemical. They are carried out in a stable, but stressful environment, which means that only robust species can be used as more sensitive species will not survive the laboratory conditions. Generally, only adults are used   and these tests do not reflect the natural variability of the real environment where salinity, temperature and

▶

Box 8.2 (continued)

other conditions may change following daily, tidal or seasonal cycles. In these assays the effect of only one chemical is observed, while in the environment animals will be exposed to a range of different pollutants which may act together to enhance or diminish their individual toxicity. Therefore, the **statistical domain** (see p. 23) of these laboratory studies is limited; field conditions, where animals may be exposed to a range of pollutants, are not easily related to laboratory tests (Matthiessen et al. 1993).

A further problem with the LC_{50} test is that it only considers death within 96 hours as an outcome. In the real world there are many pollutants which do not kill outright and immediately but give rise to sub-lethal effects such as changes in behaviour or reduced reproductive success. In the longer term these may have just as serious an impact on a population, but these effects may not be reflected in the LC_{50}. This is why Byrne includes a chronic toxicity parameter.

The EC_{50} (effect concentration) is the concentration of a pollutant that causes a certain sub-lethal effect and this is determined in the laboratory over a longer time (possibly weeks). These assays are still single chemical, single species tests but a variety of effects, ranging from behavioural to biochemical changes, may be chosen as the endpoint. For the third category of toxicity assessment, toxicity to higher animals, the most common test used is the oral LD_{50} (lethal dose) in rats who are given the pollutant in their feed.

So routine assessment of toxicity is not sophisticated. The methods used to determine persistence and tendency to bioaccumulate are similarly limited. Do the results of such tests enable us to identify the chemicals that represent the greatest threat? One can imagine that if these criteria were properly applied they would enable many individual chemicals to be ranked approximately in order of threat posed in laboratory conditions. However, there is one final problem that must be addressed – the lack of data to support an analysis of this type. As discussed by Byrne (1988) and Matthiessen et al. (1993), while there may be data available about the LC_{50} for some chemicals, information about the EC_{50}, persistence and tendency to bioaccumulate is scarce. Usually, in the absence of an EC_{50}, the LC_{50} is divided by a 'safety factor' of 10 or 100, which appears to negate the purpose of an effect concentration whose value lay in its ability to reflect an endpoint other than death. The long times and high costs involved in obtaining the data described here has led to consideration being given to the use of quantitative structure–activity relationships. These QSARs are mathematical equations, which correlate the biological effects of a set of chemicals with their physicochemical and structural properties, and a description of their use can be found in Dearden et al. (1994).

In summary, while the principle of using these three properties to assess the risk posed by chemicals appears reasonably sound, the methods used to quantify the threat are poor and the data are scarce. The sheer number of chemicals in production and in waste mean that it is not possible to use a scheme such as this rigorously.

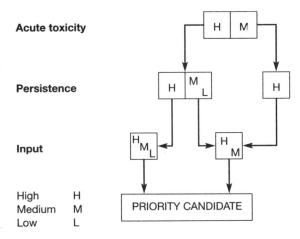

Figure 8.2 An example of a flow chart which may be used to select priority pollutants. The boundaries for high, medium and low are determined (e.g. for acute toxicity a high LC_{50} = < 1 mg per litre and a low LC_{50} = > 100 mg per litre) and the values for the contaminant are compared to enable a decision to be made. Input is derived from the quantity of the contaminant manufactured and its mobility in the environment.

Adapted from Byrne (1988).

processes. Monitoring has shown some effluents to contain over a hundred individual chemicals and the composition of the effluent can change from day to day (Johnston et al. 1991). So how can a complete assessment of such wastes be carried out? Whilst little may be known about most of the products, most by-products will not even be named in computer-based chemical dictionaries and so virtually nothing will be known about whether or not they represent a threat to the environment. A complete assessment of the waste cannot, therefore, be made, and only a few selected properties (such as pH and Biological Oxygen Demand (BOD)) will be measured, along with selected metals and other known contaminants.

What is at greatest risk?

The marine environment contains a vast range of species and habitats. Some of these, such as coral reefs, are very sensitive to pollution and disturbance whilst others, such as sandy bottoms, are more resistant. However, little is known about the vulnerability of most marine species, especially those in the deep oceans, and even less about the possible knock-on effects on ecosystem structure and function of impacting individual species (see Chapter 6).

Behaviour in the environment

What will happen to the waste once it is dumped? Will it settle rapidly in the area or be moved elsewhere? If it is transported will it simply accumulate in the nearest estuary? Will the contaminants remain strongly adsorbed to particles and thus be unavailable to biological systems or will they be more likely to accumulate in organic material? All these questions can be difficult to answer, especially when wastes persist for long periods in the environment without being degraded. Thus, the practicality of carrying pout a prospective analysis of the likely effects of waste dumping can be seen to be a complex and expensive task which in reality will not be comprehensively carried out.

8.2.2 Retrospective assessment of waste

Physical impacts

Physical impacts will occur in the water column, with increased concentrations of suspended sediments, and on the seabed. As the dumped material is released into the water column the larger, more dense particles will settle fairly rapidly while fine material (e.g. muddy particles) or those that have a low density (e.g. organic material) may remain in suspension for hours or days and be transported by the tidal currents. High concentrations of suspended solids may be avoided by some swimming fish but sedentary animals, such as mussels and others, may be stressed by high turbidities (Lack and Johnson 1985).

On the seabed, if the material dumped differs substantially from that found locally, it may change the available substrate, altering the local benthic (sea bottom) environment. An example of such change can be seen in work carried out by the UK Ministry of Agriculture, Fisheries and Food after the cessation of dumping in an area off the Tees Estuary in north-east England (MAFF 1992a).

Chemical impacts

As material is dumped its chemical environment will alter as salinity, pH and oxygen concentrations change. Generally the effect on pH will be short-lived as seawater has a very high buffering capacity. The oxygen concentrations in open seawater are near to 90–100% most of the time but they may decrease, especially towards the bottom of the water column, during periods of high productivity. The dumped material often has a high organic content but under normal circumstances, such as those described in Liverpool Bay by Head (1980) only a small depression in oxygen concentrations (say 10–20%) would be expected. This is usually a transient effect and it is unlikely to be monitored routinely.

Dumped wastes often contain a wide range of trace metals, including cadmium, lead, copper and zinc. There are difficulties in identifying the impacts of these metals on the environment. First, they are already naturally present in seawater, sediments and indeed, all compartments of the environment. How can the contaminant metals be identified? How important is, say, a 10% increase in trace metal concentration, and is this importance the same for all metals? Second, they are mobile and will partition between the dissolved (in water) and particulate (attached to particles) phases and this process will continue after dumping as a result of the changing chemical conditions, which may alter their bioavailability.

Within particulate material some of the metal may be bound in the matrix of the particle whilst another fraction may only be loosely bound to organic material or the surface of very fine particles. In the UK, when assessing the metal content of sediments, it is common to measure the total trace metal concentration (by completely dissolving the sediment in strong acid) of the fraction of sediment containing particles with a diameter of less than 63 micrometres. The importance of particles of this size is that the small particles are the ones that tend to accumulate contaminants on their proportionately large surfaces. However, around the North Sea this is not accepted as a standard. Other countries use the whole sediment sample or other fractions such as that less than 20 micrometres, or attempt to measure only surface-bound metals as they consider these to represent the bioavailable fraction more closely (Balls et al. 1993). So comparing metal concentrations measured in different laboratories and countries is often difficult, because of different methodological values (see p. 56).

For trace organic (carbon-based) compounds the picture is, if anything, more complicated. The concentrations are lower, the analytical techniques are more difficult and there are many more compounds. Routine monitoring for only a few of these was introduced in the 1980s. For example, the statistics about dumped wastes published in the North Sea Quality Status Report only details PCBs and lindane (NSTF 1993).

Biological impacts

As waste is dumped some organisms may be affected by the waste as it falls through the water column, reducing light penetration and increasing turbidity. Once the waste reaches the seabed benthic organisms may be smothered. The changes in the character of the sediment may have long-term effects on the types of animal that can survive there (MPMMG 1996). Highly organic wastes may increase the food supply for some animals causing an explosion in their populations at the expense of other animals. The frequency and extent of the dumping, the nature of the site (dispersive or containment – see p. 222) and the sensitivity of the ecosystem (e.g. originally a coral reef or cobbles) will determine the severity of these effects. The sort of procedure required to assess the likely impacts of dredge spoil dumping is given in MPMMG (1996) and is a very costly and time-consuming operation.

Levels of metals in biota are often monitored in order 1. to identify any changes (unacceptable or otherwise) in the contaminant concentrations in biota; and 2. to determine whether or not the current concentrations leave food species safe for human consumption. The latter should be a relatively simple procedure if acceptable limits are known but the former is more complicated. Very often the data are not collected in a sufficiently rigorous programme to enable trends to be identified. For example, the 1993 Quality Status Report for the North Sea concluded that in spite of an extensive monitoring programme, over more than five years, the data gathered were inadequate and did not enable upward or downward trends in trace metals in biota to be identified (NSTF 1993). Nicholson and Fryer (1992) consider the results collected in an international monitoring programme on mercury in fish. They conclude that, while there would be a 90% chance that an abrupt change of 20% in the mercury concentration would be identified, there was only a 50% chance that a similar change would be detected if it occurred over a 10-year period. In retrospective monitoring such as this, low **power** resulting from high **variability** (see p. 25) is a common problem.

In addition to metals, synthetic organic compounds or xenobiotics are also associated with wastes dumped at sea and many are toxic, persistent and liable to bioaccumulate. However, the range of organic contaminants is very large, their concentrations are often very low (as are their toxicity thresholds) and their analysis is very difficult and expensive. They are not commonly monitored in either the environment or in the biota and so there are few long-term data sets to discuss.

8.2.3 Summary

From the above discussion it can be seen that applying the assimilative capacity is not simple. The definition of 'unacceptable impact' must be identified and then the waste and/or the environment examined to see if this boundary has been or will be exceeded. Krom and Cohen (1991) conclude that while the assimilative capacity is a valid scientific concept 'it is too complex and expensive to use as a basis for legislation'. In reality, the implementation of the assimilative capacity relies on the environment showing obvious signs of harm occurring or harm increasing before action to alleviate the damage is taken. Because of the low power of many monitoring exercises, and the impossibility of applying proper experimental design (involving replication and controls; see p. 21) to most of them, even major impacts can be missed. This is almost the opposite of the precautionary principle. Instead of requiring those who wish to discharge waste to provide evidence of safety, with the assimilative capacity it is often up to the environment, or those who represent it, to show evidence of damage. Of course, by the time damage can be shown, it could be considered to be too late. Scientific risk assessments, either prospective or retrospective, also do not consider wider issues which are sometimes seen as more important than the risks associated with individual cases (see Chapter 4 for more examples). This was very apparent in the case of the Brent Spar (Box 8.3).

Box 8.3 Risk assessment and the Brent Spar

In the summer of 1995 the oil company Shell attempted to dispose of its redundant oil storage platform, the Brent Spar, by dumping it in the North East Atlantic. The Greenpeace campaign against this dumping, and the subsequent U-turn by Shell, pushed the sea dumping debate onto the front pages of the press. Was Greenpeace right to oppose the dumping? A prospective waste assessment (following a UK policy of identifying the Best Practicable Environmental Option – BPEO) had shown that there were relatively small quantities of toxic chemicals on the Spar, and that its disposal was likely to have no greater immediate impact than the sinking of any ship at sea.

Although Greenpeace had campaigned on the issue of toxic chemicals in the Spar, its main argument did not rest on a scientific risk assessment. Instead, Greenpeace was concerned that dumping the Spar would set a precedent for future decommissioning. It also wanted to make a political point about the 'throwaway society' – companies should consider the safe and ecologically sound disposal and recycling of their products before they make them, rather than assume that dumping them into the environment will always be possible. The public outcry showed that many people were sympathetic to these points.

The Brent Spar case exposed the limitations of 'scientific' risk assessments, such as the BPEO, which do not consider wider 'non-scientific' issues such as the dangers of setting poor precedents. For further discussion, see Huxham and Sumner (1999).

8.3 Sewage sludge

By 1990, 30% of the UK's sewage sludge was dumped at sea. During the 1980s the Department of the Environment had defended the practice, stating that it caused only transient changes in the water column, reversible changes in the benthos and did not present a public health risk (OSCOM 1989). Nonetheless, dumping of sewage sludge at sea in the UK ceased at the end of 1998. Likewise in the US sludge dumping has stopped in spite of suggestions that sludge could have a beneficial, fertilising effect on the oceans (Segar et al. 1985). Why? The debate about whether these were good environmental or political decisions continues.

8.3.1 Content of sewage sludge

Sewage collection networks are not only connected to individual households but also to surface water drains and some industries. This means that sewage contains not only human waste products but also wastes from businesses, such as laundries and garages, as well as road runoff which will include litter, partially burnt fuel, oils, and rubber and metals released as tyres wear. In addition, all sorts of household cleaning products, cosmetics, medicines, plastics and other 'disposable' products will be flushed into the sewer system. This means that there are many contaminants contributing to sewage and the resulting sludge.

Sewage sludge, resulting from primary or secondary treatment of sewage, is over 90% water, and the solid material is mostly made up of organic matter like cellulose fibres, fatty acids and oils. Most of this organic material will be biodegraded by microorganisms over time in the right conditions, but this breakdown will have a high demand for oxygen. In addition, nutrients, such as phosphate and nitrate, will also be present (the problems associated with this and eutrophic conditions are discussed in Chapter 9). Faecal bacteria and viruses are also present in sludge in very high numbers, even after some forms of secondary treatment, and although most are harmless, some (e.g. *Salmonella* sp.) may be pathogenic.

The metals in sewage may come from domestic sources, including copper dissolved from pipework; from road runoff (for example zinc used to strengthen tyres); and from industrial sources (for example, garages where metals may be associated with paints and oils). Trace organic compounds include pesticides, which are widely used around town centres and in the home; medicines that have been discarded or excreted; and polyaromatic hydrocarbons (PAHs) which result from fuel burning and will be deposited on roads. The majority of these contaminants will partition into the solid organic phase during treatment and thus be present in the sludge.

8.3.2 Behaviour and impacts

Sewage sludge was pumped from purpose-built vessels which discharged it into the wake as the ship was underway over the dumpsite. On most sites this began the process of dispersion, which would continue for hours afterwards as the sludge fell down through the water column. Monitoring the final distribution of sludge-borne materials can involve assessment of concentrations of organic matter, trace metals or even tomato pips, which are resistant to the best efforts of both our gut and sewage treatment processes! However, the results from such monitoring programmes are not always clear.

Barrow Deep, London's sewage sludge dumpsite, is a dispersive site. Monitoring of the area in 1990, when it was still in use, found trace metal and organic carbon concentrations that were not generally elevated, although pockets of higher concentrations, for example, up to 3% organic carbon, around 100 milligrams per kilogram of zinc and 40–50 mg kg^{-1} of lead, were found (MAFF 1992b). Surveys of the biota, which were carried out at the same time, showed some changes in the numbers of animals as a result of organic enrichment but overall the composition and distribution of biota were similar to previous years (MAFF 1992b).

In contrast, much higher concentrations of zinc, lead and organic carbon were reported for Garroch Head, Glasgow's dump site (Mackay 1986). Garroch Head is called a containment or non-dispersive site, which has very slow currents so that the sludge remains where it was dumped. Here, in 1983, an area of over 10 km^2 around the active dump site was found to have sediments that contained 4–8% organic carbon, 300–400 mg kg^{-1} of zinc and 200–300 mg kg^{-1} of lead. Sampling showed that the species composition in the area varied significantly, with a high biomass near the centre of the dumpsite, where opportunist species fed on the organic-rich sediments (Mackay 1986).

The contrast between these two sites is stark, but both were considered to be within the realm of acceptable levels of harm and dumping continued in both areas until it was banned in 1998. This example shows how wide the definition of acceptable harm in the environment can be. It could be said from these data that anything goes!

Sewage sludge is generally well characterised, and so prospective assessment of the likely impacts of dumping can be carried out. Table 8.2 compares the inputs of metals to the North Sea with sludge with the inputs from all rivers discharging into the North Sea. The UK's sludge contributed between 2% and 5% of the metals discharged by the rivers (NSTF 1993). A similar analysis of nutrient input shows that sewage sludge contributed between 5% and 10% of nitrogen and phosphorus delivered to the North Sea by pipelines.

8.3.3 Why was sewage sludge dumping banned?

We can now begin to see why the dumping of sewage sludge at sea was not considered acceptable. Although scientific observations of the dispersive dumpsites did not show evidence of extensive pollution, the monitoring programmes involved were not able to demonstrate clearly a lack of impact, often because of their situation amongst dumpsites for other materials and near polluted estuaries – that is, there were no suitable control sites (p. 22). Monitoring for far-field effects was not routinely carried out. Containment sites did show harm and although the area affected was considered by some to be small, others disagreed.

Programmes such as the North Sea Project involved all adjacent states in the collation of statistics about pollutant inputs, and the proportion contributed by such dumping to the sea as a whole seems significant. In particular, nutrient releases and eutrophication of coastal waters are high-profile issues (Chapter 9). Therefore, dumping of sludge at sea was opposed by many countries around the North Sea as it was seen as a practice which could be relatively easily stopped. It was felt that such a ban would benefit the North Sea as a whole, not just the area in the immediate vicinity of the dumpsites where most monitoring was concentrated.

Environmentalists had additional reasons for opposing sludge dumping at sea. They argue that we should not dump our wastes out of sight and out of mind, as this provides no incentive for environmental improvement. They felt that continuing the sea dumping of sludge provided a back-door route by which the industrial wastes contained in the sludge could also be dumped. However, if the sludge was to be converted into a product, for use say on agricultural land or forestry, then this would drive the water industry to avoid contamination wherever possible. Therefore, the argument goes, by pushing for the abolition of sea dumping of sludge an additional benefit is gained for the environment in that these wastes will be treated before discharge to the sewers.

On a wider international stage there were calls for dumping of many waste types at sea to end. One of the key features noted in many of the agreements about dumping at sea is that it may only occur if there is no acceptable alternative on land. Considering sludge specifically it was difficult to argue that there was no land-based alternative given that only 30% of the UK's sludge was disposed of at sea. There were particular problems with sludge created in towns – no one wants to see hundreds of lorries carrying sludge through the centre of their town on a daily basis – but these were not regarded to be insurmountable problems as they had been tackled elsewhere. And so, sewage sludge dumping ended and most UK sludge is now being used on land.

8.4 Dredge spoil

In total 36 million tonnes of wet dredge spoil was dumped around the UK's coast under 121 licences in 1990. Table 8.2 shows the quantity of certain metals within that spoil. This is a very large source of metals to the North Sea and Belgium, France, the Netherlands and Germany also dump

Table 8.2 The quantity of trace metals associated with sewage sludge and dredge spoil dumped by the UK into the North Sea in 1990 compared with the total input of certain metals via all the rivers around the North Sea

Metal	Sewage sludge	Dredge spoil	Riverine input
Cadmium	2.06	4.18	43
Copper	147	607	1200
Mercury	1.06	4.14	25
Lead	129	882	1000
Zinc	288	8113	6400

Source: NSTF 1993.

substantial quantities. Dredge spoil dumping represents the biggest source to the North Sea of arsenic, copper, lead and zinc (NSTF 1993). So why is dredge spoil dumping still allowed?

8.4.1 Source of dredged material

In many coastal areas harbours and channels need to be dredged to be kept open for commercial, naval and pleasure craft. In addition, capital works may require large-scale dredging of a new area to enable, for example, the building of a new harbour. These two operations will result in different environmental impacts. Routine dredging and the associated dumping of the spoil may be carried out on a timescale ranging from daily to once every few years. Capital projects will require massive dredging and dumping as a one-off, although maintenance may begin once the project is completed. The type of material dredged will vary from project to project, with maintenance dredgings tending to consist of silty sands while the bulk of capital dredgings will be coarser, including shingle, cobbles, rocks and heavy clay (MPMMG 1996).

Dumping dredge spoil from capital projects can be considered to be the relocation of sedimentary material and rock with a relatively low pollutant burden. Maintenance dredging involves relocating continuously accreting sediments in the estuarine environment. These latter wastes are the ones with which this section is most concerned, although some of the impacts they have will also be encountered following dumping of dredge spoil from capital projects.

River waters contain a host of naturally derived materials including weathered rock particles and organic detritus. As this enters the estuarine environment, the increasing salinity causes fine particulate material and dissolved colloidal material to flocculate to form larger particles, which may precipitate and settle in quiescent areas such as docks and harbours. The tides will also bring particles of marine origin into the estuary. All these materials will contribute to areas in and around estuaries which are accumulating sediments.

It may be assumed from the above that dumping this material would not represent a source of 'pollution'. However, dredge spoil does cause contamination of the marine environment. Industrial effluents, road runoff and diffuse discharges of pollution (such as pesticide runoff, effluent from disused landfill sites and contaminated water from old mines and spoil heaps) will all contribute to the pollutant burden carried in estuarine sediments (because estuaries trap such sediments, removal of pollutants is one of the 'ecosystem services' that they provide – see p. 150).

Trace metals are of course natural but the high concentrations of metals found in some dredged materials are not. Many of the trace organic compounds of concern are not natural. Organic compounds such as PCBs, DDT or TBT are extremely difficult to analyse but are toxic at very low concentrations. However, they too are often accumulated in the sediments within an estuary and so will be associated with dumped dredge spoil.

8.4.2 Impacts of dredge spoil disposal

Unlike sewage, which is gradually discharged into the wake of the vessel, sea disposal of dredge spoil generally takes place by instantaneous discharge. As the spoil falls from the ship the fine particles, which represent a small proportion of the total (1–5%), will remain in the water column while the bulk will fall to the seabed rapidly. This results in the formation of a mound on the seabed which may flatten over time if the material dumped is mobile and the receiving environment is dispersive, but in some cases, particularly with coarse material, it may remain almost indefinitely. This can bury animals and the change in sediment texture can result in a change in the biological community that can be supported.

The fines, which contain the highest proportion of contaminants, may remain in suspension for a considerable time and be transported large distances. While far-field affects are likely there is little evidence to say whether or not they occur. Accumulation of fine material in muddy areas, such as the Dogger Bank in the North Sea (NSTF 1993), may lead to relatively highly contaminated areas, but determining the source of the fine particles is not generally possible.

8.4.3 So why is dredge spoil dumping still allowed?

Dredging operations are critical to the development and operation of ports and harbours for commercial businesses, sports and recreation, fishing and a range of other activities. The importance of these activities in economic and political terms is such that no country is likely to call for a complete end to dredging in the near future. The OSPAR Commission has produced detailed guidelines for the management of dredged materials (OSPAR 1992).

To the environmentalists dredging is not really a source of pollution; it is rather a relocation of polluted material. Therefore, in general, environmental groups concentrate their opposition on the original sources of the contaminants to the rivers and estuaries. There are concerns about the most damaging dredged material, say if it is highly contaminated with the antifouling paint TBT or contains a high concentration of organochlorine pollutants, but this is a minority of the waste and the opposition is not vociferous.

The size of the industry is such that land-based alternatives are technically difficult and very expensive. The sea dumping of particularly contaminated spoil should not be permitted by the relevant national authorities and so other methods of disposal must be considered. For example, the Netherlands has developed containment facilities for highly contaminated sediments (Hayward 1998).

Aside from these examples for treating highly contaminated dredge spoil, one of the principal reasons for the continuation of dumping must be that there are few alternatives to dumping at similar cost. All coastal countries face similar problems and from an international perspective it is unlikely that any one country will wish to rock this particular boat.

8.5 Conclusions

In the UK the original decision to dump waste at sea was based more on perceived common sense than on science; there was a widespread belief that wastes would be assimilated harmlessly into the vast oceans. Later, attempts were made to support the presumption that it was causing no or only acceptable levels of harm by monitoring the waste and the environment. However, convincing evidence of this was not found.

One reason for this is that dumping of wastes at sea is not completely harmless and there are impacts. These range from the short-term, small-scale effects associated with turbidity or oxygen depletion to long-range and long-term contamination by persistent pollutants. The monitoring programmes used, whether to characterise the waste or determine the extent of the impacts in the environment, were inadequate and not able to describe the full range of likely or actual consequences of dumping.

However, a further key point is that scientists and scientific work cannot alone determine the difference between acceptable and unacceptable harm. Indeed, sometimes, the environmental science does not seem to be very helpful when considering such decisions. Theoretical and empirical knowledge does not answer such questions and value-based knowledge, contributed by a wider audience including politicians, industrialists and the public, is required to define limits. However, this does not necessarily lead to entirely consistent decision making as is demonstrated by O'Connor (1998).

Of the two case studies presented perhaps the decision to stop dumping sewage sludge at sea was most clearly based on scientific principles, although this was driven at an international political level. The concerns in this case were to reduce wherever possible the contaminant loading entering the North Sea.

The continued acceptability of dredge spoil dumping, and the harm which may result, is based on practical considerations. It does not contain new contaminants; they are merely being relocated. The quantity of dredge spoil around Europe and elsewhere is enormous and the economic imperative of keeping ports and harbours open and working means that treatment or containment is only seen as an option for highly contaminated dredge spoil. There is no reason to suppose that dumping dredge spoil on land would be an improvement, indeed the opposite is likely to be true. Therefore, it is likely that dredge spoil dumping will continue well into the 21st century.

8.6 Summary

- The assimilative capacity approach to waste management was important in guiding sea dumping practices. It assumes that it is possible to calculate what quantities of waste can be discharged into the environment without causing unacceptable harm.
- Prospective or restrospective assessments can be used to attempt to determine these acceptable quantities, but conducting these assessments thoroughly is often very difficult and expensive.
- Retrospective assessment of sewage sludge dump sites was not powerful enough to rule out unacceptable harm. Concerns about the long-term impacts of pollution on the North Sea, political pressure to reduce these inputs and the availability of alternatives all led to the end of sea dumping of sewage.
- Dredge spoil dumping is economically important to many states, and there are few alternatives. Although it does cause environmental damage, it is still permitted.

Further reading

Alder, J. and Wilkinson, D. (1999) *Environmental Ethics and Law*, Macmillan, London.

Preston, M.R. (1989) Marine pollution. In: Riley J.P. (ed) *Chemical Oceanography*, Academic Press, London.

Also the International Maritime Organisation's website is a useful source of information about the implementation of the London Dumping Convention; see http://www.imo.org

The website of OSPAR gives up-to-date information and access to its reports about marine pollution and its sources; see http://www.ospar.org

References

Agg, A.R. and Zabel, T.F. (1990) Red list substances: Selection and monitoring. *Journal of the Institute of Water and Environmental Management*, 4 , 44–50.

Angel, M.V. (1992) Deep abyssal plains: Do they offer a viable option for the dispersal of large bulk low-toxicity wastes? In: Smith, H.D (ed) *Advances in the Science and Technology of Ocean Management*, Routledge, London.

Angel, M.V. and Rice T.L. (1996) The ecology of the deep ocean and its relevance to global waste management. *Journal of Applied Ecology*, 33, 915–26.

Balls, P., Cofino, W., Schmidt, D., Topping, G., Wilson, S. and Yeats, P. (1993) ICES baseline survey of trace metals in European shelf seas. *ICES Journal of Marine Science*, 50, 435–44.

Birnie, P.W. and Boyle, A.E. (1992) *International Law and the Environment*, Clarendon Press, Oxford.

Byrne, C.D. (1988) Selection of substances requiring priority action. In: Richardson, M.L. (ed) *Risk Assessment of Chemicals in the Environment*, Royal Society of Chemistry, London.

Dearden, J.C., Calow, P. and Watts, C. (1994) A predictable response? *Chemistry in Britain*, October 1994, 823–26.

GESAMP (1986) Environmental capacity: an approach to marine pollution prevention. IMO/FAO/UNESCO/IAEA/WHO/WMO/UN/UNEP Joint Group of Experts on the Scientific Aspects of Marine Pollution, Reports and Studies no. 30.

Hayward, K. (1998) Storage solution. *Water Quality International*, April 1998, 15–17.

Head, P.C. (1980) The environmental impact of the disposal of sewage sludge in Liverpool Bay. *Progress in Water Technology*, 13, 27–38.

Huxham, M. and Sumner, D. (1999) Science, emotion and rationality: the case of the Brent Spar. *Environmental Values*, 8, 349–68.

Johnston, P.A., MacGarvin, M. and Stringer, R.L. (1991) Regulation of effluents and implications for environmental policy. *Water Science and Technology*, 24, 19–27.

Krom, M.D. and Cohen, Y. (1991) Environmental capacity of the ocean margins: reality or myth? In: Mantoura, R.F.C., Martin, J.M. and Wollast, R. (eds) *Ocean Margin Processes in Global Change*, John Wiley, London.

Lack, T.J. and Johnson, D. (1985) Assessment of the biological effects of sewage sludge at a licensed site off Plymouth. *Marine Pollution Bulletin*, 16, 147–52.

Mackay, D.W. (1986) Sludge dumping in the Firth of Clyde – a containment site. *Marine Pollution Bulletin*, 17, 91–5.

MAFF (1992a) Benthic studies at dredged material disposal sites in Liverpool Bay. *Aquatic Environment Monitoring Report*, 28, MAFF Directorate of Fisheries Research, Lowestoft.

MAFF (1992b) Fourth report on the group co-ordinating sea disposal monitoring. *Aquatic Environment Monitoring Report*, 31, MAFF Directorate of Fisheries Research, Lowestoft.

MAFF (1994) Monitoring and surveillance of non-radioactive contaminants in the aquatic environment and activities regulating the disposal of wastes at sea, 1992. *Aquatic Environment Montoring Report*, 40, MAFF Directorate of Fisheries Research, Lowestoft, 83 pp.

Mance, G., Brown, V.M. and Yates, J. (1984) Proposed environmental quality standards for list II substances in water; copper. Water Research Centre, technical report no. TR 210, Medmenham.

Matthiessen, P., Thain, J.E., Law, R.J. and Fileman, T.W. (1993) Attempts to assess the environmental hazard posed by complex mixtures of organic chemicals in UK estuaries. *Marine Pollution Bulletin*, 26, 90–5.

McIntyre, A. (1995) The Brent Spar incident – a milestone event. *Marine Pollution Bulletin*, 30, 578.

MPMMG (1996) Monitoring and assessment of the marine benthos at UK dredged material disposal sites. Prepared by the benthos task team for the Marine Pollution Monitoring Management Group co-ordinating sea disposal monitoring. Scottish Fisheries Information Pamphlet, 21. The Scottish Office, Agriculture, Environment and Fisheries Department, 35 pp.

Nicholson, M.D. and Fryer, R.J. (1992) The statistical power of monitoring programmes. *Marine Pollution Bulletin*, 24, 146–9.

NSTF (1993) *North Sea Quality Status Report 1993*, North Sea Task Force, Oslo and Paris Commissions, London.

O'Connor, T.P. (1998) Comparative criteria: Land application of sewage sludge and ocean disposal of dredged material. *Marine Pollution Bulletin*, 36, 181–184.

OSCOM (1989) *Review of Sewage Sludge Disposal at Sea*, Oslo Commission, London.

OSPAR (1992) *Ministerial Meeting of the Oslo and Paris Commissions, Paris, 21–22 September 1992*, Oslo and Paris Commissions, London.

Segar, D.A., Stamman, E. and Davis, P.G. (1985) Beneficial use of sewage sludge in the ocean. *Marine Pollution Bulletin*, 16, 186–191.

Stebbing, A.R.D. (1992) Environmental capacity and the precautionary principle. *Marine Pollution Bulletin*, 24, 287–95.

Chapter 9

Marine eutrophication and the use of models

Paul Tett

Editors' introduction

If you've been to the seaside recently you may well have seen long pipes (or maybe not so long) taking the waste from houses near the shore and putting it in the sea. Until a few years ago it was common to discharge untreated sewage into the sea around Britain. However, a European Community Directive of 1991 laid down a standard level of waste water treatment. At the very least the lumps had to be removed (the primary treatment), and there should usually be an additional stage of biological treatment to remove smaller organic particles and dissolved organic matter. There was, however, an escape clause – this secondary treatment need not be carried out for 'less sensitive' waters. But how do we decide which waters are 'less sensitive'? And what are the main problems when we do discharge sewage?

Clearly, lumps of untreated sewage are not good for the image of a seaside town. But the problem can be more than just an aesthetic one if the levels of nutrients in the sea (principally nitrogen and phosphorus) are significantly increased. Under certain conditions the growth of phytoplankton and seaweed is stimulated, sometimes producing unusual and toxic types of plankton which can kill fish and make shellfish poisonous to humans.

But not always ... if the sewage is discharged into waters where rapid distribution occurs, no secondary treatment is necessary. Sewage treatment is expensive, and cost–benefit considerations (see p. 59) may work against its adoption.

To decide how 'sensitive' the waters are in a particular case, we need to build a model – a mathematical one, not a 'real' physical one (see p. 11 and p. 42). The model, using assumptions about the rate at which the waters exchange with the surrounding waters, estimates how much the nutrient concentration will increase for a given discharge. We then have to make a further assumption about how much of the extra nutrients are used by the phytoplankton; and we need to decide on a maximum acceptable level of plant growth. In short, several methodological value judgements need to be made (p. 56), and this chapter presents a case study of how such judgements influence the modelling process. In the models described in this chapter, the concentration of chlorophyll is used as the indicator of plant growth, with a maximum acceptable concentration of 10 milligrams per cubic metre in the case of UK waters, as this concentration of chlorophyll is sufficient to cause a visible discolouration of the sea.

If we follow strictly the falsification procedure first proposed by Popper (p. 5), one of the models described in this chapter (the Riley+) would have to be rejected, as it does no better than a null model in which the concentrations of chlorophyll and nutrients do not change at all. A more sophisticated model than the Riley+ is likely to need more parameters which may not be very well known (see p. 31); moreover, testing of such a model will be limited to some extent by the quality and quantity of data that are available (see p. 30).

Rather than develop more complicated models with more uncertainties, a practical solution is to invoke the precautionary principle (see p. 84). A model is adopted which is simple (reducing the danger of mistakes) and which assumes the worst – that the extra nutrient is *completely* used to make extra phytoplankton. There are still methodological value judgements to be made (such as *how much* chlorophyll is produced from a given quantity of nutrient), but not as many as with the Riley+ or more complicated models. The simple model can then be tested to see whether the observed concentrations of chlorophyll are always less than those estimated by the model. If it always errs on the safe side, the model will be useful even though it lacks precision (see p. 42).

9.1 Introduction

Humans shit. I'm sorry to start like this, but it's a fact essential to my argument. We also use large quantities of plant-stimulating chemicals each time we do the laundry, and wash dishes with bits of half-eaten food on them. For several reasons, some good, we don't like to keep all this crap around the house, so we flush it away, and pay the city, or the water company, to get rid of it for us.

In Seattle, the original remedy was to pipe it into the freshwater Lake Washington. But there it began to stimulate the growth of noxious water plants (commonly called 'blue–green algae', but, in fact, bacteria), so, from 1963, the stuff was sent down a longer pipe to the sea, where the currents in Puget Sound swept it away. Hopefully, this diluted it sufficiently for the growth-stimulating compounds to be absorbed into natural cycles of nitrogen and phosphorus; and, in any case, allowing the lake to recover a healthier state (Edmondson 1961; Edmondson and Lehman 1981).

Human excreta is only one of the things that humans put into natural waters. Some industries produce effluents that are, likewise, rich in organic matter and plant nutrients. The region around the *Seton Aikai*, the Inland Sea of Japan, became urbanised and industrialised during the 1950s and 1960s, and so the Sea became the recipient of much of this sort of waste. The result (Figure 9.1) was a large increase (Prakash 1987) in water discolourations caused by an abundance of microorganisms and called **Red Tides**. Before the waste discharges were treated, the Red Tides in the Inland Sea caused many problems, including the death of farmed fish.

During the 1980s some Europeans began to be concerned that their coastal seas were at similar risk. For example, Lancelot et al. (1987) related pollution of bathing beaches by nuisance algal blooms to enrichment of North Sea coastal waters with plant nutrients. Problems with the quality of drinking water and the state of freshwater fisheries had been identified somewhat earlier (Lund 1972; Rodhe 1969). These concerns lay behind the **Urban Waste Water Treatment Directive** (UWWTD) enacted by the Commission of the European Communities in 1991, which aimed to protect the environment by controlling discharges of plant nutrients and oxygen-consuming waste.

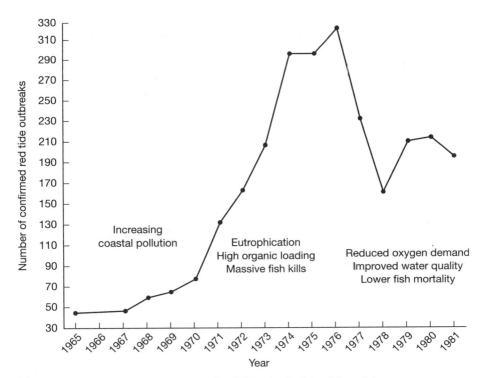

Figure 9.1 Changes in the frequency of Red Tides in the Inland Sea of Japan.
From Prakash 1987.

The UWWTD (Box 9.1) laid down a standard level of waste water treatment. This must be intensified in 'more sensitive' waters and can be relaxed in 'less sensitive' waters. Although the Directive applies to discharges to all the waters of what is now the European Union, I will focus on its application to the estuaries and coastal seas of the United Kingdom.

Box 9.1 The Urban Waste Water Treatment Directive

Summarised below are some of the articles of the European Communities Council Directive of 21 May 1991 concerning urban waste water treatment (91/271/EEC).

Article 1 The objective of the Directive is to protect the environment from the adverse effects of ... waste water discharges.

Article 4 Member States shall ensure that urban waste water entering collecting systems shall before discharge be subject to secondary treatment or an equivalent treatment ...

Article 5 Member states shall ... identify sensitive areas ... [and] shall ensure that ... discharge[s] into sensitive areas be subject to more stringent treatment than [secondary] ... for all discharges from ... more than 10 000 [persons or equivalents]. ...

Article 6 Member States may ... identify less sensitive areas ... Urban waste water discharges from agglomerations of between 10 000 and 150 000 [persons or equivalents] to coastal waters[,] and those from agglomerations of between 2 000 and 10 000 ... to estuaries[,] situated in [less sensitive areas] may be subject to treatment less stringent than prescribed in Article 4 providing that:
  – such discharges receive at least primary treatment ...
  – **comprehensive studies** indicate that such discharges will not adversely affect the environment.
Member states shall provide the Commission with all relevant information concerning [these] studies. ...

Definitions (from Article 2, Table 2 and Annex 1)
Primary treatment means treatment of urban waste water by a physical and/or chemical process involving settlement of suspended solids, or other processes in which the [biological oxygen demand] of the incoming waste water is reduced by at least 20% before discharge and the total suspended solids of the incoming waste water are reduced by at least 50%.
Secondary treatment means treatment of urban waste water by a process generally involving biological treatment with a secondary settlement or other processes ... [resulting in a reduction of biological oxygen demand by 70–90% and a reduction of total suspended solids by 90%].
More stringent treatment [means a reduction of total phosphorus by at least 80%, or of total nitrogen by at least 70%, or both, depending on local conditions].

At the time that the Directive was made, the UK government wished to identify some of its coastal waters as 'less sensitive', so that treatment levels could be relaxed. According to Article 6 of the Directive the United Kingdom therefore had to provide the European Commission with 'all relevant information' concerning 'Comprehensive Studies' in order to show that these waters were not harmed by less stringent treatment of waste. The UK government therefore set up the **Comprehensive Studies Task Team** (CSTT) and charged it with defining the environmental quality issues that needed to be addressed in a Comprehensive Study. I was a member of the Team, and in this chapter I use the CSTT's treatment of **eutrophication** to exemplify the use of **mathematical models** in environmental impact assessment.

9.2 Eutrophication

The Red Tides in the Japanese Inland Sea, and the algal blooms in Lake Washington and the North Sea, are examples of **eutrophication**, defined by the UWWTD as the

> **enrichment of water by nutrients, especially compounds of nitrogen and phosphorus, causing an accelerated growth of algae and higher forms of plant life to produce an undesirable disturbance to the balance of organisms and the quality of the water concerned.**

Sometimes the plants are water weeds or seaweeds. More often they are phytoplankton – tiny floating algae or photosynthetic bacteria. They grow by using the energy of sunlight to assemble the simple inorganic molecules of water, carbon dioxide and nutrient salts into the complex organic molecules of living protoplasm. Nutrient salts – usually in the form of nitrate and phosphate ions – are the least abundant of the raw materials. Phytoplankton are small because larger and heavier plants would sink into the dark depths of lakes or oceans. Being small helps the absorption of plant nutrients, but it also makes phytoplankton easy prey for planktonic animals. The consequence of naturally scarce nutrients and intensive grazing is that the biomass of phytoplankton is, typically, much less than that of land plants. Adding human-generated nutrients can increase this biomass to a level that perturbs aquatic ecosystems.

Under natural conditions, nutrient salts derive mainly from the breakdown – called **remineralisation** – of organic matter that was made by an earlier generation of plants. Other natural sources include the chemical breakdown of some rocks, releasing phosphate into rivers; and the capture – called **nitrogen fixation** – of dissolved nitrogen gas, N_2, by certain bacteria. These bacteria use the nitrogen in organic matter which subsequently mineralises.

Clearly, the remineralisation of organic matter made from previously existing phosphate or nitrate does not add any extra nutrient to the world's total. Nitrogen fixation, and the release of phosphate from rocks, does increase the total; but these processes are offset by denitrification and the permanent burial of organic matter. **Denitrification** takes place mostly in the beds of lakes, estuaries and coastal seas where decay has used up all the oxygen, and bacteria convert nitrate to N_2. In ways not yet fully understood, these natural processes regulate the gains and losses so that they balance at a low concentration of nutrients in natural waters.

And the consequence is that phytoplankton are often prevented from growing due to a lack of nutrients. So when humans deliver extra nutrients into the sea, the plants react (Box 9.2). They take up the nitrates or phosphates. They grow. They divide. They produce oxygen (a good thing). But then they decay, consuming oxygen (a bad thing, especially if the oxygen they made earlier is no longer around). Their decay puts mineral nutrients back in the water, fuelling another cycle of growth and decay – until the extra nutrients are removed by natural processes.

Box 9.2 Eutrophication FAQs (frequently asked questions)

What are 'nutrients'?
They are substances that plants need for growth, the most important being inorganic compounds of nitrogen and phosphorus usually found ionised when dissolved in water, hence as ammonium (NH_4^+), nitrate (NO_3^-) or phosphate (PO_4^{3-}).

What kind of plants?
All kinds – that's why gardeners and farmers use fertilisers to provide extra nitrogen and phosphorus for cultivated plants. In lakes and the sea, however, the main plants are the microscopic algae and photosynthetic bacteria of the **phytoplankton**. Many of these tiny floating green, cyan, yellow or brown organisms are single cells, reproducing by division into two.

Where do nutrients come from?
Their main natural source is the breakdown of organic material, but compounds of nitrogen are formed from nitrogen gas by lightning, and erosion of some rocks releases phosphate. Although most plants cannot use N_2, some bacteria can: they are called 'nitrogen-fixers'. Humans have increased inputs of nitrogen and phosphorus to the bio-sphere by manufacturing fertilisers, cultivating plants which carry symbiotic nitrogen-fixers, and through acid rain. Drainage from lowland farming, and the waste water produced by the concentration of people and industries into cities, contain large quantities of such **anthropogenic** nutrients.

▶

Box 9.2 (continued)

Does adding nutrients to the sea cause eutrophication?

Not necessarily. Tidal or other currents can carry nutrients away as quickly as they arrive. Even if the concentration of nutrients does rise to a level denoting **hypernutrification**, lack of light may retard the growth of phytoplankton, or the plants may be eaten by animal members of the plankton, or by animals (such as mussels) living on the seabed.

Lack of light?

In winter, for example. Or the sea could be turbid, full of suspended particles which absorb light. Turbidity is often the result of turbulence – stirring by waves or tidal currents, which pick up silt and clay from the seabed.

So marine eutrophication is a myth?

No, adding plant nutrients to clear coastal waters in summer does stimulate the growth of phytoplankton (and sometimes, also, the green seaweeds that festoon leaking intertidal sewage pipes). Worse, the mixture of nutrients in sewage, and other human wastes, is often different from the natural mixture, and so encourages unusual types of phytoplankton, which may be toxic.

Tell me more

There is another nutrient element I did not mention: silicon, found in seawater as dissolved silica – the mineral opal, a kind of glass.

And?

Silica (also called silicate) is needed by a type of phytoplankton called **diatoms**, which use it to strengthen the walls of their cells. Diatoms are the good guys of the phytoplankton; they provide food for planktonic animals and rarely harm anyone. But human waste contains little dissolved silica, and when the diatoms have used up the natural supply they stop growing. When conditions are hypernutrified, this leaves a lot of nitrate and phosphate for use by the bad guys. Amongst these are species of **dinoflagellates** and **flagellates** which contain toxins. The job of the poisons is to discourage planktonic animals from eating the dinoflagellates – which can then increase in numbers until they give rise to a **Red Tide**.

And this is a bad thing?

Sometimes. The toxins have been known to kill farmed fish, or to be harvested by shellfish which then become poisonous to humans. When the organisms of the Red Tide die, their decomposition can use up all the oxygen dissolved in seawater, resulting in further deaths – for example, of seabed animals.

I see.

Eutrophication is a *chain* of cause and effect; the *effect* of each link may (but need not) become the *cause* of the next.

So much phytoplankton can be produced that the sea turns red or brown (a Red Tide). Decaying products of Red Tides, carried ashore, can render beaches unusable by holidaymakers. Worse, some species of plants may be better fitted than others to make use of these human-supplied nutrients. Natural increases in phytoplankton growth usually consist of organisms that make good food for planktonic animals, so the increases, or **blooms**, are rapidly grazed. But if the nutrient balance is 'wrong', toxic species can grow which are unpleasant to grazers, and potentially poisonous to humans or to the fish or shellfish we farm.

It is these effects, and the excessive consumption of oxygen that can follow a bloom, that makes **anthropogenic** – human-caused – eutrophication a potential hazard to natural ecosystems and to human society. Nutrient enrichment can be beneficial: for example, eutrophication may have provided more food for young brown shrimp in Dutch coastal waters, resulting in a better shrimp fishery (Boddeke 1996). Nevertheless, ecologists cannot reliably predict the outcome of enrichment, and so it is thought wise to try to avoid it.

In the preceding sentence, 'it' could mean 'enrichment' or 'outcome'. Those who draw the first meaning would want always to avoid adding extra nutrients to the sea. Indeed, the original concerns about marine eutrophication followed from the assumption that added nutrients always resulted in extra biomass and harmful consequences. These concerns were not unwarranted. The case of Lake Washington demonstrated that increasing phosphorus input led to eutrophication, and studies in Canada (Schindler 1977) and elsewhere have found a strong link between the amount of phytoplankton and the amount of phosphorus in a lake.

However, the sea is not just a large lake with added salt. Phosphorus is the element that most commonly limits plant growth in fresh waters. In the sea, it is more often nitrogen. The beds of estuaries and coastal seas provide good conditions for bacterial denitrification. Compared with lakes, coastal seas tend to be more *dispersive* (because of tidal and other currents), more *turbulent* (because of eddies generated by tidal currents and stronger winds), and more *turbid* (because of light-absorbing particles lifted from the seabed by currents). The consequence is that some coastal waters can receive large doses of human-waste nutrients without becoming excessively nutrient-enriched. And even when nutrient concentrations reach high levels, the extra nutrients are converted into biomass only if there is sufficient light for phytoplankton growth, and only if what grows is not eaten or flushed away.

So the conclusion is that we need to avoid the harmful outcomes of enrichment, rather than enrichment itself. Given the present organisation of society and the concentrations of large numbers of people (and their work) in cities, it is no longer feasible to recycle waste locally. Aquatic, especially marine, environments can safely handle a certain amount of organic waste and inorganic nutrients. Sewage treatment is expensive, and has environmental as well as economic costs. Sometimes it makes sense to let the waters take the shit.

9.3 Sewage disposal in the sea

A few years ago it was common for untreated sewage to be discharged into the sea around Britain from short pipes, producing what was politely called 'an aesthetic problem'. **Primary treatment** of waste water solves this problem by removing the large lumps (which have then to be buried or burnt). The effluent from primary treatment contains many small organic particles and also much dissolved organic matter. The organic particles can, potentially, smother seabed animals, and their microbial-driven decay, together with mineralisation of the dissolved organic matter, consumes the oxygen dissolved in water. The potential for this consumption is routinely measured during water quality surveys and is called **Biological Oxygen Demand** (BOD). In lakes, slow-flowing rivers and poorly flushed coastal waters, addition of even small amounts of BOD can result in complete deoxygenation of water or bed, killing most animals and releasing harmful gases such as methane and hydrogen sulphide. This is why the UWWTD calls for removal of most BOD in a **secondary treatment** as a standard procedure.

Rapid-flowing rivers and tidally flushed coastal seas, however, can deal with more BOD. They disperse it over a wider area, and their turbulence stirs in more air, maintaining higher oxygen levels. Most secondary sewage treatment plants rely on microbial action to remove BOD. Either they cover a wide area, or they use a large amount of energy in stirring air or oxygen into tanks of sewage. Furthermore, they produce a **sewage sludge**, which must be disposed of. There is, therefore, a good case for using natural microbial processes to do for free what would otherwise be carried out expensively in treatment plants, so long as the receiving water has the capacity to handle the BOD discharge. This is the justification for allowing waste water to receive only primary treatment before discharge into waters able to absorb a high biological oxygen demand safely.

Secondary treatment removes little of the nitrogen and phosphorus from urban waste water. The remineralisation of sewage organics that takes place artificially in a treatment plant, or naturally in rivers or the sea, converts organic forms of nitrogen and phosphorus into dissolved nitrate and phosphate, adding to those already present in sewage. Eutrophication is, thus, the remaining hazard of waste water discharge. Where receiving waters are already eutrophic, or are thought likely to become eutrophic, the discharge may need what the UWWTD calls 'more stringent' treatment: the removal of nutrient elements.

223

9.4 Predicting eutrophication

The Urban Waste Water Treatment Directive definition of eutrophication does not provide an unambiguous yardstick with which to measure nutrient impact. Chlorophyll is the green pigment contained in all phytoplankton (Box 9.3). The UK's Comprehensive Studies Task Team therefore laid down the **operational definition** that a water body is eutrophic if, in summer, its **chlorophyll** concentration regularly exceeds a **Water Quality Standard** (WQS) of 10 milligrams per cubic metre (CSTT 1994).

Given this standard, it is in principle simple to decide if an estuary or coastal sea is eutrophic by measuring its chlorophyll content. However, the amount of phytoplankton in the sea is highly variable, even when nutrients are plentiful. So it would, in many cases, be necessary to make numerous observations during several years in order to see if the WQS were regularly exceeded. The CSTT therefore thought it useful to provide a simple procedure for deciding if a water body were potentially eutrophic. The procedure, derived from work by Gowen et al. (1992), requires a minimum of measurements, and can be applied either to existing inputs or to take account of a proposed new discharge of waste water. It includes a sequence of calculations which make up a **mathematical model**, and which I will call the 'CSTT model'.

The CSTT procedure answers four questions about the effects of a discharge:

- How much will the receiving-water concentration of nutrients increase as a result of the discharge, given the rate at which these waters exchange with the surrounding waters?
- If all the extra nutrients were used by phytoplankton, would the resulting concentration of chlorophyll exceed the WQS of 10 mg m^{-3}?
- Can phytoplankton in fact use these nutrients (that is, might the receiving water be too turbid to allow plant growth, or diluted too fast to sustain an increase in the abundance of plankton)?
- Would any of these answers be much different if the discharge received primary rather than secondary or more stringent treatment?

The model is shown diagrammatically in Figure 9.2. Box 9.4 illustrates its application to a case based on the Inverness Firth in north-eastern Scotland. The conclusion is that this Firth is not eutrophic, and will not be made eutrophic by receiving the waste water from a population of 150 000, even if this waste receives only primary treatment. The main reason for this happy state of affairs is that water in the Inverness Firth exchanges freely with the waters of the adjacent North Sea, which thus dilutes the sewage nutrients. It is also fortunate that the Firth's rivers drain mountainous regions which are poor in nutrients. In contrast, the model has predicted substantial nutrient enrichment in cases where coastal waters receive rivers draining fertilised farmland.

Box 9.3 Chlorophyll

Phytoplankton consist of many species, mostly very small. Estimating phytoplankton abundance by microscopy is time-consuming. For practical purposes it often suffices to measure the amount of **chlorophyll** contained in a given volume of seawater. This can be done by (i) passing a water sample through a glass-fibre filter, which retains the phytoplankton, (ii) placing the filter in an organic solvent so that the photosynthetic pigments, including chlorophyll, dissolve, and (iii) measuring the concentration of the chlorophyll in the extract using a spectrophotometer.

In fact, such extracts contain a number of pigments: not only **chlorophyll a**, the central agent of photosynthesis, but also accessory pigments including chlorophyllide c and carotenoids, and breakdown products called pheopigments. Studies requiring exact concentrations of chlorophyll a would introduce an extra step between (ii) and (iii), in which pigments would be separated by High Performance Liquid Chromatography (HPLC). When this is done, it is found that chlorophyll a is typically between 40% and 80% of that which is measured by the routine methods. I have, therefore, chosen to use the imprecise term 'chlorophyll' for the results of routine measurement. These measurements are quick and well suited for routine monitoring.

The CSTT thus decided to recommend chlorophyll concentration as a measure of phytoplankton abundance. Although it is an index of biomass rather than of growth, and although the CEC definition of eutrophication refers to 'accelerated growth', we further decided to set a chlorophyll **Water Quality Standard** (WQS) for eutrophication. This recognised that (a) chlorophyll is the key part of the photosynthetic mechanism, so indicates the potential for producing new biomass (which we took as the key aspect of growth), and (b) neither growth rate nor production of phytoplankton is easily measured routinely.

In deciding on a WQS of 10 mg chlorophyll m^{-3} during summer as the threshold for eutrophication, we had in mind that this concentration of chlorophyll is sufficient to cause a visible discolouration of the sea. Some UK coastal waters regularly exhibit chlorophyll concentrations in excess of 10 mg m^{-3} during the spring, the period of the Spring Bloom, without stimulation by anthropogenic nutrients. However, seasonally increasing populations of planktonic animals commonly graze down the Spring Bloom, and under normal circumstances the concentration of chlorophyll during the summer should be much less than 10 mg m^{-3}. Anthropogenic hypernutrification might allow summer phytoplankton to make a growth spurt ahead of the grazers, or it might result in a change in the balance of phytoplankton species, favouring forms which were not grazed. In either case the regular occurrence of high biomass in summer would indicate a disturbance of natural conditions.

The effect of phytoplankton pigments on the colour of the sea can be measured remotely, by 'ocean colour sensors' in aircraft or earth-orbiting satellites. Although there are some difficulties in relating the colour change to the amount of chlorophyll, remote sensing is likely to be used increasingly for detecting eutrophication.

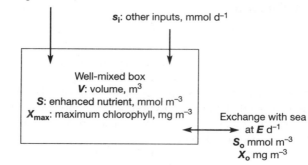

1. obtain data
2. calculate equilibrium enhanced nutrient $S = S_o + (s_i + s_d)/(E.V)$
3. calculate maximum chlorophyll $X_{max} = X_o + q.S$
4. calculate phytoplankton light-controlled growth rate: $\mu = \alpha.(I - I_c)$
5. **eutrophic** if $X_{max} > 10$ mg m^{-3} and $\mu > L + E$

Figure 9.2 Principles of the CSTT model for predicting eutrophication. The 'receiving waters' of a waste water discharge are treated as a box. The exchange rate, E, is the volume of new seawater which daily displaces water from the box, divided by the volume of the box, d = day; q = yield of chlorophyll from nutrient.

Box 9.4 An example application of the CSTT model

The model of steps 1 to 4 is that given in the report by the UK Comprehensive Studies Task Team (CSTT 1994), but the decision making procedure of steps 5 and 6 has been expanded to take account of Article 5, as well as Article 6, of the Urban Waste Water Treatment Directive (UWWTD). The example has been simplified from a study of the Inverness Firth, a coastal water in north-east Scotland. The contents of the Firth are treated as if they were the well-mixed contents of a box.

Step 1. Obtain data.

V: volume of the Inverness Firth at midtide:	450 million cubic metres
E: dilution rate, obtained from physical measurements:	0.1 litre per day
I: light for photosynthesis, averaged over depth and summer month:	50 micromoles of photons per square metre per second
S_0: summer concentration of nitrate in sea:	1.0 micromolar
X_0: summer concentration of chlorophyll in sea:	1.0 milligram per cubic metre;
s_i: daily input of nitrate from rivers Ness and Beauly:	79 kilomole per day
l: local loss rate of phytoplankton, unknown so assume:	0.0 per day

Box 9.4 (continued)

Step 2. Calculate the maximum nitrate concentration in the absence of urban waste water.

$$S_m = S_o + s_i/(E.V) = 1.0 + 79/(0.11 \times 450) = 2.6 \text{ micromolar nitrate}$$

Step 3. Calculate the potential maximum concentration of chlorophyll assuming all nitrate is converted to phytoplankton at yield q of 1.1 grams of chlorophyll per mole of nitrate.

$$X_m = X_o + q.S_m = 1.0 + 1.1 \times 2.6$$
$$= 3.9 \text{ milligrams chlorophyll per cubic metre}$$

Step 4. Compute light-controlled phytoplankton growth rate, taking photosynthetic efficiency α as being 0.015 per day per unit of light and the minimum light level I_c for growth as 12 micromole of photons per square metre per second.

$$\mu\,(I) = \alpha.(I - I_c) = 0.015 \text{ x } (50 - 12) = 0.57 \text{ per day}$$

Step 5. Ask some questions.

$\mu > E + l$: does the light-controlled growth rate exceed losses?

No: phytoplankton can't use nutrients, so only primary treatment is necessary;

Yes: true in this case (0.57 > (0.13 + 0.0)) so continue.

X_m > WQS for eutrophic conditions: does the maximum predicted amount of phytoplankton exceed 10 milligrams of chlorophyll per cubic metre?

Yes: receiving water is potentially eutrophic, so more stringent treatment is needed;

No: water is not eutrophic. True in this case (3.9 < 10) so continue.

Step 6. Repeat steps 2–3, taking into account waste water with various treatments. The waste water comes from a population of 150 000. The effects of three treatment levels are given (but should not be taken as definitive).

Treatment	Primary	Secondary	More stringent	Units
daily waste water nitrate input s_d	68	61	18	kilomoles per day
S_m	4.0	3.8	3.0	micromolar
X_m	5.4	5.2	4.3	mg chlorophyll m^{-3}

Conclusion. Even with only primary treatment of waste water, the example will not become eutrophic. Secondary treatment provides little extra benefit, and so primary treatment would be allowed under Article 6 of the UWWTD, subject to continued monitoring.

227

Because the CSTT model was designed for use as part of a national procedure to protect the marine environment, it had to be reliable. In our view this meant it had to be both *safe* and *simple* to use. Related to the issues of safety and simplicity are two further matters. The first concerns the scientific knowledge that the model employs. The second concerns the difference between the way this knowledge was obtained and the way it should be employed in a safe model. So I want to continue by comparing the CSTT model with a model used in scientific research. The gist of the comparison is that research models are not intended to be safe. Their purpose is to fail in an instructional way, because science advances by refuting hypotheses.

9.5 A research model

The research model is a modification of the first-ever mathematical model for marine phytoplankton (Riley 1946), and is pictured in Figure 9.3. Like the CSTT model, this 'Riley+' model deals with the content of a box, in this case the **Surface Mixed Layer** (SML) of the ocean. The model is for-

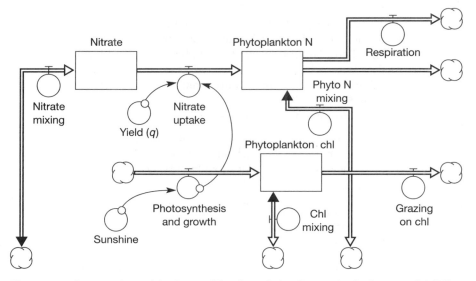

Figure 9.3 A research model: the modification of the first–ever plankton model (Riley 1946), known as Riley+ and used by Tett and Wilson (2000), drawn according to the conventions of the Stella™ modelling software. The rectangles show stocks of chlorophyll (chl) or nitrogen (N), and the thick arrows show flows. The clouds denote a source or a sink of material outside the model. Circles control flows: note, in particular, the circle representing the yield, q, of chlorophyll from nitrate. Riley+ divides the amount of newly produced phytoplankton by the value of q to compute how much nitrate has been used, whereas the CSTT model multiplies the supply of nutrient by the value of q to predict the amount of phytoplankton that could be made if all nutrient were used.

mally defined by equations which describe how the following will change with time:

- the amount of phytoplankton chlorophyll, which is assumed to increase in proportion to biomass as a result of photosynthesis, and to decrease because of respiration and grazing;
- the amount of organic nitrogen in phytoplankton, which increases because of uptake of nitrate from seawater and decreases because of grazing;
- the amount of nitrate dissolved in seawater, which decreases as it is absorbed by phytoplankton: when all the nitrate is used, the growth of phytoplankton is halted.

Each of these quantities is, in modelling jargon, a **state variable**: Riley+ is thus a model with three state variables. Everything else contained within the equations of the model is either a **parameter** or a **forcing variable**. Parameters are numbers that have a constant value during any one set of calculations made with the model. An example that we shall meet again has the symbol q: this stands for the **yield of chlorophyll from nutrient**, the amount of chlorophyll that is made by phytoplankton after intake of a unit of nitrate. An example of a forcing variable is sunshine. Model calculations require a value for sunshine on the day for which predictions are to be made. In the case of the application of the CSTT model in Box 9.4, it was necessary only to supply a typical value of sunshine on a summer's day in Scotland, whereas in the case of calculations with Riley+ it is necessary to supply a different value for each day of the year.

Figure 9.4 shows results obtained with Riley+, and two other models, for the North-East Atlantic Ocean, where the surface mixed layer is 300 metres deep in winter and 30 metres deep in summer. The continuous lines are values obtained for each day with the aid of a computer program that used the model equations to predict tomorrow's phytoplankton and nitrate from today's, taking into account today's sunshine and mixed layer thickness. In fact, 'predict' is not quite the right word, since the calculations were made with the intent of imitating, or **simulating**, data that already existed. Figure 9.4 shows **numerical simulations** that may be compared with the observed concentrations of phytoplankton chlorophyll and dissolved nitrate.

At first glance, the model results look good: they show a **spring phytoplankton bloom**, ended by nutrient depletion; a seasonal cycle typical of temperate oceans. But a critic would say that many of the observations, shown by black squares, do not lie on the lines representing the simulations. So, how can we know if the Riley+ model's predictions are correct? Alternatively, following Popper's method (see p. 5) what might tell us to reject a model?

A standard method is to assess the **goodness of fit** of a numerical simulation (hence, of a model) to a set of observations, by calculating the **Sum Of Squared Differences** (SOSD) for the results in Figure 9.4. The SOSD is

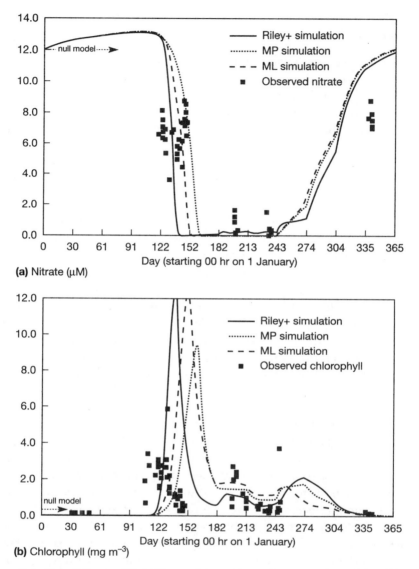

Figure 9.4 Use of the modified Riley model, and two other research models of Tett and Wilson (2000) to simulate seasonal cycles of (a) dissolved nitrate, and (b) phytoplankton chlorophyll, in the N.E. Atlantic, west of Scotland. Black squares show Surface Mixed Layer (SML) mean concentrations obtained by sampling during 6 cruises, each of 2–4 weeks, during 1995 and 1996, and the lines show the results of simulations with three models 'forced' by sunshine (described by a sine wave with period 1 year) and the thickness of the SML taken from the 1994 *World Ocean Atlas* of the US National Oceanographic Data centre.

the total, for all observations, of the squares of the differences between the actual concentrations and the concentrations simulated by the model. The SOSD enables the performance of the Riley+ model to be compared with two other models, which employ more complicated descriptions of plankton biology. It turns out that, in this case, the other models 'fit' better: their predictions differ less from the observations and so have a smaller SOSD. In addition the SOSD arising from a particular model can be compared with that due to a **null model**. This second type of comparison gives an absolute measure of the goodness of fit of a simulation to observations. And the news is bad. The predictions of the Riley+ model are worse than the null model's assumption that the concentrations of chlorophyll and nitrate, used to start the calculation sequence, do not change during the simulated year.

One interpretation of Popper's method would require us to abandon the Riley+ model. However, this is too strict. It may be this particular simulation which is no good. Changing some of the values of parameters such as the chlorophyll yield, q, might result in a new simulation which agrees better with the observations. Alternatively, it may be that the model's science is wrong.

9.6 Simplicity

Whilst writing this chapter, I alternated between using a word processor and a high power microscope. It was spring bloom time, and the microscope showed me chains of diatoms: capsular cells of *Skeletonema costatum*, joined like the coaches of a subway train; skewered discs of *Thalassiosira rotula*. Moving about the brightly lit circle of the field of view were **protozoa** – unicellular planktonic animals: cells of a species of *Strobilidium* looking like a cross between an ice-cream cone and a shaving brush and darting like a humming bird; the gracefully gyrating pointed ovoid of a species of *Gyrodinium*. Both protozoa contained remains of the *Skeletonema* cells that they had eaten. So the biology of the real phytoplankton, and of the pelagic bacteria and protozoa intimately associated with them, is much more complicated than that represented in the CSTT or Riley+ models, and this may explain why Riley+ simulations do not correspond well to observations. Is the solution to the failure of Riley+ to make a more complicated and therefore more realistic model?

Not necessarily. More complicated models have more parameters, for which accurate values must be found. Simulations with a complicated model using imprecise parameter values will quite likely be more inaccurate than simulations with a simple model using a few well known values. Of course, it is possible to keep adjusting the parameter values of a complicated model until its simulation is in good agreement with a set of observations – and, used in this way, a complicated model will almost always agree better than a simulation made by a simple model. But the adjustment must be carried out for each location that the model is to mimic, a time-consuming and expensive process.

Another aspect of simplicity concerns the physical space represented in the model. In Riley+ this space is the mixed surface layer of the ocean, and simulations take no account of spatial variability. Similarly, the CSTT model views the receiving waters as a single well-mixed region. Complex patterns of water movement, which replace parts of the receiving waters by unpolluted sea water, are summarised by a single number, called the exchange rate. Sophisticated models would describe water movements more exactly, by means of calculations carried out for each mesh of a net of points laid (metaphorically) over the receiving waters. Such models are available. In skilled hands they are reliable and can be used in impact studies to estimate the exchange rate.

'State of the art' models link exact simulations of water movement with detailed descriptions of biological processes. Some environmental scientists think that we should use these models in order to predict the impact of anthropogenic nutrients in coastal waters. I don't agree. Even our best biological models seem insufficiently reliable for prediction: they are designed as research tools and thus intended, if not for heroic defeat in their confrontation with reality, at least as the basis for further tinkering. Furthermore, the complicated models have many parameters for which values must be supplied but which are not well known.

The Comprehensive Studies Task Team, therefore, opted for simplicity. We tried to identify the essential features of the eutrophication process, and to include these, and only these, in the eutrophication prediction model. Descriptions of most of these features exist in the Riley+ model, but Riley+ is **dynamic**: it deals with variability in time. The CSTT model jettisons time by considering only the worst case.

For example, the nitrate equation in Riley+ predicts changes in this nutrient as a result of removal by phytoplankton and re-supply by mixing across the bottom of the ocean's surface layer. The CSTT model describes a mixed box receiving a nitrate-rich discharge of waste water and perhaps also of river water. In typical applications of the model, exchange with nutrient-poor sea water removes nitrate. Suppose there to be no phytoplankton, and a starting condition in which the box is filled with sea-water. Then the discharge begins. At first, nitrate concentration increases; but, as this happens, so more nitrate is lost by exchange. After a while, a state is reached in which the exchange loss exactly balances the rate of supply of nitrate by waste water and river discharge. This is the greatest nitrate concentration that can possibly occur, and its value, and the amount of phytoplankton it can engender, is all that concerns the CSTT model.

9.7 Safety

The safety of the CSTT scheme stems in part from the scheme's simplicity, which reduces the danger of making mistakes in calculations. In contrast, the calculations necessary for simulations using dynamic models are, typically, hidden from view because they are made by complicated computer programs. Although computers compute reliably, their programs are prone to 'bugs' – programming mistakes of various kinds. It is very difficult to eliminate all such 'bugs', especially those resulting from bad translation of a model's equations into program statements.

The other, and more fundamental, contribution to safety in the CSTT model comes from the use of the **precautionary principle**. The worst outcome of nutrient enrichment is when the added nutrient is completely used to make extra phytoplankton. If this worst case is not bad, because it is less than the WQS of 10 milligrams of chlorophyll per cubic metre, or if it will not happen because phytoplankton growth is prevented by high turbidity, then there is nothing to worry about.

Whereas the Riley+ and other models try to predict, accurately, the actual amount of phytoplankton likely to occur in a given circumstance, the CSTT model aims only to predict the maximum amount. Returning to Figure 9.4, it might be said that someone using the CSTT protocol is only interested in knowing the size of the bloom's peak. They don't care *when* the bloom occurs, or about the pattern of growth that precedes the maximum, matters that are crucial in considering the success of the Riley+ model.

Both the CSTT and Riley+ models are said to be **sensitive** to chlorophyll yield, q, because changing its value can lead to quite different predictions. In the case of the CSTT procedure, using a low value would result in few cases in which potential eutrophication was predicted. Someone concerned purely about protecting the marine environment might argue that the values chosen for yield should be the maximum known to occur. A spokesperson for the sewage disposal industry could counter-argue that a typical value should be used, as using a maximum value would lead to the requirement to install secondary, or even more stringent, treatment when it was, in fact, not needed – with consequent higher charges to city residents, and extra land and energy costs in providing the treatment and disposing of the extra solid waste that results.

The CSTT might have required local measurement of the yield, just as it did for exchange. However, this would have demanded skills, experience and equipment unlikely to be available in most environmental impact assessment studies. Furthermore, many measurements would be needed to provide an appropriate maximum value for use with the CSTT protocol, and there might be a bias towards selecting particularly high or low values of this maximum depending on the customer for the results. The CSTT therefore concluded that it should lay down standard values for the biological parameters. Box 9.5 shows how these values were obtained for the chlorophyll yield.

The reader will see that there is a range of values of q, and might expect the model to use the largest value in order to predict the worst outcome. However, circumstances in which all nitrate is converted to phytoplankton

---

Box 9.5 Chlorophyll yield

The results of the CSTT model depend, especially, on the values used for q, the **yield** of chlorophyll from **DAIN**. DAIN is **Dissolved Available Inorganic Nitrogen** – the compounds of nitrogen, especially in the forms of the ions nitrate and ammonium, that are found in, or added to, seawater, and which are available for assimilation by phytoplankton. For simplicity the text refers to nitrate instead of DAIN.

Although many studies have shown a strong relationship between the amounts of phosphorus and chlorophyll in lakes (Schindler 1977), the relationship between nitrogen and chlorophyll in the sea is by no means as easy to demonstrate (Hecky and Kilham 1988)

The CSTT used the results of Gowen et al. (1992), who examined 60 sets of chlorophyll and nitrate concentrations measured during research cruises in the fjordic waters of western Scotland. In 38 of these sets, there was a significant negative correlation between the two variables: high values of chlorophyll corresponded to low concentrations of nitrate. Gowen et al. argued that this was the result of phytoplankton growth after assimilation of nitrate, and hence that the slope of a graph of chlorophyll against nitrate was an estimate of the yield of chlorophyll from nitrate. Their estimates of the yield were between 0.12 and 5.4 g chl (mol N)$^{-1}$. As summarised by CSTT (1994), the **median** value was 1.1 g chl (mol N)$^{-1}$, and 90% of the values were less than or equal to 2.8 g chl (mol N)$^{-1}$. The '90th percentile' value serves as an estimate of the 'true' maximum, because the actual greatest value is likely to be too high due to addition of errors.

The CSTT recommended the median for use in routine assessment of eutrophication, and the '90th percentile' as a maximum value for use in cases where there might be a particular risk from blooms. Such a case might be a water body containing fish farms, where the farmed fish take several years to reach maturity but could be killed quickly by one short-lived toxic bloom.

---

are, generally speaking, few even in potentially eutrophic waters. Factors such as dilution or predation militate against complete conversion. In most cases, a very occasional and short-lived non-eutrophic bloom is unlikely to have serious consequences. Hence a rare failure of the CSTT model is tolerable, and so the team recommended the use, in normal conditions, of a typical rather than a maximum yield.

Exceptions, however, are cases in which farmed fish might be killed by such a short-lived bloom. Because fish take several years to rear to a marketable size, the acceptable risk for a fish farmer is lower than in the general case, and so it might be wise to use the higher value of yield in these special cases. I might add that in such cases, the fish farm is often the main source of anthropogenic nutrients as well as the most likely sufferer from the effects of eutrophication.

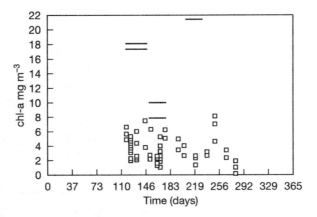

Figure 9.5 A test of the CSTT model with data from Kirkcaldy Bay in the Firth of Forth, Scotland. Points show chlorophyll concentrations measured in 1991–1993. Lines show maximum chlorophyll concentrations predicted by the CSTT model according to two sets of values of nitrate concentration in sea water supplying Kirkcaldy Bay.

From the MSc thesis of Fernando Pérez Castillo (*Screening for 'less sensitive areas' using an eutrophication model*, 1994, University of Wales, Bangor).

Figure 9.5 shows a test of the CSTT model for part of the Firth of Forth in Scotland. The crucial point, for the test, is that observed concentrations of chlorophyll are all *less than* those calculated by the model – as is required for a tool capable of worst-case predictions.

9.8 Discussion

The Council of the European Communities made the Urban Waste Water Treatment Directive, but it is left to member states to oversee implementation. Like the governments of other states, that of the UK had to provide 'all relevant information' about Comprehensive Studies to Brussels in order to make use of the Article 6 derogation in favour of primary treatment. In Britain, individual discharges are controlled by regional public bodies such as the Scottish Environmental Protection Agency, who give 'Consents to Discharge' in response to satisfactory applications by private or public companies. Despite what might be thought, these companies often prefer to build plant with a high level of treatment, in the interests of a wholesome public image and because they can pass the costs on to their customers. Although they are, on the whole, monopoly suppliers of sewage services, a UK public body called OFWAT regulates water and sewerage prices, and can require a waste water company to explore cheaper treatment options in order to protect the customers. And, while 'Surfers against Sewage' press for more treatment of waste water, there is a counter pressure to minimise the area and activity of treatment works from citizens who don't want these works in their backyards.

As an academic scientist I tend to shrug my shoulders at these interactions and concentrate, instead, on the complexity of the system called the 'plankton'. Asked to suggest a simple means for measuring the amount of plankton, or a simple method for predicting its abundance, I would say 'well ... it's complicated ... you would need to take samples with tow-nets and water-bottles, and examine them under a microscope, and identify the most important species, and count them ... and as for modelling ... I use it more as a research tool, to identify my areas of ignorance, than for prediction.'

However, as the Chair of the CSTT pointed out, if we, relatively unbiased, experts failed to come up with a usable scheme for predicting eutrophication (and carrying out other aspects of 'Comprehensive Studies'), we would allow the ball to pass to those who were, conceivably, less expert or more biased. So the job involved ceasing to use science as a method, and instead treating it as a body of knowledge to be applied with the aid of the precautionary principle. But the principle had be used with precision. Unless we wanted to bring about universal secondary treatment of waste water, we had to devise a scheme which did not predict eutrophication for all receiving waters. On the other hand, a scheme that failed to predict potentially harmful algal blooms would fail the requirement to protect the environment and would destroy our credibility as experts.

The CSTT scheme was first published in 1994. Later that year I gave an account of the box model approach at an international meeting in Canada. Some of the scientists and marine resource managers in my audience told me that the simple approach seemed right. Others argued for 'state-of-the-art' models, that would take account of uncertainties by including error predictions in the model output. I have tried, in this chapter, to explain why the CSTT chose a simple model. And, finally, making enquiries as I wrote this chapter in spring 1999, I found that few UK waste water treatment companies still wanted to make use of the derogation provided by Article 6 of the UWWTD. Most new plant is being designed to apply (at least) secondary treatment. The precise utility of the CSTT scheme, which was to help identify 'less sensitive' waters, has, therefore, largely ended. Nevertheless, the use of models in environmental management, which I have illustrated with an account of the CSTT scheme, remains an important and controversial issue.

9.9 Summary

- Eutrophication results from the enrichment of water by plant nutrients, and is excess growth of phytoplankton that causes changes in the balance of organisms and a decrease in water quality.

- In order to satisfy the requirements of the EU's Urban Waste Water Treatment Directive, the UK established a Comprehensive Studies Task Team to provide a eutrophication-predicting methodology for use in identifying 'less sensitive' waters.
- The CSTT chose to recommend a simple model, based on the precautionary principle approach of worst-case conversion of added nutrient into phytoplankton, rather than more complicated models which are designed for research use and thus likely, and perhaps intended, to fail.

Further reading

Jorgensen, B.B. and Richardson, K. (eds) (1996) *Eutrophication in Coastal Marine Ecosystems*. Coastal and Estuarine Studies, vol. 52. American Geophysical Union, Washington DC. A comprehensive introduction to coastal eutrophication.

Rykiel, E.J. (1996) Testing ecological models: the meaning of validation. *Ecological Modelling*, **90**, 229–44. A look at the problem of how complicated models can be tested.

Want to try some modelling yourself? Search the High Performance Systems Inc site at www.hps-inc.com for details of the Stella software.

References

Boddeke, R. (1996) Changes in the brown shrimp (*Crangon crangon* L) population off the Dutch coast in relation to fisheries and phosphate discharge. *ICES Journal of Marine Science*, **53**, 995–1002.

CSTT (1994) Comprehensive studies for the purposes of Article 6 of DIR 91/271 EEC, the Urban Waste Water Treatment Directive. Report published for the Comprehensive Studies Task Team of Group Coordinating Sea Disposal Monitoring by the Forth River Purification Board, Edinburgh, Scotland.

Edmondson, W.T. (1961) Changes in Lake Washington following an increase in nutrient income. *Proceedings of the International Association for Theoretical and Applied Limnology*, **16**, 153–8.

Edmondson, W.T., and Lehman, J.T. (1981) The effect of changes in the nutrient income on the condition of Lake Washington. *Limnology and Oceanography*, **26**, 1–29.

Gowen, R.J., Tett, P. and Jones, K.J. (1992) Predicting marine eutrophication: the yield of chlorophyll from nitrogen in Scottish coastal phytoplankton. *Marine Ecology – Progress Series*, **85**, 153–161.

Hecky, R.E. and Kilham, P. (1988) Nutrient limitation of phytoplankton in freshwater and marine environments: a review of recent evidence on the effects of enrichment. *Limnology and Oceanography*, **33**, 796–822.

Lancelot, C., Billen, G., Sournia, A., Weisse, T., Colijn, F., Veldhuis, M.J.W., Davies, A. and Wassman, P. (1987) *Phaeocystis* blooms and nutrient enrichment in the continental coastal zones of the North Sea. *Ambio*, **16**, 38–46.

Lund, J.W.G. (1972) Eutrophication. *Proceedings of the Royal Society of London*, B **180**, 371–82.

Prakash, A. (1987) Coastal organic pollution as a contributing factor to red-tide development. *Rapport et Procès-verbaux des Réunions, Conseil international pour l'Exploration de la Mer*, **187**, 61–5.

Riley, G.A. (1946) Factors controlling phytoplankton populations on Georges Bank. *Journal of Marine Research*, **6**, 54–73.

Rodhe, W. (1969) *Crystallization of Eutrophication Concepts in Northern Europe*, National Academy of Sciences, Washington DC, pp. 50–64.

Schindler, D.W. (1977) Evolution of phosphorus limitation in lakes. *Science*, **195**, 260–2.

Tett, P. and Wilson, H. (2000) From biogeochemical to ecological models of marine pelagic systems. *Journal of Marine Systems*, in press.

Chapter 10

Radiation protection: science and value

David Sumner

Editors' introduction

The nuclear industry had its origins in the Second World War, in the Manhattan project to make atomic bombs; bombs which were eventually dropped on the cities of Hiroshima and Nagasaki in 1945. The Nagasaki bomb was made of plutonium, and it was plutonium that turned out to be the best material for nuclear weapons. The manufacture of plutonium requires the complex technology of reprocessing the fuel rods which are removed from nuclear reactors.

Given these origins, the nuclear industry was inevitably surrounded by considerable secrecy. As its civil dimension grew, the coating of secrecy continued to stick and has proved rather difficult to shake off. Even today complete information about some of its activities is difficult to obtain.

In parallel with the development of the nuclear industry, both civil and military, there has been more than half a century of research into the health effects of ionising radiation. Our most important source of data remains the survivors of the Hiroshima and Nagasaki bombings. However, these were acute exposures at high doses, so we have to extrapolate (see p. 46) to estimate the risk at low doses, and just how this should be done continues to be controversial. The present consensus is that the relationship between dose and risk of cancer (the principal long-term effect of exposure) is a straight line down to zero dose; that is, however small the dose there is a small increased risk of cancer. This is usually referred to as the linear no-threshold model (LNT). There are dissenters from this view, at both extremes, all implying that there are strong contextual values at work (see p. 56). Those who think the risk has been overestimated claim that the LNT model is used simply because it makes the 'book keeping' easier; those who think that the risk has been underestimated suspect that the nuclear industry has considerable influence behind the scenes on new regulations and legislation. It is very difficult, if not impossible, to test the LNT at low doses, because very large samples would be needed to achieve adequate statistical power (Box 1.4, p. 25). The confidence intervals on the risk at low doses are very large (see p. 40); this chapter, above all others in the book, stands as an illustration of the problem of low power in scientific studies.

If the LNT model is true, it raises ethical and moral questions which are not part of scientific knowledge (see p. 55). There can be no 'safe' dose, only an 'acceptable' one. But who decides what is acceptable, and how? A very elaborate system of radiation protection has evolved, driven mainly by the International Commission on Radiological Protection (ICRP), an international body of scientists who review the science and also make the value judgements. These value judgements are now incorporated in the very fabric of radiation protection, being built in to the unit of radiation dose, the sievert.

Because any practice involving radiation exposure of the public – such as the discharge of radioactive waste into the sea – will involve some risk, ICRP has a principle of 'justification' which states that any radiation detriment must be offset by some benefit. This leads to the use of apparently 'objective' types of decision making, such as cost–benefit analysis (see p. 59).

The discovery of an excess of childhood leukaemia around the Sellafield nuclear reprocessing plant in 1983 was hailed by opponents of the nuclear industry as a clear indication of the dangers of discharging radioactive waste. However, estimates of the radiation doses that might have been received by the children seemed much too low to account for the excess. But the models used are very complex, with many uncertainties. Maybe there are pathways of which we are completely ignorant? (p. 48).

After more than 15 years of research the issue remains controversial. 'Mindsets' have grown up (p. 56), and not just in those openly supporting or opposed to the nuclear industry. While uncertainty remains, campaigning organisations such as Greenpeace invoke the precautionary principle (see p. 84) and call for an end to all discharges. Supporters of the nuclear industry continue to proclaim their faith in the models and point to the economic benefits of reprocessing.

10.1 Introduction

... today, radioactive waste is being piped directly into the sea. Prevailing ocean currents spread this radioactive material northwards throughout the coastal waters of Western Europe, the Nordic nations and the Arctic. Radioactivity collects in seafood and seaweed, and radioactive material washes up on beaches and invades river estuaries, leaving its toxic legacy throughout the environment. Once in the food chain or air it can cause cancer and genetic damage.

From *Save our Seas*, a leaflet produced by Greenpeace International in 1998

240

What is the 'radioactive waste being pumped into the sea' referred to by Greenpeace? Does it leave a 'toxic legacy in the environment'? If so, why is it allowed?

Nuclear power is an important source of power in many countries. But nuclear power stations in themselves discharge relatively small quantities of radioactive substances into the environment. The reference in the Greenpeace leaflet is not to nuclear power stations, but to reprocessing plants, which extract plutonium and unused uranium from fuel rods removed from nuclear power stations. Reprocessing was originally carried out first at Hanford in the USA during the Second World War and then after the war at Sellafield in the UK, primarily to make plutonium for nuclear weapons. Plutonium was also produced for eventual use (it was hoped) in Fast Breeder Reactors, which have not proved to be commercially viable. Both military and civilian reprocessing have now ceased in the USA, and there are now only three commercial reprocessing plants in the world (at Sellafield and Dounreay in the UK, and Cap La Hague in France). A feature of all reprocessing plants is that they discharge radioactive material to the sea and air, in significantly larger quantities than nuclear power stations. Who decides, and how, what level of discharges are permissible?

This chapter will not attempt to discuss the complex and many-faceted arguments for and against nuclear power and reprocessing, but will concentrate on the ways decisions are made about **radiation protection** – essentially, decisions about how much exposure to radiation is permissible for members of the public. In turn, these decisions are related to further decisions about how much radioactive waste is allowed to be discharged to the atmosphere and to the sea.

10.2 Ionising radiation and its effects

10.2.1 Radiation dose

First we must summarise the science needed to understand the decisions. Box 10.1 explains what we mean by radiation, in particular the different types of ionising radiation and how they can damage cells. We need some measure of the biological damage caused by ionising radiation; such a measure is the **radiation dose**, which is related to the energy deposited in tissue by different kinds of radiation (see Box 10.1). The unit of radiation dose most commonly used is the **sievert** (symbol Sv). In the USA the old unit – the **rem**, equal to one hundredth of a sievert – is still in widespread use. The radiation dose in sieverts is obtained by multiplying the energy deposited in tissue (in joules per kilogram) by a factor to take account of the way the energy is deposited – this factor is 20 for alpha particles and 1 for X-rays, gamma rays and beta particles. So, for a given energy deposition, alpha particles are about 20 times more damaging than X-rays.

241

Box 10.1 Ionising radiation

The term **radiation** should really be used for visible light and other forms of light which are invisible to us – radio waves, microwaves, infrared, ultraviolet, X-rays and gamma rays. However, the term is often used to include the particles that are emitted by radioactive substances.

Radiation is said to be **ionising** if it has enough energy to ionise atoms, that is, remove electrons from them. Ionising radiation includes X-rays and gamma rays, and also the particles that are emitted from radioactive substances, but does not include light, infrared, microwaves or radio because they do not have enough energy to ionise atoms.

There are three main types of radioactive decay:

- emission of an alpha particle (two protons and two neutrons bound together)
- emission of a beta particle (an electron or positron [the positively charged anti-particle of the electron])
- emission of a gamma ray (a high-energy photon)

When they have sufficient energy, alpha particles, beta particles and gamma rays can ionise atoms. When ionisation occurs, bonds between atoms can be broken and the chemical constitution of the system can be changed. Through the process of ionisation, therefore, radiation is capable of damaging the cell.

There is a considerable difference in the damage to cells that can be caused by alpha particles on the one hand, and beta particles and gamma rays on the other. An alpha particle has about 2000 times the mass of a beta particle; it also moves much more slowly. The resulting ionisation per unit distance travelled is therefore much greater for an alpha particle than it is for a beta particle, and consequently the alpha particle only travels a very short distance in tissue – usually much less than 100 micrometres (μm). Since most animal cells are about 50–100 μm across, an alpha particle can deposit all its energy in just one cell. Alpha particles can therefore be much more damaging than beta particles and gamma rays.

Box 10.2 Radiation doses to individuals and populations

The radiation dose to an individual is measured in millisieverts or microsieverts. It is sometimes useful to calculate radiation doses to a population, by summing all the doses to individuals in that population. A population dose has the units **man sievert** (or, to be gender neutral, **person sievert**) and is referred to as the **collective dose** to that population. So

collective dose = average dose to an individual in the population ×
number of people in the population

The sievert is a large unit (single doses of more than about 10 Sv are almost invariably fatal), so more usual units are the **millisievert** (mSv, one thousandth of a sievert) and the **microsievert** (μSv, one millionth of a sievert).

The dose to a population is called the collective dose (see Box 10.2).

10.2.2 Sources of radiation

We are continuously exposed to radiation from natural sources – particles from the sun and outer space, radioactive materials in the soil, radioactive gases (mainly radon, a decay product of uranium) in our homes, and radioactive substances in our bodies. In addition to these natural sources of radiation, we are now exposed to radiation from various artificial sources, such as fallout from the atmospheric nuclear weapons tests of the 1950s and 1960s, fallout from the 1986 Chernobyl accident, and discharges from nuclear installations. Table 10.1 shows the average annual dose to an individual in the UK from various natural and man-made sources. Note that these are all averages; the range of doses is high, and depends on each individual's place of residence, habits, occupation and health.

Average doses from natural background radiation worldwide are similar to the figures given in Table 10.1, although, as might be expected, the range is wide – from 1500 μSv up to 6000 μSv per year (and this range does not include places where the background is unusually high, for example parts of the coast of Brazil and the south-west coast of India) (UNSCEAR 1988; Eisenbud 1987).

Table 10.1 Annual radiation doses to the UK population

Source	Average (μSv)
Natural sources	
Cosmic rays	250
External radiation from terrestrial sources	350
Internal radiation from terrestrial sources	300
Exposure to radon and thoron, and their decay products	1300
Artificial sources	
Medical[1]	300
Fallout	10
Occupational exposure	5
Radioactive discharges	< 1
Miscellaneous[2]	10
Total dose from all sources	2500 μSv or 2.5 mSv

[1] Diagnostic only – does not include radiotherapy.
[2] Includes air travel, luminous watches, and exposure to naturally occurring radionuclides released during the burning of coal.

243

10.2.3 Effects of ionising radiation

The biological effects of ionising radiation depend on the total dose received and also the rate at which the dose is received. In general, a given dose received in a very short time is more damaging than when it is spread out over a long period. A bottle of whisky drunk in half an hour is likely to be highly toxic, even fatal, but if consumed slowly over several weeks is harmless (and might even be beneficial!). Doses of ionising radiation greater than about 1 Sv, given as a single dose in a short time, can cause radiation sickness, with damage to the gastrointestinal tract, bone marrow and central nervous system. A single dose of more than about 10 Sv is almost invariably fatal.

Radiation sickness occurred on a large scale following the dropping of the atomic bombs on Hiroshima and Nagasaki in 1945, as graphically described by the American psychiatrist Robert Jay Lifton:

> **Survivors began to notice in themselves and others a strange form of illness. It consisted of nausea, vomiting and loss of appetite; diarrhea with large amounts of blood in the stools; fever and weakness; purple spots on various parts of the body from bleeding into the skin ... inflammation and ulceration of the mouth, throat and gums ... bleeding from the mouth, gums, throat, rectum and urinary tract ... loss of hair from the scalp and other parts of the body ... extremely low white blood cell counts when those were taken ... and in many cases a progressive course until death.** (Lifton 1967)

Dramatic symptoms such as these are the result of large numbers of cells being killed by radiation. Low doses of radiation, or low dose rates, are much less likely to kill cells. Nevertheless important damage can be produced at low doses. Radiation can damage all biological molecules including DNA, which although usually repaired, may not be repaired correctly, so that the cell continues to survive and reproduce with a built-in 'error message'. Such a cell may eventually become a cancer many years or even decades later. There is ample evidence that people exposed to high doses of ionising radiation are at greater risk of developing cancer. More than 50 years after the bombings, the survivors of Hiroshima and Nagasaki are still developing cancers as a result of their exposure to radiation.

Radiation can also affect future generations, by damaging egg or sperm cells. Diseases or abnormalities in children caused in this way are usually referred to as **genetic effects**. Cancers and genetic effects are together often referred to as **stochastic effects** of radiation. For the doses usually encountered in the environment (see Table 10.1), only stochastic effects need be considered, and it is with these that we will be concerned for the remainder of this chapter.

10.3 The risks of ionising radiation

10.3.1 Estimating the risks

The risks of cancer and genetic effects resulting from exposure to ionising radiation can be estimated from two complementary disciplines:

- **radiobiology** – the study of radiation effects in molecules, cell cultures and also in whole animals
- **epidemiology** – the study of disease patterns in populations exposed to ionising radiation

Radiobiologists investigate the effect of radiation at a cellular or subcellular level or in animals such as mice. Radiobiology can provide important insights into basic mechanisms, although the behaviour of isolated cells may not always correspond to what happens in entire living organisms. A wealth of information has been obtained from animal experiments, although these require large numbers of animals to be studied for long periods of time – an expensive and very time-consuming business, to say nothing of the ethical objections.

The importance of epidemiological studies is that they give us some information on the effects of radiation in human populations. Epidemiological studies can involve high doses (e.g. the survivors of the atomic bombings in Hiroshima and Nagasaki) or low doses (e.g. studies of workers in the nuclear industry), and high and low dose studies each have their problems.

From high dose studies we can sometimes obtain a relationship between cancer risk (i.e. number of excess cancers) and radiation dose. This is called a **dose–response curve**; an example is shown in Figure 10.1. However, if we then want the risk at low doses we have to extrapolate from the high doses. This means we have to make assumptions about the form

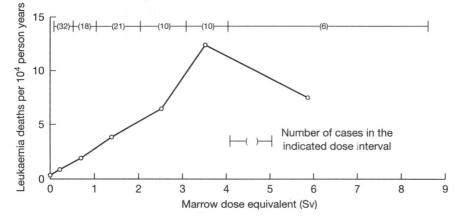

Figure 10.1 Cumulative leukaemia mortality in Hiroshima and Nagasaki as a function of the estimated radiation dose to the bone marrow.

245

of the dose–response curve at low doses. Because of the uncertainties on the data points, there are many different ways in which the dose–response curve for high doses can be extrapolated to low doses (see Figure 10.2). At present it is usually assumed that the dose–response curve is a straight line at low doses, curving upwards as the dose increases.

But is the dose–response curve a straight line right down to zero dose? In other words, is there a threshold for cancer induction? The absence of a threshold for cancer is certainly plausible radiobiologically, because tumours have their origins in single gene mutations in single cells, and just one gamma ray is capable of ionising an atom in a strand of DNA. The combined assumptions of a linear relationship between cancer risk and dose, and the absence of a threshold, are usually referred to as the '**linear no-threshold model**' (LNT). If the LNT is correct, the risk of cancer at low doses is directly proportional to dose, and any dose of ionising radiation, however small, will increase the risk of cancer. This means that we can't talk about 'safe levels' of radiation; decisions have to be made about what levels of risk are acceptable.

Unfortunately, low dose studies are no more successful at estimating the risk of cancer. This is because cancer is a common disease with many causes, and it is often very difficult if not impossible to distinguish a small excess of radiation-induced cancers from the high 'natural' background incidence of cancer (see Box 1.4, p. 25).

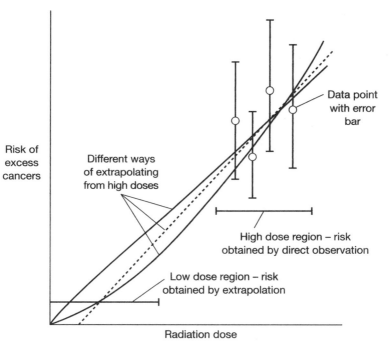

Figure 10.2 Extrapolating for risk at low doses from data at high doses.

Estimating the risk of genetic effects from radiation is even more diffi-cult. As with cancer, the main source of our information is from the survivors of Hiroshima and Nagasaki. The incidence of congenital abnor-malities, stillbirths and child deaths has been examined in about 70 000 pregnancies in the survivors, and compared with pregnancies in a control group of people who were not exposed to the bombs. No statistically sig-nificant difference between the groups has been seen, but this does not mean that there is in fact no difference. Animal studies have shown beyond doubt that there are genetic effects of radiation, so there is no reason why they should not occur in humans too. If we assume that the production of genetic effects per sievert is the same in humans as it is in mice, then it can be shown that, given the doses at Hiroshima and Nagasaki, an effect would be very difficult to detect given the inevitable fluctuations in the background incidence of congenital abnormalities and stillbirths. In other words, the failure to detect any effect may be a Type II error (see p. 16 and p. 57).

10.3.2 Present estimates of cancer risk

Data on radiation hazards are regularly reviewed by the International Commission on Radiological Protection (ICRP). On the basis of these reviews, ICRP then makes recommendations for radiation protection.

In its most recent (1990) review and recommendations, ICRP endorses the linear no-threshold model at low doses and estimates the risk of fatal radiation-induced cancer to be 0.05 per sievert; in other words, if 20 people received a dose of 1 sievert (or 20 000 received a dose of 1 mSv) there would probably be one additional fatal cancer. There are some dis-senters from this view: at one extreme, there are those who say that because there is no direct evidence for the linear no-threshold model, the risks may have been overestimated. They also highlight studies which claim to show a protective effect at low doses (Doll 1998; Clarke 1998). At the other extreme, there are claims that the risks have been underesti-mated: for some time it has been claimed by the radiation epidemiologist Alice Stewart that cancer risk should not be estimated from the Hiroshima and Nagasaki survivors because they are not 'representative human beings'; many of those exposed to radiation had died of acute injuries before systematic study of the survivors was underway (Stewart 1998).

As mentioned previously, low dose studies cannot resolve this issue. If 100 000 people each received a dose of 1 mSv we might expect (if the ICRP risk factor is correct) about five additional deaths from cancer. Even if the risk factor was ten times higher than ICRP think it is, the resulting 50 addi-tional deaths would be submerged in the 20 000 or so cancer deaths that would eventually occur in our sample of 100 000 people (see Box 1.4, p. 25). Inevitably, therefore, estimates of risk obtained from low dose studies have large uncertainties. A recent study of cancer mortality among nuclear industry workers in Canada, the UK and the USA concluded that the estimated cancer risk was compatible with a range of possibilities, from a reduction of risk (in other words, radiation is good for you!) up to about double the ICRP value (Cardis et al. 1995).

10.4 Radiation protection

10.4.1 Policies and legislation

On the international scene, the main player in radiological protection is the International Commission on Radiological Protection (ICRP), which, as already mentioned, periodically reviews the literature on the effects of radiation exposure, and provides estimates of the risks of cancer and genetic effects at low doses.

ICRP was established in 1928, with the name at that time of the International X-ray and Radium Protection Committee. It was set up originally in response to the deaths of many early radiation workers – for example, medical radiologists who worked with X-ray machines and radium sources. In 1950 it was restructured and given its present name, and since then has made recommendations on radiation exposure for both occupational and public exposure. At present it consists of 28 scientists.

For governments, policy makers and the nuclear industry, ICRP is widely regarded as the foremost authority in the field of radiological protection. However, ICRP has often been criticised for being a self-appointed and non-accountable body, overly influenced by the nuclear industry.

Rosalie Bertell, a veteran anti-nuclear campaigner and persistent critic of ICRP, has said that the members of the main Committee of ICRP, the 'decision makers, are either users of ionising radiation in their employment, or are government regulators, primarily from countries with nuclear weapon programs' (Bertell 1998).

The translation of ICRP's recommendations into laws is left to other national or international organisations. In the UK, recommendations on radiological protection are made by the National Radiological Protection Board (NRPB), but its recommendations (generally, but not invariably, in line with ICRP) are not legally binding. We shall look more closely at how the recommendations are translated into legislation later on in this chapter. First we examine the ICRP approach in more detail.

10.4.2 The principles of radiation protection: science and value judgements

ICRP states three fundamental principles of radiation protection:

- **Justification**. No practice involving exposures to radiation should be adopted unless it produces sufficient benefit to the exposed individuals or to society to offset the radiation detriment it causes. Note that the justification principle balances all benefits against radiation detriment only.
- **Optimisation**. All exposures to radiation should be kept as low as reasonably achievable (ALARA), economic and social factors being taken into account.
- **Dose limitation**. The exposure of individuals should be subject to dose limits. The dose limit is usually specified as an annual limit which is additional to natural background.

The implementation of ICRP's three principles involves some science, but all three also involve value judgements. Of the three the most problematic is justification, which obviously must involve many considerations other than scientific ones. The process of justification, in which the benefits of some practice involving radiation are balanced against the harm that might result from it, is really a form of **cost–benefit analysis**, a tool for decision making in which all the supposed benefits and detriments are given a financial value (see p. 59). The preferred option is then the one in which the difference between benefits and detriments has the largest value. Attempts have been made by the nuclear industry to use cost–benefit analysis in the justification of particular projects (UKAEA, 1995); this involves assigning a cost to radiation doses that are likely to be received by workers and members of the public. Discussion of the 'cost' of radiation dose is essentially a discussion about the value of life, although this point is not usually made clear.

We shall return to a discussion of the justification principle later in this chapter, when we discuss the specific example of Sellafield discharges. But what about value judgements in the other two principles, optimisation and dose limitation? Value judgements are clearly involved in optimisation – the expression 'reasonably achievable' can have no universally agreed 'objective' definition.

On the face of it the third principle, of dose limitation, doesn't seem to contain value judgements. But if the linear no-threshold model is correct, there is no 'safe' dose – the dose limit corresponds to the maximum 'acceptable' dose. Bodies such as ICRP and NRPB not only review the science but also decide what is 'acceptable'.

In its 1977 recommendations, ICRP set dose limits at 50 mSv per year for those occupationally exposed to radiation (workers in the nuclear industry, for example) and 5 mSv per year for members of the public. ICRP based the limit for workers on a comparison of the average fatal cancer risk in radiation work with the rates of accidental death in industries not associated with radiation, and the limit for members of the public with risks that 'an individual can modify to only a small degree ... an example of such risks is that of using public transport' (ICRP 1977). In the 1990 recommendations, the occupational and public limits have been lowered to 20 mSv (strictly speaking, 100 mSv over a five-year period) and 1 mSv per year respectively. However, ICRP no longer relates these simply to the risks of fatal cancer, but also makes allowance for the years of life lost due to cancer (which will vary greatly with the type of cancer) and the poor health resulting from non-fatal cancer. Clearly there are a number of difficult value judgements to make here. ICRP has taken the step of actually incorporating these value judgements into the unit of **effective dose**, the **sievert** (see Box 10.3). Rather confusingly, the sievert is the unit of both the effective dose and the more straightforward radiation dose introduced at the beginning of this chapter.

Box 10.3 Effective dose

Radiation doses to workers and members of the public are usually given as **effective doses**. The effective dose is obtained by summing the radiation doses to different organs of the body, multiplying each dose by a weighting factor.

In the 1977 recommendations of ICRP (ICRP Document 26), the weighting factor for a particular organ (lung, bone marrow, etc.) was proportional to the risk of radiation-induced fatal cancer in that organ. In the 1990 recommendations (ICRP Document 60), the weights now include not only the risks of fatal cancer and serious hereditary defects (as before), but also a factor to take account of years of life lost for each cancer and a factor to take account of the ill-health caused by non-fatal cancers.

The unit of effective dose is the **sievert**. The change in recommendations has meant that the unit has changed its size, so that (in some cases) the same radiation exposure now gives rise to a different dose. During the changeover some documents gave doses according to both the new and old recommendations. For example, here are the estimates of public radiation exposure from discharges of liquid radioactive waste from Sellafield in 1993:

Exposure pathway	Group	Dose (mSv)	
		ICRP-26	ICRP-60
Fish and shellfish consumption: local fishing community		0.15	0.10
Fish and shellfish consumption: fishermen (Scottish coast)		0.18	0.11
External: houseboat dwellers		0.26	0.26
External: fishermen (Whitehaven)		0.13	0.13
Handling of fishing gear: local fishing community		0.61	0.61

Source: Data from MAFF: Radioactivity in Surface and Coastal Waters of the British Isles, 1993.

The members of ICRP themselves acknowledge that their recommendations are a mix of science and value judgements. In the words of the current Chairman of ICRP, Roger Clarke:

> **The Commission must ... supplement its scientific knowledge with value judgements on the relative importance of different kinds of risk and balance the risks and benefits, and it must make clear how these judgements are made.** (Clarke 1998.)

These comments raise an important question: are a body of radiation experts the most appropriate people to make these value judgements? At least one former member of ICRP, Roger Berry, thought not:

> **I do not think that the scientist, by virtue of his science, has any right to believe that he is better at making moral and social judgements. By presenting knowledge in a clear and understandable way, he can, however, assist the moral decision.** (Berry 1987.)

How are the recommendations of the ICRP, value judgements and all, translated into national legislation? Box 10.4 summarises the processes in the UK, Europe and the USA. Case studies that follow will explore some of the themes that have emerged so far.

Box 10.4 Radiation protection legislation in the EU, the UK and the USA

The European Union

Radiation Protection in the EU is driven primarily by **EC Directives**, issued by the Commission of the EC but based on guidance from a group of experts established under Article 31 of the Euratom Treaty of 1957. A Commission proposal is submitted first to the Economic and Social Committee, and then to the Council of Ministers and the European Parliament. The Parliament can propose amendments to the proposal, but ultimately it is the Council which decides on the content of the Directive.

Basic standards for the protection of the health of workers and the general public against the dangers arising from ionising radiation were laid down for the first time by the European Community in 1959. The Directives were revised in 1962, 1966, 1979, 1980, 1984 and (most recently) in 1996. This last directive (96/29/Euratom) is based essentially on the 1990 recommendations of ICRP, and must be transposed into national legislation by May 2000.

The UK

Draft legislation based on the 1996 EC Directive has been drawn up in the UK by the Health and Safety Commission (HSC), but its room to manoeuvre is severely restricted by the Directive. Although the HSC legislation has been made available for public consultation (in the first half of 1998), the original EC/Euratom Directive appeared in its final form without any similar opportunities for public participation. We will look at this problem in more detail in a case study later in this chapter.

▶

Box 10.4 (continued)

The USA

Regulations governing how much ionising radiation the public can be exposed to are set by a joint process involving the Nuclear Regulatory Commission (NRC) and the Environmental Protection Agency (EPA). Although the 1990 ICRP recommendations are adhered to in practice, legislation has not yet been prepared.

10.5 Childhood leukaemia around Sellafield

This case study is of particular interest because it illustrates the continuing uncertainties in the science and how these uncertainties may have a bearing on decisions about radioactive discharges.

In 1983 Yorkshire Television presented a programme which dealt with the incidence of childhood leukaemia in the village of Seascale, near Sellafield in Cumbria (a nuclear fuel reprocessing plant run by British Nuclear Fuels, BNFL). The incidence of leukaemia was, it seemed, much higher than would be expected in a village of this size. Using census data they estimated that there was approximately ten times more leukaemia among children under 10 in Seascale (based on five cases) than would be expected from national incidence figures. This prompted the government to set up an Independent Advisory Group, chaired by Sir Douglas Black, to investigate whether the leukaemia could be due to the discharges from Sellafield.

The Group reported in 1984 that the incidence of leukaemia in Seascale was indeed much higher than would be expected. These findings were seized upon by opponents of the nuclear industry, and Sellafield in particular, as evidence that radioactive discharges from Sellafield over a period of 30 years or so (discharges were much higher in the 1970s than they are now) were the cause of the leukaemia cases. In order to try to establish whether the increase was related to the discharges from Sellafield, the Advisory Group commissioned a report from NRPB. NRPB was asked to estimate what radiation dose the children of Seascale might have received over the period 1950–1970, as a result of the discharges from Sellafield. As there were insufficient data from environmental monitoring, the radiation doses could not be measured directly, so a complicated computer model had to be constructed which made assumptions about the children's diet, how much time they spent on the beach, and so on. On the basis of what BNFL had said about the level of the discharges, NRPB was able to estimate radiation doses to the children. Using conventional risk factors, the estimated doses came nowhere near explaining the raised incidence of leukaemia actually observed – the discrepancy was a factor of several hundred. So if the leukaemias were due to radiation, there must have been errors in the reported discharges, the estimated radiation doses, or the risk factor. Alternatively, of course, the explanation for the excess might not involve radiation at all.

A surprising twist to the story occurred in 1990, when Martin Gardner and colleagues released the results of a case–control study (Gardner et al. 1990) which suggested that there was an association between the risk of leukaemia in a child and the radiation dose received by the child's father. This finding generated speculation that radiation could damage sperm cells and so pass on genetic damage to the next generation. However, further study of the leukaemias in children of Sellafield workers has shown that the association between paternal radiation dose and leukaemia risk is restricted to children born in Seascale. Moreover, the finding has not been confirmed by other studies of workers in the nuclear industry. Sir Richard Doll, reviewing the issue recently (Doll 1998), concluded that 'Gardner et al.'s finding was a statistical fluke.'

After more than 14 years and many studies, there is general agreement that the excess of leukaemia is real, but the explanation for this (continuing) excess is still unclear. The view of NRPB has continued to be that the doses likely to have been received by children in Seascale could not account for the observed incidence of leukaemia (Simmonds et al. 1995). An alternative explanation is that the leukaemia is due to the spread of infection in susceptible people brought about by the mixing of urban and rural populations, a hypothesis originally due to Leo Kinlen. The government Committee on Medical Aspects of Radiation in the Environment (COMARE), set up in 1985 on the recommendation of the Black Advisory Group, has now issued four reports, the latest of which (COMARE 1996) is a comprehensive review of the possible causes of the excess of leukaemia and cancer cases in young people in the Sellafield area.

COMARE concludes that

> it is probable that population mixing is a factor in the increase in childhood leukaemias described in some population groups ... however, it is not possible to quantify this effect in a satisfactory way in order to relate it to the effect of population mixing on leukaemia incidence in Seascale since no areas in the published studies are directly comparable with Seascale. The evidence available at present does not convince us that such a large relative risk persisting over more than three decades could be wholly attributed to population mixing.

However, COMARE also conclude that it seems 'highly unlikely that radioactive discharges from Sellafield have been the sole cause of the the excess Seascale cases.'

COMARE's reasoning, that the doses are too small to explain the excess cases, assumes of course that the doses have been correctly estimated, and that the risk factors relating dose to leukaemia incidence are correct. The doses are estimated using complicated models, which are subject to various uncertainties, as described on pp. 42–44.

As well as many uncertainties in the science, there are a number of important contextual values here. In 1993, the families of two Seascale children who had suffered from leukaemia presented a lawsuit against BNFL; lawyers for these families contended that the two fathers had experienced germ cell damage as a result of exposure to radiation. The case lasted several months and a large number of distinguished scientists were called on both sides. In the end, the judge concluded that the case against BNFL had not been convincingly established. It would have been damaging financially to BNFL if it had been shown that the leukaemia cases were due to Sellafield.

A glance at Table 10.1 shows that, on average, individual doses from artificial sources of radiation are much less than those from natural sources. The idea that this is not just true on average, but invariably true, has widespread currency and gives rise to an almost instinctive reaction (from most scientists, at least) that environmental radiation could not possibly be the cause of the leukaemias. This prevailing culture does have some influence on the funding available for research, and therefore the direction of the research. In the language of Chapter 2, contextual values are at work here. A recent article in *New Scientist* suggested that the European Commission recently rejected proposals to investigate the link between radiation and genetic damage, because the 'bureaucrats at the heart of Europe are dedicated to the nuclear cause: their mission is to prevent the untimely demise of the nuclear power industry.' (Edwards 1998.)

It seems likely that the jury will be out on the causes of childhood leukaemia around Sellafield for some time yet. In the meantime, all sides in the debate can exploit the uncertainties in the science, as we shall see in the next section.

10.6 Sellafield discharges, THORP, and public consultation

10.6.1 Background

This case study – which concerns the public consultations on Sellafield discharges prior to the opening of THORP in 1994 – illustrates the process of decision making in detail, with particular reference to the difficult question of justification.

In 1992, BNFL applied for new authorisations to discharge radioactive waste from Sellafield, as a result of the commissioning of its new Thermal Oxide Reprocessing Plant (THORP) and the treatment of waste stored on site. In its application, BNFL proposed a reduction in the discharge limits for some radioactive materials, although it later became clear that it was intending to utilise a higher proportion of the limits than previously – in other words, actual discharges of many substances would increase.

Extensive public consultations were held on these proposals in 1992 and 1993. Of the many important issues arising from these consultations, three are particularly worthy of note.

10.6.2 Doses to individuals

The discharges to sea and air were deemed to be acceptable because the estimated doses to **critical groups** were less than the dose limit recommended by NRPB. A critical group is a small homogeneous group of individuals who, due to their habits of life, represent the most highly exposed individuals in the population. In the Sellafield area the critical group are thought to be members of the local fishing community who eat large quantities of locally caught fish and shellfish. Many official pronouncements were made during the consultation period along the lines that 'all populations ... are protected provided the critical groups are protected'. There are a number of problems with a statement like this, some of which overlap with the childhood leukaemia problem discussed in the previous section.

- The critical group may not have been correctly identified.
- Even if we have identified the correct critical group, how can we be sure that their habits will not change? Predictions over very long timescales are involved.
- Complex models, with many uncertainties, are used in the estimation of dose. How do we know that all pathways have been allowed for?

These questions were brought into sharper focus by the controversy over childhood leukaemia around Sellafield, discussed in the previous section. COMARE made the comment that:

> The Committee consider that the cause of the excess rate of cancer in the 0–24 year old age range in the village of Seascale is currently unknown. There are a number of possible causes which may have led to this excess. There is insufficient evidence to point to any one particular explanation and a combination of factors may be involved. As exposure to radiation is one of these factors, the possibility cannot be excluded that unidentified pathways or mechanisms involving environmental radiation are implicated. In the light of this, proposals to increase the level of discharge of any specific radionuclide as proposed in the draft authorisations should be viewed with concern.
>
> (Bridges 1993.)

But NRPB said:

> The Board has made extensive efforts to assess doses and risks to children and young persons in Seascale. It has not been possible to account for the observed excess of leukaemia in the village ... radiation risks [for the population of Seascale] have been found to be dominated by the radiation received naturally, even allowing for past discharges from the Sellafield site.
>
> (NRPB 1993.)

10.6.3 Doses to populations

As part of the authorisation process for THORP, estimates were made of the collective doses likely to result from the discharges to air and sea (see Box 10.2 for an explanation of collective dose). Because of the long half-lives of many of the radioactive substances being discharged, and their persistence in the environment, collective doses can be summed over very long time periods – thousands or even millions of years. If the linear no-threshold model is correct, it should be possible to estimate the number of fatal cancers that would result from a given collective dose, simply by multiplying the collective dose by the risk factor (0.05 per sievert). These cancer deaths will not be detectable (as they will form a very small proportion of cancer deaths from other causes) and will occur well into the future. Greenpeace published estimates of the number of deaths that might result from Sellafield discharges, but these were criticised, not for their arithmetic, but for their (mis)use of collective dose:

> A consideration of the differing levels of collective dose (taking due account of the uncertainties, time periods, relative levels of individual dose, etc.) will form a part of the resultant decision making process ... what it will not become – at least in the hands of responsible decision makers – is a means of attempting to focus on estimated deaths. (Coulston 1994).

Again we are brought back to our theme of science and value judgements. Estimating the number of deaths that may occur is largely a matter of science; deciding whether they are acceptable, or whether they should feature in decision making, has nothing to do with science.

10.6.4 Justification

This point follows directly from the previous one. During the consultation period, Greenpeace and other objectors to THORP concentrated on the issue of justification – the first principle of ICRP. Could the benefits of THORP be said to outweigh the detriment? The point was repeatedly made that a comparison had not been carried out between the dry storage and reprocessing of spent nuclear fuel. The second public consultation (in 1993) was concerned entirely with the question of justification. When the government finally decided in favour of BNFL's application, Greenpeace and Lancashire County Council called for a judicial review. Prior to the issue being raised by Greenpeace, it had been assumed (by NRPB, for example) that justification would apply generally to a process such as the generation of electricity from uranium, or the reprocessing of spent nuclear fuel. However, Justice Potts ruled in *Rv Secretary of State, ex P Greenpeace* [1994] 4 All ER 321–416, that:

> In my view ICRP 60 and the [EC] Directive are concerned with justification of particular practices which affect particular individuals in particular circumstances. In this case the type of activity is thermal oxide reprocessing at Sellafield. There has been no justification of this activity involving the decision maker being satisfied that the benefits flowing from the activity outweigh the detriment.

This is often referred to as the 'Potts judgement' and there is some evidence that the UK government (and certainly the nuclear industry) regarded it as perverse. In 1996 the EC issued its new Directive on radiation protection; the section on justification reads as follows (emphasis added):

> 1. Member States shall ensure that *all new classes or types of practice* resulting in exposure to ionising radiation are justified in advance of being first adopted or first approved by their economic, social or other benefits in relation to the health detriment they may cause.
> 2. Existing classes or types of practice *may be reviewed* as to justification whenever new and important evidence about their efficacy or consequences is acquired.

Effectively any 'class or type of practice' being carried out already is *de facto* justified, unless 'new and important' evidence is acquired. This appears to have been composed so as to rule out the possibility of a 'Potts judgement' in future. The Directive has been incorporated into draft UK legislation with very little change. As an Annex to the draft legislation, HSC includes a long list of existing types of practice, which can continue without justification unless 'new and important evidence' becomes available. Exactly what constitutes 'new and important' evidence is, of course, open to debate. Conceivably if it were ever shown that discharges from Sellafield were a primary cause of childhood leukaemia in that area, this might be sufficient to review the justification for reprocessing. It seems unlikely, however, that the science will ever be so unequivocal.

10.7 Conclusion

We can now look back and evaluate the quotation at the beginning of this chapter. We have seen that radiation can indeed cause cancer and genetic damage, and the assumption generally made is that even low doses of radiation can increase the risk of cancer, so any level of discharge is potentially harmful. However, we have also seen that the science has many uncertainties: there is still some controversy about the size of the risk at low doses, which cannot be measured directly but has to be estimated by extrapolation from high doses. There is often uncertainty about the size of the radiation doses that people have received, and it is just possible that in some cases these estimates are seriously in error.

Given these uncertainties, many value judgements have to be made. At one level many different pieces of scientific evidence have to be evaluated and synthesised, a process common to any review of a scientific topic. But then, in addition to this, more problematical decisions have to be made – about what level of risk is acceptable and about what level of radiation dose is 'reasonably achievable'. It is frequently argued that if radiation doses from artificial sources are only a relatively small fraction of the doses from natural background (as indeed they are, on average, if the dose estimates are correct) this should in itself make the doses acceptable. A related argument compares the very small additional cancer risk from radiation with the much larger 'natural' risk of cancer which applies to all of us. On the other hand, how seriously should we take the possibility that in some cases estimates of radiation dose may be badly wrong and that radiation exposure may be partly or wholly to blame for the excess of childhood leukaemia around Sellafield? There are some who argue that, so long as this uncertainty remains, discharges must be reduced and eventually eliminated; in other words, we should apply the precautionary principle.

No one disputes that a lot of difficult value judgements have to be made here. Invoking the precautionary principle in itself is not a solution, because we then have to decide just how precautionary we should be. The problem lies not primarily in the nature of the value judgements themselves, but the process by which they are made. As we have seen, a relatively small group of experts both evaluate the science and decide on questions of acceptability. Inevitably these expert groups often perceive radiation risk in a different way from members of the public.

So how can the public be more involved in a more open discussion of the risks of radiation? There are no easy answers. Some encouraging signs are the growth of 'consensus conferences' (in which a citizens' panel, selected from the general public, is given the opportunity to question experts about a particular topic, and then has to produce a report) and 'stakeholder workshops' (in which an independent body arranges a discussion meeting between interested parties, such as representatives of the nuclear industry, trades unions, NGOs, regulatory authorities and so on). But there is a long way to go if the process of decision making is to be made more open, accountable and democratic.

Finally, we should stress that questions of radiation risk are often addressed not in isolation but as part of a much wider context which we have only touched on in this chapter. For reprocessing, it is difficult to separate a discussion of the risks of radioactive discharges from a consideration of the various risks and benefits of reprocessing itself: employment, income from foreign trade, possible diversion of plutonium into weapons, the risk of accidents and so on. However, this further reinforces the need for the decision making process to be made more open and democratic.

10.8 Summary

- The main biological effects of low dose ionising radiation are the induction of cancer and genetic effects.
- The risk is assumed to be proportional to dose, right down to zero.
- Cancer is a common disease, so sorting radiation-induced cancers from the rest is very difficult – direct measurements of the risk at low doses are difficult if not impossible.
- Estimation of cancer risk involves two main steps:
  1. Estimating the radiation dose: for occupational exposure, doses can usually be estimated for each individual worker; for members of the public, doses are usually estimated using models.
  2. Estimating the risk per unit dose: it is usually assumed that the ICRP risk factor (0.05 per sievert) is appropriate.

Both these steps have associated uncertainties.

- In the context of these uncertainties, value judgements have to be made:
  - What size of risk is acceptable?
  - What trade-off should there be between risk and benefit?
- There is a continuing excess of childhood leukaemia around the nuclear reprocessing plant at Sellafield in the UK. The possible role of radiation exposure in the cause of these leukaemias remains unclear.
- One of the central principles of radiation protection is justification, which states that the benefits of a practice involving radiation must offset the detriment. This principle came under much greater scrutiny before THORP, the new reprocessing plant at Sellafield, was commissioned.

Further reading

Beral, V. and Bobrow, M. (eds) (1993) *Childhood Cancer and Nuclear Installations*, BMJ Publishing Group, London.

NRPB *Living with Radiation*. Obtainable through HMSO. A regularly updated guide for the public.

Sumner, D., Wheldon, T. and Watson, W. (1994) *Radiation Risks: An Evaluation*, 4th Edition, Tarragon Press, Whithorn.

References

Baverstock, K. (1997) European Conference on Nuclear Safety and Local/Regional Democracy, Gothenburg, 24–26 June 1997.

Berry, R. (1987) In: Jones, R.R. and Southwood, R. (eds) *Radiation and Health*, John Wiley, Chichester.

Bertell, R. (1998) Limitations of the ICRP Recommendations for worker and public protection from ionising radiation, STOA Workshop, Brussels, 5 Feb 1998.

Bridges, B. (1993) Letter to Mr M Mardell, Her Majesty's Inspectorate of Pollution, 22 Jan 1993.

Cardis, E., Gilbert, E.S., Carpenter, L., Howe, G., Kato, I., Armstrong, B.K., Beral, V., Cowper, G., Douglas, A., Fix, J., Fry, S.A., Kaldor, J., Lave, C., Salmon, L., Smith, P.G., Voelz, G.L. and Wiggs, L.D. (1995) Effects of low doses and low dose rates of external ionizing radiation: cancer mortality among nuclear industry workers in three countries. *Radiation Research*, **142**, 117–32.

Clarke, R. (1998) Conflicting scientific views on the health risks of low-level ionising radiation. *Journal of Radiological Protection*, **18**, 159.

COMARE (1996) *Fourth Report: The Incidence of Cancer and Leukaemia in Young People in the Vicinity of the Sellafield Site, West Cumbria: Further studies and an update of the situation since the publication of the report of the Black Advisory Group in 1984*, Department of Health, Wetherby.

Coulston, D.J. (1994) Editorial. *Journal of Radiological Protection*, **14**, 107.

Doll, R. (1998) Effects of small doses of ionising radiation. *Journal of Radiological Protection*, **18**, 163–74

Edwards, R. (1998) The sins of the fathers. *New Scientist*, August 15 1998, 49.

Eisenbud, M. (1987) *Environmental Radioactivity*, 3rd Edition, Academic Press, Orlando.

Gardner, M.J., Snee, M.P., Hall, A.J., Powell, C.A., Downes, S. and Terrell, J.D. (1990) Results of case–control study of leukaemia and lymphoma among young people near Sellafield nuclear plant in west Cumbria. *British Medical Journal*, **300**, 423–9.

ICRP (1977) *Recommendations of the International Commission on Radiological Protection*. ICRP Publication 26, Pergamon Press, Oxford.

ICRP (1990) *Recommendations of the International Commission on Radiological Protection*. ICRP Publication 60, Pergamon Press, Oxford.

Lifton, R.J. (1967) *Death in Life*, Random House. Quoted in Rhodes, R. (1986) *The Making of the Atomic Bomb*, Simon and Schuster, London.

NRPB (1993) Responses to public consultation conducted by HMIP and MAFF on BNFL's applications for revision of the Certificates of Authorisation.

NRPB 1993. This is a section of a document issued jointly by HMIP and MAFF in 1993. Report on the Public Consultation conducted by Her Majesty's Inspectorate of Pollution and the Ministry of Agriculture, Fisheries and Food (The Authorising Departments) on British Nuclear Fuels plc's Applications for Revision of the Certificate of Authorisation to Discharge Liquid and Gaseous Low Level Radioactive Wastes and for a New Authorisation to Dispose of Combustible Waste Oil from the Sellafield Works at Seascale in Cumbria.

Simmonds, J.R., Robinson, C.A., Phipps, A.W., Muirhead, C.R. and Fry, F.A. (1995) *Risk of Leukaemia and other Cancers in Seascale from all Sources of Ionising Radiation*. NRPB-R276

Simmonds 1995. This is a Report from the National Radiological Protection Board (Chilton, Didcot, Oxon OX11 0RQ) published in October 1995 and available from HMSO, ISBN 0 85951 383 1.

Stewart, A.M. (1998) A-bomb survivors: reassessment of the radiation hazard, STOA Workshop, Brussels, February 1998.

UKAEA (1995) This is a document issued by UKAEA as part of the Dounreay Public Consultation. UKAEA Environment and Emergencies Department. Social and Economic Effects of Dounreay's Projected Programme of Work 1995–2005. EED(95)P28 - ISSUE 1 15 September 1995. Prepared by GW Lewthwaite.

UNSCEAR (1988) *Sources, Effects and Risks of Ionizing Radiation*, United Nations, New York.

Index